The Advertiser's Manual

OTHER BOOKS BY STEPHEN BAKER

Advertising Layout and Art Direction
Visual Persuasion: Effect of Pictures on the Subconscious
An Art Director's Viewpoint
How to Live With a Neurotic Dog
How to Live With a Neurotic Wife
How to Look Like Somebody in Business Without Being Anybody
How to Play Golf in the Low 120's
How to Live With a Neurotic Husband
How to Be Analyzed by a Neurotic Psychoanalyst
How to Get a Job Without Asking For It
Systematic Approach to Advertising Creativity
Games Dogs Play
Get-Around Guide to New York City
The I Hate Meetings Book
5001 Names For Cats
The Executive Mother Goose Book

The
ADVERTISER'S
MANUAL

Stephen Baker

WILEY

John Wiley & Sons, Inc.

New York • Chichester • Brisbane • Toronto • Singapore

Publisher: Stephen Kippur
Editor: Katherine Schowalter
Managing Editor: Andrew Hoffer
Compositor: Progressive Typographers

Masculine gender used throughout the book for grammatical simplicity is always meant to encompass both sexes with no emphasis on either.

This publication is designed to provide accurate and authoritative information in regard to the subject matter covered. It is sold with the understanding that the publisher is not engaged in rendering legal, accounting, or other professional service. If legal advice or other expert assistance is required, the services of a competent professional person should be sought. *From a Declaration of Principles jointly adopted by a Committee of the American Bar Association and a Committee of Publishers.*

Baker, Stephen, 1921–
    The advertiser's manual / by Stephen Baker.
        p.   cm.
    ISBN 0-471-63518-9
    1. Advertising.   I. Title.
    HF5823.B253 1988
    659.1--dc19   88-5892
                                                                          CIP

Printed in the United States of America

88 89 10 9 8 7 6 5 4 3 2 1

Information
Begets Inspiration

Preface

Rarely has advertising seen—and lived through successfully—as many changes as in the last few years. These have been not merely tremors on the industry's own Richter scale—they were quakes in every sense of the word.

For one thing, both marketing and advertising have grown more sophisticated in their ways. They can not afford not to. Competition has become keener than ever. New businesses have entered the arena—many that would surpass a science fiction writer's wildest dreams. They have sprung up everywhere, here and in other parts of the world—nations re-born with new ideas and new skills, not only in the making of goods but also in the ways they are marketed and advertised.

In the meantime, the United States has itself expanded to near-unwieldy proportions. As the reader will quickly surmise from reading this book, the new marketplace at home calls for new approaches, and the giving up of old, comfortable ideas. No longer is it possible to sell a product to everyone in this country. Selectivity has become the battle cry of the eighties, in products, distribution, advertising, and marketing.

It is no wonder that there is little similarity between the advertising of ten or twenty years ago and that created today. Creativity still ranks high on the priority list, but modern advertisers demand, and get, accountability as well. Responding to the pressure, advertising agencies—no slouches are they—have continued to hone their tools: words, pictures, and the ways by which they are brought to the buying public.

The advent of high technology makes for accurate targeting. Today's advertiser knows almost as much about the person he is selling to as he did a century ago serving his customers from behind a counter at the neighborhood corner store.

It is hoped that the reader will find much information — and inspiration — in this overview of recent happenings. Advertising is getting smarter. As should those who are creating and using it.

Stephen Baker
New York City

Acknowledgments

It is said that authors celebrate their books on three separate occasions: first when they get the final nod from their publishers, second when the work is completed, and third at the first whiff of success (critical, commercial, or both). At the time of this writing, I am delighted to report that we have arrived at the second plateau at long last, and champagne is flowing freely.

My happiness, I am sure, is shared by many others who now can find comfort in the fact that their experience and talents are no longer at the whim of an author calling them on the telephone either too early in the morning or too late at night.

It should be mentioned here that few books just "happen", contrary to what seems to be the case. Compilation of reference material is a tedious and involved process, rarely the work of a single individual. A lot of hands — not to say, brains — are at work here feeding material.

More than a hundred professionals — old friends, new friends — have helped with their expertise in putting this book together. Credits are accorded to as many as space allowed. Those — art directors, copywriters — whose names are conspicuous for their absence we humbly apologize. We tried to include as many in the captions, or in the index at the end of the book, as we could. We thank all the contributors for permitting us to reproduce their outstanding work for review purposes.

The reader may notice that the names of certain agencies — Fallon McElligott, Chiat/Day, Hal Riney & Partners, Hill Holliday Connors Cosmopulos, Ogilvy & Mather, Ammirati & Puriss, Della Femina McNamee, to mention a few — appear more frequently throughout the book than do others. This does not intend to be a reflection of preference. An attempt was made simply to find samples of work best dramatizing points made in the text.

The contributions of a few individuals should receive special mention here. Such a person is Gretchen Bader, secretary/editorial assistant who actually reads all the word sequences while in the process of committing them to paper; a talent comparable to, say, that of simultaneously playing a Bach Three-Part Invention on the piano with one hand and making sushi with the other. Katherine Schowalter and Andrew Hoffer of John Wiley & Sons are two other very special people when it comes to this book; she for her support when it all appeared to be coming apart at the seams; he for getting so profoundly involved as to have instantaneous recall of any page in the book sight unseen.

Contents

1

Advertising on Both Sides of the Brain

The owner of a chain of cleaning establishments in a large city has a brilliant promotional idea: a 24-hour "We Clean While You Sleep" overnight service. In true entrepreneurial spirit, he has an award-winning free-lance creative team design a full-page color ad to appear in a magazine covering not only his immediate trading area but the suburbs and beyond. However, his advertising, though highly praised by everyone, fails to produce results until a space salesman calls on him with a proposal to concentrate his advertising in the city's major newspaper. The same campaign but in a different type of media. This time it works.

The brand manager of a large packaged goods company conceives what he considers an airtight marketing plan, based on distribution of the product and other solid criteria. His proposal passes the various approval stages in his company. Left pouting are the people in his advertising agency. "Wrong creative premise," they mutter collectively, and submit their own creative platform — diametrically opposite to the brand manager's.

A group of dedicated engineers develop a new type of drum brake for cars for roughly half of the production cost of any other on the market. By all accounts, they have come up with a "better mousetrap." A major automobile manufacturer buys the patent. He markets it to car owners on the basis of its quick braking power, not lower price as the inventors thought he would. "Safety beats savings," the advertising manager explains.

Sound Familiar? Of Course

The examples just given are based on true case histories. Instances like these occur every day in the field of advertising or in other creative fields, for that matter, like publishing, entertainment, and fine art. They are but a reflection of the difficulties we so often face in separating facts from fancy, practical knowledge from poetic imagination.

All of which only proves that by nature's fiat, human beings have come to use the brain not one but two ways. Too late to change — so we might just as well take maximum advantage of what God giveth.

One plus One Makes Two: The Duality of the Human Brain

The fact that our cerebrum is divided into two distinct halves (literally), each of which goes about solving problems in its own preordained way, is hardly a revelation. For centuries, philosophers, scientists, psychologists, and even alchemists have pondered the phenomenon and applied it as a ready explanation for much that is going on inside and outside our heads. Chinese Taoists, known for their remarkable insights, referred to the two-sidedness of nature as *Yin* and *Yang*. The former was to represent the emotional, more feminine side of the human soul: warm, compliant, passive, the moon floating across the sky. The latter had more positive, rational, and masculine (this all happened before the women's liberation movement!) connotations, symbolized by the sun.

A more scientific examination of the two-sidedness of the brain was taken up at the California Institute of Technology during the 1960's under the leadership of Nobel Prize-winner Roger W. Sperry. Through a series of tests he and his staff proved there are two separate hemispheres, each of which processes the *same* information in a *different* way.

Rudyard Kipling more fancifully yet accurately described this state of affairs. His poem written some fifty years ago about the "Two-sided Man" explains:

> I would go without shirt and shoe,
> Friend, tobacco or bread,
> Sooner than lose for a minute the two
> Separate sides of the head!

Like most creative people with the ability for introspection, Kipling was conscious of the workings inside his brain. And no wonder. To write a poem (or any piece of literature, including advertising copy), one must know *what* to say before figuring out *how* to say it.

Those chuckling at the left vs. right hemisphere theory may be surprised to learn that as late as in the 1930's and 1940's, the shapes of children's heads were still being examined in this country for purposes of predicting their propensity for learning.

In the context of this book (aimed not only at the everyday practitioners of advertising but also the men and women held accountable for the final results), the two-sidedness of the human mind takes on a special significance. *For advertising created exclusively on one side of the brain is almost always flawed.*

The Right Half: Create I Must

This side of the brain contains "such stuff as dreams are made on." Not surprisingly, nearly all measurable electrical activity during a sleeper's REM (rapid eye movement) state occurs in this area. For the most part, it is here that hazy thoughts take on tangible form (i.e. designing a layout), and words metamorphose into pictures. This hemisphere tends to think nonverbally, substituting symbols and musical notes for mere locution. (Hence the popular notion that art directors rarely win spelling bees.) Predictably, this side of the brain has little patience with rules of grammar — or any fixed rules, for that matter.

In dealing with creative people it is important to understand their approach to problem solving. Right-brainers are more likely to take a subjective, holistic, time-free approach to problems, one which often appears a bit helter-skelter to those more accustomed to listening to the left side of the brain — such as a more "pragmatically" inclined business executive. A right-brainer will examine a problem "horizontally"; i.e. flit from one idea to another with all the logic of a bee searching for the nectar. It is no simple matter for the average left-brainer to follow the mental histrionics of his right-brained friends. But this is precisely how right-brainers hit on sudden, unexpected discoveries. When this happens, they exclaim "Got it!" or "Now I see the picture!" or even "Eureka!"

This is in keeping with the postulation of Dr. Morris I. Stein, a professor at New York University, who has found that most

2

of the so-called "creative process" occurs almost entirely in the subconscious. Often the person doesn't even know he is approaching the solution, though his body may give him clues to that effect. Research shows that the heart rate changes during different phases of problem solving, beating faster as the solution nears.

The Left Half: Let Reason Be

The left-brainers are as puzzling to the right-brainers as the right-brainers are to them. "It takes them forever to get to the problem," said the creative director of a major New York agency after a meeting with the account group. "They're nuts."

In point of fact, the left side of the brain is eminently capable of solving problems but with an important difference. The left hemisphere deals with facts, verifiable evidence. This part of the brain analyzes, counts, verbalizes, marks time (is conscious of approaching deadlines and closing dates of publications), and thrives on structure. It much prefers to follow a vertical thinking pattern.

At the risk of indulging in generalities, it could be said that the majority of people in business and commerce go about their tasks with the grim determination of a left-brainer. Their jobs demand it. Seat of the pants thinking is not particularly welcomed at the oval conference table; chimerical thoughts are rarely allowed to take the place of well-documented (and thus less risky) facts.

Who's Who in the Professions

Few people are "pure" left- or right-brainers, particularly in the field of advertising, as we shall see later. Nevertheless, a study made by brain researcher Ned Herrman of 7000 people showed definite relationships between hemisphere dominance and the way subjects earned a living. Here are some of the occupations that seem to have their goodly share of left-brainers:

Accountants	Engineers
Airplane pilots	Lawyers
Car mechanics	Media buyers
Bankers	Administrators
Bookkeepers	Research analysts
Doctors	Statisticians

And these occupations make full use of right-brainers:

Actors	Musicians
Artists	Photographers
Composers	Politicians
Editors	Psychologists
Entertainers	Social workers
Entrepreneurs	Top executives

For the most part, it is the restless (and sometimes reckless) right-brainers who supply many of the original "breakthrough" ideas; left-brainers refine, implement, and help these ideas enter the mainstream. Both contributions are important.

Much has been written about the two halves of the human brain. Each functions automatically, if need be. Most activity, however, is shared by both, and so the brain still operates in a remarkably holistic fashion.

3

When young children set out to create, they do so by instinct. They are eager to express themselves, to let the world—their parents—know how they feel. They allow all five senses to switch into high gear. The result is imagination at its wildest—and sometimes at its most eloquent.

It is only as we go through life that we put increased demands on our left brain—the more rational (and therefore more controllable) side. We try harder to avoid making "mistakes," to avoid being proven "wrong." This may be for the better in most instances, but not all. Giving the right brain its due later in life often spells the difference between "creative" and "non-creative." Attitudes formed early in life are difficult to shake off, and as Betty Edwards points out in her best-selling book *Drawing on the Right Side of the Brain*, few schools are equipped to teach the right hemisphere mode. Says she:

Teaching is sequenced: students progress through grades one, two, three, etc. in a linear direction. The main subjects learners study are verbal and numerical: reading, writing, arithmetic. Time schedules are followed. Teachers give out grades. And everyone senses something is amiss.

The right brain—the dreamer, the artificer, the artist—is lost in our school system and goes largely untaught. We may find a few art classes, a few shop classes, something called "creative writing," and perhaps courses in music; but it is unlikely that we would find courses in imagination, visualization, in perceptual and spatial skills, in creativity as a separate subject, in intuition, in inventiveness.

These drawings were put on paper by a four-year-old. Simple, confident strokes show the lack of inhibitions of a child. Not yet hampered by the artistic dictates of society, these sketches may be short on accuracy but not in expression. They convey the emotions of an artist, perhaps even more so than illustrations created for commercial purposes.

Redesign the American flag to make a personal statement about a political or social issue in the United States. In order to maintain a connection between the traditional flag and your new design, you must use stars and stripes and the colors red, white, and blue. These limitations provide experience in using purely graphic elements to resolve a design problem.

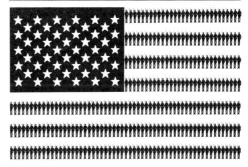

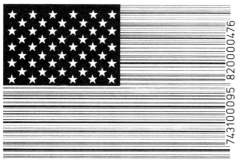

STEVEN KAUFMAN

TOM OZGA

ELAINE A. RUSSELL

LESLIE KIRSCHENBAUM

WENDY BALBO

JANE TARALLO

Putting the emphasis on personal interpretation, Richard Wilde, Chairman of the Graphic Design and Advertising Departments at the School of Visual Arts, regularly turns his students loose on a wide range of hypothetical and real problems in graphic design, typography, illustration, and advertising. The result is an amazing combination of craftsmanship and imagination — the two sides of the brain working in harmony.

PROBLEM: I DON'T FIT IN
SOLUTION:

Carlos Alden

Stephen Silvestri

Christine Zepf

Wendy Kassner

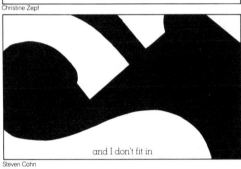
Steven Cohn

Clyde Henriques

PROBLEM: I HAVE A SPLIT PERSONALITY
SOLUTION:

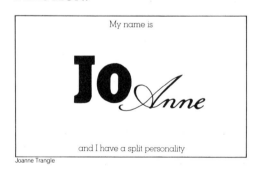
Joanne Trangle

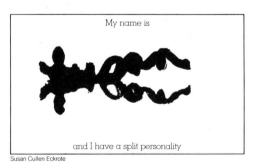
Susan Cullen Eckrote

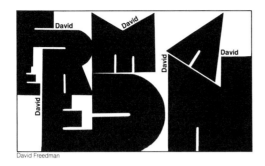

David Freedman

Henry Yee

Left Side, Say "Hello" to the Right

Domination by one side of the brain (usually the left, as pointed out earlier) over the other is not a hard biological fact. During the first few years in our life, we tend to use mostly the right hemisphere. Visceral emotions—the desire to eat and sleep, and the urge to play—make their beginnings here. That is why it is relatively simple to tell how infants feel at the moment. If they are unhappy, they let out a howl. When they are happy, they giggle.

Left-Brain to Right-Brain Talk: How to Make It Happen

Some of us shut off our right side by using *only* logic and reason in problem solving; others are just as guilty in allowing the right hemisphere to do all the talking. The latter happens all too commonly in the field of advertising. Art directors, copywriters, and other "creatives" place so much emphasis on their intuitive sensibilities that they ignore the valuable contributions of the left side of their brains.

All is not lost, however. Our brain can be programmed; it is in fact one of the most flexible organs in the human body, always amenable to change.

In his previous book entitled *Systematic Approach to Advertising Creativity*, this author had set out to motivate art directors and copywriters to let facts lead them to fancy, and not the other way around. Readers were encouraged to combine "vertical" with "horizontal" thinking, to converge (a left-brain activity) as well as diverge (a right-brain activity). For want of a better name, the process espoused in the book came to be known as the "pyramid principle": a simple and easy-to-follow, three-step system that begins with (1) *information* at the base of the structure (the widest part), progresses to (2) *analysis*, and ends as the (3) *big idea* at the apex as the solution to a well-researched problem. The beginning of the book sets the tone:

> Many people, perhaps most, think that ideas fall from heaven like manna: all one has to do is look up and pray. Unfortunately, creativity does not work quite that way. Ideas rarely happen as if by divine revelation. More often than not, they are the end product of arduous and well-organized intellectual activity. The final thought, referred to here as the *idea*, is the result.
>
> Once you are willing to concede that creativity is not a haphazard but a purposeful exercise, things fall into line with surprising ease. Remember that logic encourages, *not* discourages, inspiration. Use it and you will never again experience a paucity of ideas.

Make Peace, Not War

Dissension between clients and their advertising agencies more often than not can be traced back to the inherent problems of thinking pattern differences. As a rule, the former are more left-brain oriented than the latter. Involved in the manufacturing process, they are often more *product* oriented (focusing on product attributes but not from the consumer's point of view) than *people* oriented (focusing on public reaction to the product).

Ability to develop empathy with *both* left-brain and right-brain approaches to the same problems is key to developing a productive relationship between clients and agencies. In the next chapter we will deal with this important question.

To Sum It Up

Advertising ideas are the result of input from both hemispheres of the human brain; the "intuitive" (right side) and the "rational" (left side). Too much emphasis on insights at the expense of information may produce campaigns far off the mark. Conversely, overdependence on facts (however well researched) leads to messages lacking that most important ingredient of attention-getting advertising: originality.

Thinking patterns are habit-forming. Most people tend to favor one side of their brain over the other. If that's the case, you can either (1) learn to use the full potential of your mental resources or (2) work closely with those who use the "other" side of their brains.

2

How to Work with an Advertising Agency — and Like It

The vast majority of companies in the United States employ agencies to create their advertising. Each of the Fortune 500 has at least one agency on its roster. Over two-thirds of clients make use of several agencies, each of which handles a different brand, or different aspects of the company's advertising. Their agencies may be located in the same city, different cities in this country or all over the world.

Must a Company Have an Advertising Agency?

The answer is "not necessarily." There are several viable alternatives to having the advertising done by an agency. The client can, if he so chooses:

1. Have an "in-house" agency prepare the advertising.

2. Use specialized services like printers, typographers, production houses, writers, artists, direct mail specialists, fulfillment houses, and so on. More about the specific nature of such services in Chapter 5.

3. Hire an advertising consultant (individual or an organization) to create and/or administer advertising.

4. Not do any major media advertising at all (television, radio, newspaper, magazine, posters). Though agencies much prefer to do business with advertisers who advertise in "regular" commissionable media, they usually maintain flexibility in their working arrangements with clients. Many have facilities to provide a wide spectrum of professional services, including direct response advertising, sales promotion, package design, marketing research, telemarketing, exhibits, catalogue design, corporate literature, annual reports, graphic assignments, public relations, and even complete film and video production.

Some clients manage to have the best of all possible worlds, augmenting agency contributions with those of "outside" specialists. They may, for example, have an agency work on creative assignments yet retain their own media service to place time and space at less than the usual 15% agency commission rate. Or they may turn to a package design studio, a telemarketing firm, or a sweepstakes contest expert on special projects. The days of consolidating all work under the roof of one advertising agency are over.

Advantages of Having an Advertising Agency

With so many advertisers having an agency to do their bidding, there must be a reason for their taking this route. That certainly is the case. Consider the following:

1. An advertising agency provides an *outside point of view*. It is not inhibited by inside office politics of the client, personality clashes, fixed habits, concepts that have long become relics of the past ("it has worked for us before").

2. An advertising agency has first-hand experience in *advertising*. Let's face it: turning out a widget is one thing, selling it to the world is another. It is particularly skilled in mass media selling. That is the reason that most agencies are more people than product oriented.

3. An advertising agency has access to a variety of *outside specialized services* best suited for the job. Keeping track of the forever changing pool of experts can be an awesome task, and certainly not one that a business executive can hope to fit into his schedule offhandedly. An agency art director, for example, may have dozens of photographers he works with on a continuous basis, each with a "style" of his own. The print production department may have had a working relationship with hundreds of printers, engravers, typographers, whose cards are kept on file. Media buyers keep a close watch on print and air buy opportunities and various last-minute discounts. Such work calls for total concentration.

4. A large part of the staff in an advertising agency consists of *professional creative talent*. Agency atmosphere encourages original thoughts. Status depends on creativity; salaries and promotions are often decided on creative performance. Interoffice competition to get an ad approved borders on the brutal; instant stars are made on the basis of a single award-winning campaign.

In this way, an advertising agency serves as a "collective right-brain hemisphere" for the client. While agencies too have their share of left-brained "scientists," there *always* is present that large and vociferous bunch of renegades whose lives center around pictures and words. In the more structured environment of a large corporation, these people would quickly become worn down and creatively inhibited.

The Disadvantages

Nobody is perfect, not even advertising agencies: For one thing, like people, agencies too have an ego. Sometimes that's all to the good; it drives them to excell, beat the competition. Other times, pride stands in the way of an open mind, of recommendations made by other than members of the inner circle.

It is important to remember that an agency's definition of "good work" may be in the eye of the beholder, namely the creator of the campaign. Few would deny that there is a tendency to measure success in terms of creativity on the part of agencies. The end product—TV commercial, print ad—is proof of the pudding; what you see is what you get.

Many clients agree with the value their agency puts on the creative product. Creative excellence ranks on the top of clients' lists of attributes affecting their choice of agencies, above—in order of importance—account service, media, top management involvement, research and strategy, long-range planning, and even employee morale.

There can be no question about the fact that the creative product of the agency is one of the most important yardsticks an advertising manager can use in evaluating an agency. As we shall see later in this book, this factor easily overpowers all else offered by way of "services."

Who's Who in an Advertising Agency

Described here are the functions of people you are most likely to encounter in your day-to-day dealings with an advertising agency. Though the "personality profile" that follows each description tends to reflect stereotypes — in reality no two people are exactly alike — it will be useful in serving as a basic guide.

The *CEO (Chief Executive Officer)* is responsible for the operation of the advertising agency — in a general way. His strengths may lie in client contact, financial, marketing, administration, or creative. Rare is the chief executive who combines all these talents.

This person may or may not be the founder of the company. It should be noted that more than half of the advertising agencies today are less than a generation old; they grew within the lifespan of the individuals who started them.

When selecting an advertising agency, it pays to keep in mind the basic orientation of the founder or founders of the organization. That individual's (or group of individuals) personal philosophy is likely to have a strong influence over others in the agency.

The most usual combination of agency founders consists of a writer, an art director, and an account executive. That is why so many agencies' stationery features not one but two or more names.

The *management director* or *account executive* will probably be your direct line (and at times, lifeline) to the agency. He manages a wide variety of responsibilities including but not limited to overall marketing and advertising strategy, new product introductions, budgets, timetables, and coordination of the myriad and often bewildering functions of the agency — anything from network advertising to "put out the fire" sales promotions. Of all people in the agency, this person is most likely to be familiar with the daily problems of *your* business.

This person is also likely to be a supreme diplomat, sensitive to the client's personal likes and dislikes, perhaps overly so at times. Long lunches, golf games with "gimme" putts, season boxes at hometown football stadiums have all been the brainchildren of this important agency representative.

Should you judge your account executive by his creative brilliance? Buyer beware. If his is the mind to dream, his presence would better serve the agency sitting behind a typewriter or drawing board. Creative minds rarely have the patience to oversee the mundane details that are part and parcel of every project. In fact, it is better to be skeptical of the account executive bearing his own self-made creative gifts. Ideas do not come swiftly — not even to those making a living at it. And remember, you are paying for the professional talents of an art director and a copywriter. Why not make the most of it?

The *marketing executive* (he may or may not be the account executive or account planner) is the bottom-line person from the agency who listens and understands your field, including your distribution problems.

He knows your customers, if not for their soul, then for their statistics. He is also familiar with your competitors, your sales figures, and lo and behold, may even have in his pocket a handy little black book containing a precious list of retailers he has had dealings with on a first-name basis.

Not so long ago agencies often got accounts on the basis of their account or marketing executives' intimacy with their clients' everyday problems — including such esoterics as manufacturing and distributing the product, (the word *product* in this book may also be interpreted as "service"), the latest on costs, the breakdown of sales territories. No doubt, such information speaks the language of the advertiser. But do not allow marketing razzle-dazzle to overshadow the true calling of an agency which is to create advertising.

What was just said is not to minimize the contributions the agency's *research analyst* brings to an advertiser. Your marketing experience is one thing. Having insights about customers is quite another.

Members of the research department of an agency have the unique capacity to mix study of the human race with pure mathematics. Their findings can be immensely helpful in evaluating advertising campaigns, though their evaluations must always be tempered with the knowledge that research — especially posttesting — is better in defining a problem than in offering solutions to it.

Breakthrough ideas usually come from the *art director* and the *copywriter,* or as agencies like to refer to them, "the creative."

It is one of the truisms in the industry that not every art director can work with every copywriter — or vice versa. The two must share the same convictions about advertising approaches; i.e., "hard-sell," "emotional," "intellectual," "big picture," "long copy," "humorous." Eclectic combinations of the various approaches are possible but still, deep down, the two hearts must beat as one.

Art directors and copywriters therefore often come in pairs. They usually stumble upon one another quite by accident while pursuing their respective careers and then become virtually inseparable. In fact, "Positions Wanted" classified ads in trade publications often specify art-copy teams with proven track records. You either hire the whole show or nothing at all. Agency managements are usually fully aware of the spiritual affinity between art and copy and will go out of their way to play matchmaker.

At times you may find lack of agreement between account executives and the creative, even from the same agency. Not to worry. It goes with the territory.

Both art directors and copywriters — with their right brains in high gear — can make significant contributions all through the development of a campaign. Their antennae are different from those of us ordinary human beings; they are tuned in to a different frequency. Logic, as we pointed out before, is not the only way of arriving at a solution.

For example, the idea of using a Chaplinesque figure to sell IBM computers occurred some time ago to an art director of all people. Graphically oriented, he was intrigued by the juxtaposition of a human figure in a dark suit against a white background. The "little tramp" had a five-year run and sold millions of products. In similar vein, the thought of combining the luxury of leather upholstery and the scent of "new leather" (courtesy of Webcraft Technologies) in advertisements for Rolls-Royce (with the headline: "This, in essence, is Rolls-Royce") came up in a conversation between the executive vice president of the company (himself of creative bent) and the creative head of Della Femina, Travisano & Partners. They were having some scent-strip thoughts on behalf of a Perry Ellis fragrance (an agency client) and as advertising history would have it, one thing led to another.

Dealing with a *media supervisor* after you have just spent time with the creative people can be an eye-opening and perhaps even mind-boggling experience. It is hard to imagine that they are both on the same team. The media buyer has an exacting occupation with hard facts and numbers dominating the scene. A bewildering amount of data on circulation, exposure, costs, and other criteria on media effectiveness passes the desk of this executive. Nothing must escape his attention.

This person is likely to take a keen interest in the breakdown of the annual advertising budget, your marketing strategy,

An advertising agency may consist of anywhere from a few, up to three thousand people. Flow of work follows the same basic pattern, regardless of the size of organization. Client's instructions are passed on to account management, and then to various departments: "creative" (copy and art), research, media, and production.

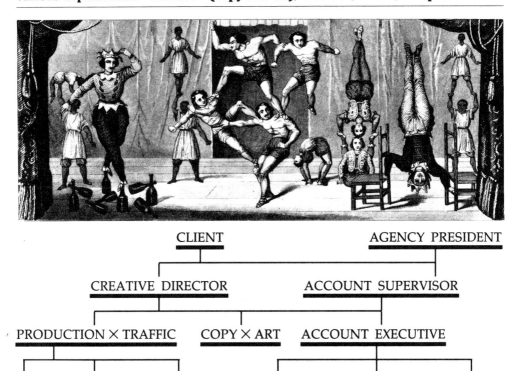

CLIENT   AGENCY PRESIDENT

CREATIVE DIRECTOR   ACCOUNT SUPERVISOR

PRODUCTION × TRAFFIC   COPY × ART   ACCOUNT EXECUTIVE

TV   PRINT   MEDIA   RESEARCH   LEGAL   CLERICAL

and time schedules. It is his job to design a media mix that best suits the purpose of getting your message to just the right people at minimum expense. In meetings that involve planning of advertising, participation by one or more media experts is absolutely essential. Without their input, no realistic budgetary allocations can be made.

The *production manager* of an agency tends to be a less frequent guest at clients' meetings. If he is there, it is usually after the fact; i.e. the advertising campaign has already been approved and is now in the production stage. The major focus of the production department in an agency is to follow through on client-approved storyboards and layouts. Perhaps he should be invited more often, for the production manager plays an important role in the final outcome of advertising—as the consumer will experience it.

The primary responsibility of the *print production department* is to oversee reproduction, typography, printing, binding. Their decisions involve such esoterics as choice of paper stock, reproduction methods (offset, letterpress, rotogravure, computer-generated), typefaces and colors (with the art director)—elements having a great deal to do with the final appearance of an ad. Most of all, they keep the production budget under control.

Just as complex is the task of the agency's *television and radio production department.* Unlike their counterparts in print production, broadcast production people often participate in the creation of a campaign from the outset. Their expertise is invaluable in casting, following up the audio, staging, creating special effects, editing, finding the right production house to execute the commercial, and making cost projections. Estimates on a television commercial are usually long and highly detailed.

Accompanying the production manager might be the **traffic supervisor** of the agency. This person keeps track of the work, making sure that deadlines are met. He deals with all the departments in an agency. While he is not expected to provide creative input at clients' meetings, he may yet prove to be a welcome addition. No one is better qualified to report on the exact status of a job than this administrator.

You may or may not encounter the **attorney** from the agency. He could be a member of the organization or be an outside counsel providing services on a retainer basis. This person can make important contributions in untangling the myriad legal problems an advertiser faces in today's marketplace. An attorney should be able to advise the client on validity of product claims, postal and other regulations that affect content of advertising, television and print censorship in the United States and other countries, protection of symbols, trademarks and copyrights, rules for contests and sweepstakes, special state regulations affecting sales promotions. In many agencies today, the legal department checks and approves *all* advertising. Much misunderstanding (and litigation) can be avoided this way.

It is better to work with a lawyer whose instincts propel him to suggest *alternatives* to problems. Legal precedents notwithstanding, court decisions are rarely based on absolutes. The law is a fluid, constantly changing entity reflecting current thoughts, and providing not one but usually a number of solutions to a given problem.

To Sum It Up

There are advantages as well as disadvantages to having your advertising done by an agency. Weigh both carefully, and decide on whatever suits you best. No two advertisers have exactly the same needs; do not rely on formula solutions.

To get the most out of your advertising agency, it is essential that you be familiar with all the "players" servicing your account. The key departments are administration, creative (art and copy), research, media (print and broadcast), production (print and broadcast), traffic, and legal. Their relative position in the power structure on the organization chart tells much about the agency's advertising philosophy.

ORGANIZATION BY FUNCTION

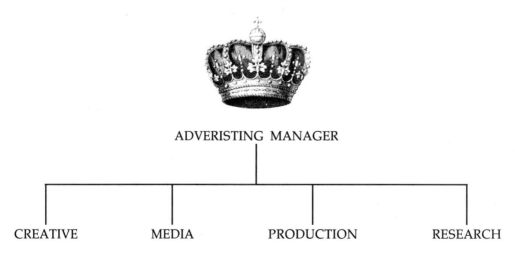

ADVERISTING MANAGER

CREATIVE MEDIA PRODUCTION RESEARCH

ORGANIZATION BY PRODUCT

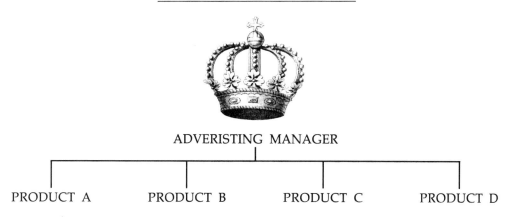

ADVERISTING MANAGER

| PRODUCT A | PRODUCT B | PRODUCT C | PRODUCT D |

ORGANIZATION BY END USER

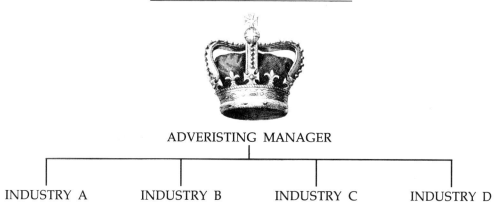

ADVERISTING MANAGER

| INDUSTRY A | INDUSTRY B | INDUSTRY C | INDUSTRY D |

ORGANIZATION BY GEOGRAPHICAL UNITS

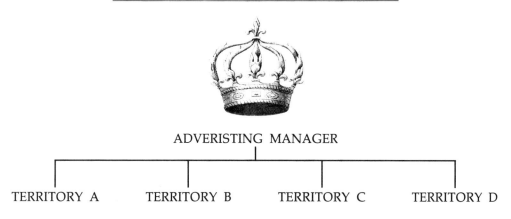

ADVERISTING MANAGER

| TERRITORY A | TERRITORY B | TERRITORY C | TERRITORY D |

In-house departments may be an adjunct to outside services (including advertising agencies) or an independent unit. They are organized to satisfy the needs of the parent corporation.

"ROUGHS"

"COMPREHENSIVES"

FINISHED PROOF

This magazine advertisement for Proctor & Gamble, prepared by Saatchi & Saatchi DFS Compton, journeyed through the agency in typical adlike fashion. Based on a specific creative platform and copy, the art director had first sketched out several "roughs" (in black and white). No attempt was made at this point to simulate the ad as it would eventually appear. A color comprehensive was drawn from this for a client presentation in this case. (Some agencies go from roughs right into finish.) Once approved, the layout was returned to both art *and* production, with much of the work farmed out to outside talent. Humorous illustration and lettering was done by one artist, product rendition by another. Type was set with two departments working in concert. At every step of the way traffic kept tally on progress to make sure all pieces came together on time and no deadlines were missed.

PROJECT INITIATION

- PROJECT TITLE

Date_____   Code No._____

Project Originator_____   Section_____

- SPECIFICATIONS   - COST ESTIMATES (including tax)

Quantity_____ No. of Colors___   Est. Production_____

Page Size_____ No. of Pages _____   Est. Art _____

Paper Stock_____   Est. Total _____

Cover Stock_____   - COMMODITY

Method of Printing _____   _____

Printer_____   _____

Composition_____   _____

Mechanical_____   _____

Packaging_____   - BUDGETARY REMARKS

Delivery to_____   _____

Transportation_____   _____

Mailing Requirements_____   _____

- DATES	Schedule	Actual	- PRODUCTION/SCHEDULE REMARKS
To Agency	_____	_____	_____
From Agency	_____	_____	_____
Revise Out	_____	_____	_____
Revise In	_____	_____	_____
OK Date	_____	_____	_____
Art Start	_____	_____	KEY
Art Finish	_____	_____	White, Section Mgr.
Prod. Start	_____	_____	Buff, Budget Control
Prod. Finish	_____	_____	Blue, Attach to Project
Dist. Start	_____	_____	Green, Production
Dist. Finish	_____	_____	Pink, Order & Inquiry
			Gray, Adv. Design Services.

All projects going through an advertising agency or a department are — or should be — accompanied by written records. This information is usually kept in a "job envelope" that acts as a point of reference of work in progress.

- INSTRUCTION COVERING ART PRODUCTION

_____
_____
_____
_____
_____
_____
_____
_____
_____
_____
_____
_____
_____
_____
_____
_____
_____
_____
_____
_____
_____

• ART

	Date out	Art rec.	Inv. rec.	Est. cost	Cost

STATUS REPORT

(NAME OF AGENCY OR COMPANY)   No._____

• PROJECT TITLE

Date_____   Code No._____

Present (agency, client, suppliers, etc.) _____

_____

_____

Place _____

_____

Topics _____

_____

_____

Instructions (type of work, general purpose, media, time schedule, plan for another meeting, approvals needed, comments by agency and clients, payments, firm commitments to be made at this point, etc.) _____

_____

_____

_____

_____

_____

_____

_____

_____

_____

Signed _____

Status reports are issued to reflect discussions with client. Copies are often sent to the advertisers to avoid future misinterpretations.

19

PRODUCTION ESTIMATE: PRINT MEDIA/COLLATERAL

Date: _____

Client/Division: _____ A/E _____ Job No.: _____

NOTE: This estimate is as of the above date; it is specifically agreed that the below estimates may change if specifications are materially altered. Client signed authorization is considered by agency as permission to initiate services and purchase materials listed below. Actual costs may vary by _____ % from estimated costs.

	Original Estimate	Revision #1	Revision #2	Total
Copy				
Layout				
Photography				
Finished Art				
Model Fees/Special Effect Required				
Retouching				
Lettering				
Mechanical				
Photostatting				
Prints, Velox, Dye Transf.				
Typography/Proofs				
Publication Materials				
Mats				
Printing				
Misc./Contingency Costs:				
TOTAL COSTS				
Sales Tax (1)				
Shipping				
Agency Commision/Fees (2)				
TOTAL, this Estimate				

A/E Approval: _____ Date: _____ Client Approval _____ Date: _____

(1) Applies to specific cost elements, per individual state sales tax laws.

(2) Determined by agency-client agreements.

Production estimates are filled out to keep costs under control along the way. They may be initiated after or even before layouts are prepared.

PRODUCTION ESTIMATE: BROADCAST

Date: _____

Client/Division:_____ A/E_____ Job No.: _____

NOTE: This estimate is as of the above date; it is specifically agreed that the below estimates may change if specifications are materially altered. Client signed authorization is considered by agency as permission to initiate services and purchase materials listed below. Actual costs may vary by _____ % from estimated costs.

	Original Estimate	Revision #1	Revision #2	Total
Artwork, internal agency				
Scriptwork, internal agency				
Music				
Talent fees				
Special Effects				
AFTRA, SAG Costs				
On-location or Studio costs:				
a.				
b.				
Tapes				
Prints				
Editing/Dubbing				
Travel/Lodging				
Shipping				
Misc./Contingency Costs:				
a.				
b.				
TOTAL COSTS				
Sales Tax (1)				
Agency Commision/Fees (2)				
TOTAL, this Estimate				

A/E Approval: _____ Date: _____ Client Approval _____ Date: _____

(1) Applies to specific cost elements, per individual state sales tax laws.

(2) Determined by agency-client agreements.

Especially important are cost projections made for complex television shootings. Allowance is made for a minimum of 10 percent contingency fee.

CLIENT APPROVAL

Date Revised:_____

(A/E: Complete this form for each individual client division being handled by agency).

Client/Division Name: _____; A/E Name:_____

City:_____; State _____; Zip:_____

Phone No.:_____; Agency Job No. Prefix:_____

Traffic information:

1. Adv. Mgr. name (or name of person primarily responsible for client advertising matters): _____Title: _____

2. Client approval information: list names/titles of all client personnel who must normally approve all or any portion of the acency's work (include names and addresses/phone numbers of persons not directly employed by the client -- such as attorneys, consultants, etc.).

Approver Names/Titles	Stages of Agency Output, or Specific Items Requiring each Person's Approval
_____	_____
_____	_____
_____	_____
_____	_____

3. Government or other non-client approval requirements (including legal approvals):

_____

4. Individual Job Cost Estimates:

_____ Required by client for all jobs.

_____ Required only when indicated by A/E on agency Job Order.

Almost all work requires approval by the advertiser, usually by several people, in management. Familiar to everyone is the chain of command, and the time needed for approvals.

3

What Every Advertiser Should Know About Agency Costs

Traditionally, advertising agencies worked on a commission basis; their income was based largely on the 15% commission they received from media for placing advertising—a rebate on the cost of space and time. In theory, the advertiser paid only for the creation and production of advertising. Had he made the media purchase directly, he would have had to pay full price ("gross"), receiving *no* discount by way of commission. In point of fact, the agencies would receive payment for generating business for the media much as does a realtor for selling a piece of real estate.

This method of compensation had been in effect for several decades and dominated the scene until fairly recently. But now it is beginning to show signs of becoming a relic of the past for reasons explained later in this chapter. According to a recent survey conducted by the Association of National Advertising, only 43% of its 282 members still derive most of their profits from "straight" 15% commission; an additional 28% said they used some percentage other than 15% for compensation, and that was "usually less than 15%." Other compensation methods are now replacing percentage-based remuneration—sometimes to the dismay of

large agencies (with multimillion dollar clients), and other times to the delight of small shops (with clients billing under $2 or $3 million).

Frets Graham Phillips, Chairman of Ogilvy & Mather, U.S., a veteran of many client/agency feuds regarding compensation methods: "Clients are asking for more, but trying to pay less." Robert Purdstein, DDB's Chief Financial Officer, agrees: "The commission we receive often falls short." But another, smaller agency, Hill, Holiday, Connors, Cosmopulos of Boston (where overhead has not yet reached the lofty heights of New York) chose from its very inception to bill its clients on a time-cost basis, and do away with commissions altogether. Over 90% of its clients went along with the idea. Interestingly enough, the agency not only enjoys earnings substantially over industry averages but also happens to be among the fastest growing in the industry.

Why the Change in Method of Financial Remuneration?

To say that clients are getting more sophisticated in their ability to evaluate advertising service would be too quick an answer — and probably an oversimplification of a complex issue. It is of course true that advertisers demand more accountability from their agencies today. New methods of setting budgets have been gaining popularity, methods that may not be set in concrete but nevertheless act as constraints on spending.

At the same time, and as if having a life of its own, the cost of advertising has gone up in every area, thus making more money available. Over $100 billion is spent on advertising in the United States, and almost double that on promotion, and the figure keeps rising near or over 10% a year. Double-digit inflation in the seventies made salaries shoot up in one of the most labor intensive industries in the country. Television production costs rose almost 100% in the last eight years, averaging close to $100,000 for a 30-second network commercial today. High-end spenders such as travel, appliance, automobile, fast-food, and soft drink advertisers are closer to $150,000 per shoot with some the-heck-with-the-expense clients having spent in excess of $1,000,000 in the last few years (Pepsi-Cola, Apple Computer). With the director's $10,000 per diem or more, and the fees charged by some celebrities, the cost of producing a spot may approach that of a $1\frac{1}{2}$-hour feature film made for theatrical distribution, and most certainly that of the average half hour television sitcom.

But most of the increase in advertising costs is due to the skyrocketing cost of media, especially airtime. Network rate increases have jumped as much as 20% in a single year. Rising rates, a change in the law that encourages media to pass on the 15% discount to any and all purchasers of space and time (including clients making a direct purchase), and general flexibility in media costs caused advertisers to reexamine the prevailing standard agency commission system. To stay competitive, agencies had to reduce their commission percentage as media spending went up.

If Not a Straight 15% Commission — Then What?

Here are the most often-used payment systems, some of which are new:

1. *Profit-sharing.* When net profits (whatever the source) reach a certain level, agencies and clients split the excess. Conversely, they share the down-side when profits take a turn for the worse.

2. *Cost-plus.* Under this system, the fee is based on handling the account plus a negotiated profit and overhead (usually 15% to 25%). Client is invoiced for all media and production expenses. The agency keeps tab of time spent on each job.

3. *Rebate.* Client is charged a minimum fee until the point is reached when commissions equal the fee, paying for agency expenses plus mutually agreed-upon profit. Commissions are then retained as a source of revenue and the fee is discontinued.

4. *Bonus based on sales results.* The reduction of standard 15% commission is made up by bonuses paid on the basis of sales results. Both agency and client share the rewards for work well done. Such an incentive plan works especially well in direct-response advertising, where it is possible to trace sales directly to advertising.

5. *Negotiated commission.* As mentioned previously, here the percentage of commission varies with the size of billing. The larger the billing, the less the percentage of the commission.

6. *Straight-service-fee basis.* Agency and client estimate the value of each job (i.e. designing a brochure, writing a series of television commercials, researching consumer attitudes). Commissions are rebated in full to the client.

7. *Commission plus service fees.* This is still the most popular system. Client is billed for all noncommissionable expenses plus a service fee that may be either 15% or 17.65% of the expenses. Agency keeps commission.

8. *Combination of two or more methods mentioned above.* Opportunities exist to develop a compensation package that satisfies both the client and the agency. Long-term goals may be taken into consideration from the viewpoint of both the agency and the client.

You Get What You Pay for — or Do You?

Shopping for agencies is not the same as bargain hunting in a store. Rarely are the differences in quality visible to the naked eye. Unless you know in advance what is being offered and, most of all, what it is *you* want and need, you may end up with services that aren't for you.

Just as few agencies offer exactly the same kind of work, either in terms of quantity or quality, client compensation agreements rarely follow the same pattern either. We will deal with the quality aspect in the next chapter. With the focus on financing, let us first break down the cost of doing business with an agency.

All agency services must be paid for by whatever method of compensation. With so many agencies losing part or all of their income traditionally handed over to them in the past by way of commission, the definition of *billable* and *nonbillable* costs ("charged" or "not to be charged") should be decided with reasonable accuracy between the client and his agency at the beginning of their working relationship. In the absence of a clear understanding, problems are sure to arise. Normally, the advertiser pays for the following:

Cost of Media. This usually means the gross charged by the media (i.e. "billing").

The agency passes on the net cost. The difference between gross and net constitutes the commission; i.e. $100,000 gross for media (paid by client, if so agreed) leaves the agency with a $15,000 commission, and this after paying a net of $85,000 for space or time.

Most media offer cash discounts for "prompt" (10 to 30 days) payments. The discount can run anywhere from 2% to 3% of the gross, depending on the time payment is made. In large purchases, this can mean a considerable saving. The agency should keep the client posted on the amount of discount and pass it on either in the way of credit or rebate.

Work Done Outside the Agency (Out-of-Pocket Costs). Not so long ago, agencies tried providing as many in-house facilities as it was possible for them. Some still do. Large, well-financed agencies can afford to maintain art studios, photostat machines, reproduction centers, typesetting and printing facilities, test kitchens, photographer's studio, film and video production all under one roof. (One agency in Chicago even offered complete overnight accommodations to its out-of-town clients, complete with showers and breakfast delivery.) To some small and medium-sized agencies, such add-on services may represent an additional profit center, especially if they happen to be located outside major cities or in foreign countries.

The trend, however, is to cut down on such amenities. For most agencies, it is becoming less economical to keep offering specialized services on a sustained basis, given the fickle nature of the business. Besides, there is less need today for one-stop shopping centers of creative services. Advertisers have grown sophisticated enough to know it is more economical to reach out for skilled help only when needed.

Illustrations and photographs are billed to the agency and usually passed on at cost to the advertiser. Rare is the agency that prepares finished art (art ready for reproduction) in-house. It would be prohibitively expensive to have an accomplished illustrator or photographer on staff. Even fewer in number are the agencies using their own staff to produce television or radio commercials from beginning to end.

Merchandising and Advertising Allowances. Payments made to retailers for advertising for specific periods of time (co-op advertising), handling allowances (for handling merchandise requiring special attention, such as coupon redemption), discounts, and other sales incentives are the responsibility of the advertiser. If the agency is required to follow through on such activity, the client is billed for time.

If at all possible, the client should pay media by the due date. The agency should not be asked to finance its client's purchases or develop the reputation of being a deadbeat through asking for postponements. Media costs can run into several millions of dollars, and an agency's credit rating and "recognition" by media (perception of the agency) are based to a large degree on its ability to pay media on time.

Work Done Inside the Agency Other than Developing and Placing Advertising. An agency may perform a variety of advertising-related services that, as pointed out before, are usually charged to the client on the basis of time spent on them or by way of negotiated service fee. Such items as writing and designing a financial report, brochure, point-of-sale pieces, package, trademark, and direct mail—all fall into this category. Many agencies have a wide range of talent on hand, particularly in art and copy. It is best to discuss cost of agency services (as compared to other sources) before placing the assignments, since hourly rates can run high in a high-salaried business.

In the event the agency charges straight commission, the client (unless specified otherwise) does not pay for:

Selecting and Purchasing Media. This is a prime function of the agency. Monitoring purchased space or time is also an agency function; i.e. getting tearsheets from publications, or affidavits of performance (air-check) from television and radio stations that a message or program appeared on schedule.

Planning Advertising Strategy. This may involve a great deal of research, analysis, and writing of reports. While it is possible that the agency would keep time sheets on these activities (though unlikely since much of this takes place among members of top management), costs are not customarily passed on to the client.

Office Overhead. Staff salaries, office rent including equipment and furniture, and other normal expenses of running a business are not billable.

Creative Services. Conceptualizing and developing campaigns is the responsibility of the agency. Art directors, copywriters, creative supervisors, and others involved in the creation of ads are part of agency overhead. So is the preparation of layouts or storyboards or any form of creative recommendations made to the client. Unless agreed differently, it is the agency's loss if the work gets rejected.

The advertiser may or may not (depending on specific arrangements made between client and agency) be paying for:

Travel and Entertainment. This can be one of the grayest of all areas. It is usually the account executive who picks up the check when taking a client to lunch or dinner (or more in keeping with the times, to breakfast). But who pays for the account executive's trip to the client's overseas office if it was the client who requested it?

Research. The project may be the client's idea; it may be conducted to answer more of a marketing problem (product research, pricing policies, sales audits) than one that involves advertising (copy pretesting, readership studies, focus group interviews). It is best to be as specific as possible on this point in the original agreement between parties.

Legal Services. It depends on the understanding. A lot has to do with the nature of services. Do they concern advertising? Or the myriad other legal problems that really are not the agency's business? Patent application? Disputes between the advertiser and the post office? Insurance claims?

"Comprehensives." The rendering of a "tight" storyboard by a professional sketch artist (or art studio) can cost as much as $100 a frame. An "experimental photograph" in a proposed print ad can run into $1,000 or more. It is best to decide beforehand as to which party will be responsible for paying such indulgences, as well as for an animated storyboard (animatics), a "demo reel," a dye-transfer color print, typeset layouts, a videotape made of a professional model.

Other Miscellaneous Out-of-Pocket Expenses. These in some instances are passed on to the client, but by no means always. Entertainment of manufacturers and distributors doing business with the client, shipping and mailing of material, corrective advertising, retrieval of information of interest to the client (articles, references, etc.), long-distance calls (especially when made to overseas offices), concepts for new products or services fall under this heading.

A good rule of thumb to remember concerning agency compensation is that if media commissions do not cover costs and a reasonable profit, the agency must look to extra-service charges to make up the difference.

Naturally, the size of the advertiser's billing is a major criterion. Obviously, media spending of larger clients (over $10 million) leaves enough of a profit margin for the agency, with less need to charge for labor. Conversely, a client not heavily involved in media spending must find ways to pay for services other than through the usual commission route.

What Every Advertiser Should Know About Agency Overhead

Agencies spend between 50% and 70% of their income on employee compensation, be that in form of salary or bonuses, stock options, and other perks. The saying that "our overhead goes down with the elevators at the end of each office day" is based on more than a modicum of truth.

The proportion of salaries runs even higher in some agencies. If you find that is the case in your agency, be on your guard. The organization might be on less than solid financial ground. Either it is paying higher-than-average salaries to its employees (particularly its top management) or it is indifferent to showing a loss. In either case, it is a sign of poor financial planning. The day of reckoning may be not far and you, the client, could be left holding the bag. In some extreme cases, you may even discover some of your payments to media and various suppliers have yet to reach their destination.

The billing-to-personnel ratio (income based on media and service charges per employee) should be approximately $375,000 to $400,000 in an agency. With the ratio based on individuals directly involved with the account (account executives, creatives, research, media, etc.) the figure could be closer to $500,000. In that case, an agency "billing" $10 million would have anywhere from 20 to 40 people on staff, taking into account clerical help.

The smaller the agency, the more people it must proportionately employ in order to properly service its clients. An agency billing only $1 million may find it must have five to ten people on staff. But agencies with annual billings of $500 million or more (Young & Rubicam, Saatchi & Saatchi Worldwide, Ted Bates

Worldwide, J. Walter Thompson Company, Ogilvy & Mather Worldwide, just to mention a few) can — and do — "make it" with less than 3 (usually, higher paid) employees per $1 million billing. Several well-known agencies in New York manage to produce consistently outstanding advertising with less than 1 employee per $1 million in billing. Not surprisingly, they tend to hire people with long and noteworthy professional track records.

(It should be added here that these figures should be handled with circumspection. Some agencies make it their policy to farm out much of their work, both creative and noncreative, thus playing havoc with industrial averages. Others follow a program just the reverse.)

Salaries run high in the advertising agency business. As a rule, the larger the agency, the higher the take-home pay. Billing size of organization is a key factor in setting pay scales as well as bonuses. The highest-paid positions are (in this order in most cases): CEO/president, creative department head, account department head, creative director, media department head. It is interesting to note that the salaries of creative heads are often at or near the level of that of the CEO/president of the agency. In some of the smaller agencies, creative heads actually surpass presidents in salary. This again shows the value put on creative talent in the industry, and since creative talent can often double its salary by changing employers, the average tenure of such people is the shortest among the better-paid employees in advertising — less than four years.

The East is the highest-paying region for nearly all job categories, with the Midwest and West following. The Southwest pays its marketing executives well in companies but lags behind the East in the advertising sector. The lowest-paying jobs are in the Southwest.

Advertising agency staffers often earn higher salaries than those they serve, bringing about a situation where the executive entrusted to pass judgment on their work, like the advertising manager or the sales director in a company, may earn considerably less than the person who submits the work. One can only contemplate the psychological consequences of such a relationship in a culture that tends to measure personal worth on basis on income.

Incentive bonuses are paid on top of salaries, normally at the end of the year. As in many other businesses, rewards are often meted out for beyond-the-call-of-duty performances. Such payments may run from 1% to 50%, with an average of 25% of base salary, contingent on gains in "new business" and increases in current billings.

Other perks for members of top management range from the usual fare of health and life insurance packages, stock options, and supplemental retirement benefits, to such cabala as automobiles (over 80% of CEOs travel on company-paid wheels), pieds-à-terre in the city, country club membership dues, trips to faraway places (for purposes of study and research and therefore tax deductible), clothing and beauty allowances (including dry cleaning), paternity leaves, and even "crisis counseling."

Nor are agency executives reluctant to include under "business costs" a wide spectrum of golden parachute clauses. Employees enjoying six-figure salaries usually look to carefully drafted employment contracts to provide peace of mind in a business not known for its tranquility. "He who has, gets" is the maxim. Agreements may run from two to five years, and for the most part favor the employee, not the employer. While it is true that such documents usually include a "noncompetitive clause" — keeping the employee from *soliciting* accounts held by the agency up to two years following his leaving his job — that is but a small price to pay for peace of mind. He cannot be fired except for "reasonable cause" — a definition that defies strict interpretation. He must be paid, even in the face of lost business. From the employer's point of view, non-competitive clauses are difficult to enforce; the law cannot keep a disgruntled client with the agency and tell him where to take his business.

Then, too, with the spreading of corporate mergers and takeovers the price of executive buy-outs can be stratospheric. Someone has to pick up the bill, perhaps even clients.

The second-largest fixed expense of an advertising agency is rent. This may run anywhere from 5% to 15% of operating expense, depending on location, type of office space, and most of all, the agency's willingness to pay for the psychological payback of a pleasant working environment.

Real estate comes high in the business districts of large cities. Yet it is here most advertising agencies prefer to stake out their claim. Neighborhood has an important effect on clients. For an agency to exist in a warehouselike environment would be something like a lady going to an opening night at the opera in khaki coveralls — unless it wants to make cheap chic its creative trademark.

Office rents are highest in the East. In the business section, space costs about $25 per square foot in Chicago, $28 in Los Angeles, $22 in San Francisco, $21 in Boston, and $15 in Houston and Dallas. At this moment, Denver is at the bottom of the list with $10 a square foot.

According to a survey conducted by real estate investment advisors Richard Ellis, Inc., "cost of occupancy" (rent, common area maintenance, taxes and miscellaneous operating expenses) in New York has gone up almost tenfold in the last 15 years or so. In the "uptown" area of the city (north of 42nd Street), cost of space runs anywhere from $40 to $125, with an average of about $65 per square foot. Choice locations command extra premiums, with Madison Avenue no longer the only place to be. Park, Third, Fifth carry the same prestige. D'Arcy Masius Benton & Bowles are moving to Broadway. And BBDO, Interpublic Group of Companies, N. W. Ayer, Time-Life, McGraw-Hill, CBS, ABC, NBC are making the Avenue of the Americas and the Fifties the new hub of the nation's communication business.

To beat the high cost of sitting in a spacious office in the center of New York, several agencies have moved to other sections in town, even "downtown" near the Village, So-Ho, and No-Ho, which, incidentally, are home to some of the busiest and most talented photographers, illustrators, and show-biz people. Not surprisingly, the presence of agencies has given birth to a number of haute cuisine eating establishments, and groggeries catering to the young and not-so-young after-office-hours crowd.

Other business expenses in running an advertising agency come from miscellaneous sources. Office supplies (including art supplies, a relatively large expense), telephone, postage, depreciation (computers can be a major item), entertainment and travel, cost of borrowing money (i.e. to pay media) can consume another 5% to 10% of agency revenue.

Left over are profits. They average between 10% and 15%, but exceptions abound. Smaller agencies are often willing to forego earnings in the beginning. The bottom line rarely stays put even among the majors. The fourth largest agency in the world, J. Walter Thompson, made less than 9% profit on its revenues not long ago — satisfying perhaps but less than sensational. For comparison, when the average after-tax profit of the Fortune 500 drops below 10%, financial analysts shake their heads in dismay, and stockholders run for cover.

There is of course a subtle difference between profit and profitability, as any business executive (or investor) knows only too well. *Profit* is the actual return received after all operating expenses have been met. *Profitability*, on the other hand, connotes the ability to make profit — hopes, dreams, promise of a future. Much depends on the philosophy of management. It may choose to focus its energies on accumulating profits, perhaps to leverage the cash purchase of other companies, or increase its own worth for a buy-out. It may choose to compound the original sum by means of investments, or simply buy security by having money in the bank. At the other end of the spectrum is the agency willing to forego such long-range ambitions and disburse its year-end earnings by way of raises and tax-deductible bonuses.

To put it in plain business English: It may be the agency that reaps the financial benefits at the end of the fiscal year. *Or* its people may. Either way, it amounts to the same thing. Profit is profit by whatever name.

Twenty-Six Ways to Keep Your Advertising Budget on Course

Ask yourself these basic questions *prior* to signing an advertising budget:

Is this project really necessary?

Is it really necessary that the project should be done at this time?

Is there a simpler solution to the same problem?

Is the decision to run the advertisement an emotional or a rational one?

Am I being too subjective in my evaluation—or just not subjective enough?

Here is how you can make your advertising dollar go further:

1. Begin with a basic advertising strategy. If the premise of the campaign is wrong, creative execution will not set it right.

2. Basic direction eliminates expensive trial-and-error method—a "fishing expedition."

3. Keep reminding yourself that a plan—no matter how firm—is still only a plan. It can—and should be allowed to—change shape on its way to the finish.

4. Don't ask for laboriously executed "comps" unless you have a large surplus of money you need to get rid of. Tight renderings can discourage artists, photographers, television directors, actors, and other creative talent from making contributions along the way. Meanwhile, you're paying.

5. Don't wait until the eleventh hour to get the work done. Pushing panic buttons can be fun, but not all people are able to do their best under pressure. You will be paying extra for their displeasure.

6. Explain in detail what you have in mind. Invite the creatives to hear you firsthand, if you wish. But never, never offer a specific creative solution. Dwell on the problem instead.

7. Unless you enjoy meetings, have as few of them as possible. Try combining two or three separate sessions into a central one. Or try a conference phone call. Or circulate a memo. Meetings, too, can add to the overhead—the agency's and yours.

8. Institute steps of approval. That way, you stop small mistakes from growing into big. Advertising strategy comes first. Research, media, budgeting, and creative follow. Production is last on the line.

9. Get estimates before you embark on a project—any project. Build in a minimum of 10% contingency fee. Go through the numbers carefully with those who present them.

10. Don't be afraid to suggest names of suppliers with whom you yourself have worked. You just may know a printer who has always come through in the past—at less than half the cost of the agency's. Or a typographer. Or

an engraver. Tact counts, however. The agency probably has a network of vendors all its own. You're one foot in their territory.

11. Compare costs. Shop around town for, say, a display manufacturer. Then show the estimate to your agency.

12. On any large job, insist on at least three bids. But keep in mind, the cheapest is not always the best value. Nor does the highest bid guarantee quality.

13. If you work in a large city — like New York — find out how much it would cost to have the job done out of town.

The figures may pleasantly surprise you.

14. Keep experimentation down to the minimum. Don't ask the agency to submit a half-dozen "suggestions." Or one campaign after another. Don't get into the habit of trying to touch all bases. The agency may start charging you every time it picks up a pencil, just for spite. Or its people will spend much of their energies hating you.

15. Be tough on the agency about getting the best possible deal from various media. Even giants will go out of their way to give you a deal (except the *New York Times,* which can afford not to). Rate cards are the beginning, not

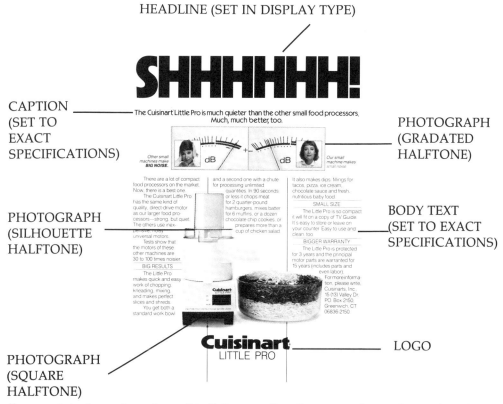

HEADLINE (SET IN DISPLAY TYPE)

SHHHHHH!

CAPTION (SET TO EXACT SPECIFICATIONS)

The Cuisinart Little Pro is much quieter than the other small food processors. Much, much better, too.

PHOTOGRAPH (GRADATED HALFTONE)

PHOTOGRAPH (SILHOUETTE HALFTONE)

BODY TEXT (SET TO EXACT SPECIFICATIONS)

Cuisinart
LITTLE PRO

LOGO

PHOTOGRAPH (SQUARE HALFTONE)

Every print ad consists of graphic "elements"—the pieces that make up the whole. The cost of each can be estimated before completion of the ad, as can the agency's overhead (art direction, preparation of "mechanical," presentation), production (engraving, typography, printing), and artwork (illustration or photography, retouching). Layout serves as a basis for estimates made by art and production departments, as well as outside suppliers.

vo: Not all artists paint, write, or play musical instruments.
Eight-hundred-flowers. Phone 24 hours a day, 7 days a week.

vo: This commercial interruption is brought to you . . .
. . . on behalf of the people who make commercial interruptions . . .
. . . as a reminder that without commercial interruptions . . .
. . . there wouldn't be anything . . .

(SFX: CLICK)

. . . to interrupt

SILENCE

The notion that the effectiveness of an advertisement is directly related to its budget has little basis of fact. It is the concepts that lend strength to the message, more so than "production values." Illustrating the point are the commercials created by Chiat/Day for 800-FLOWERS and Fallon McElligott for the AAAA's.

Imagine this page is the Atlantic Ocean.
See those black lines? That's us.

Those black lines going back and forth across the page are the number of times TWA flies across the Atlantic each week.

About four hundred times in fact. (Don't count them, they didn't all fit.)

That, by the way, is more than anyone else.

And on April 28th, we even discover three brand-new places, Copenhagen, Geneva and Bombay.

(The latter, you may feel, is something of an exciting departure from our traditional destinations.)

You'll be able to get to Copenhagen and Geneva from J.F.K. every day. And to Bombay three times a week.

We're also starting a new Gateway to Europe at St. Louis which will make your life a great deal easier if you happen to live in the West and want to go

nonstop to London or Paris or even Frankfurt.

And we'll have a new nonstop from J.F.K. to Tel Aviv. And from June 15th, a nonstop to Munich, and a 747 on our nonstop to Amsterdam.

That, of course, is on top of all the existing ones.

Twenty-eight opportunities a week to get to London from J.F.K. Twenty-one to get to Paris. Fourteen to get to Rome, Frankfurt and Athens. Twelve to get to Madrid. Daily flights from Boston to London, Rome and Paris. Three times a week to Cairo and Tel Aviv. The list is endless.

The only important thing you really need to know is that we fly nonstop from the U.S. to more places in Europe than any other airline.

Then, next time you need to go, all those little black lines will begin to make a lot of sense.

LEADING THE WAY. TWA.

Here, Fallon McElligott once again proves that inexpensive art work can go a long way if used imaginatively — here by way of a full-page newspaper ad.

How much did the art cost in these ads? Nothing for the ad conceived for MBank by The Richards Group. Very little for the ads made for The Richmond Newspapers by Westbrook Advertising Agency; art director Carolyn Tye used her own fancy-free but attention-getting "scribbles"— an excellent choice.

Hill Design Group practices what it preaches in its own house-logo — at low cost.

the end. They make great conversation pieces. (See Chapter 11.)

16. Use a media-buying service if that will help you save money at no sacrifice in quality. But consider the agency's feelings, too. You are moving in their most important revenue source. To keep them as friends, you may have to devise a payment plan that will make up for their loss — both psychological and financial.

17. Try working with media directly now and then. Their representatives may be willing to sell you net. As mentioned before, no law says they cannot do so.

18. Consider farming out work to *suppliers* other than to the agency. (More about this in Chapter 5.) But again — let your agency know what you are doing, and why.

19. Look into the advantages — and disadvantages — of having more than one agency.

20. Consider the economic benefits of consolidating all your advertising in one agency.

21. If you are a global advertiser, think about the possibility of "global advertising" — the same campaign in different countries. But don't jump to a quick conclusion. (More about this in Chapter 10.)

22. Meet with your agency at their office. For one person to travel *to* could be less expensive than, say, for six persons to travel *from*.

23. Drinks on the house are never on the house. Go easy on entertainment, even if it means being entertained less frequently.

24. Find out about advertising other than in commissionable mass media. For example, promotion, direct mail, publicity.

25. Work out compensation arrangements *beforehand*. Not after the fact.

26. Get it in writing.

To Sum It Up

Less than half the agencies are compensated by way of the full 15% media commission system today. Other payment systems used are (a) fees based on the advertiser's profits and sales, (b) the cost of servicing the account, (c) predetermined maximum or minimum income for the agency, or (d) combinations of the above. The arrangements can be quite specific; they are negotiated beforehand. Percentages vary with the size of the account, media purchases, need for collateral services, in-depth requirements other than "making ads" (research, marketing, merchandising, direct response, legal, etc.), salaries of agency personnel and other overhead, and even such intangible yet important factors as prestige of the advertiser or the advertising agency.

There are many ways to minimize costs of agency-produced advertising. Again, understanding the inner workings of an agency can be immensely helpful. An agency should be held fully accountable for the services it provides; clients must ensure a cushion of profits for all included; greed on either side can prove to be counterproductive. As much time as needed should be spent on planning. Hit-or-miss advertising is the costliest of all.

4

How to Choose the Agency Right for You

Few decisions affect the sales—and perhaps, the success—of a consumer-oriented company as much as the choice of the agency to handle its advertising. Increase in sales can be dramatic and immediate. As an example, take three outstanding campaigns currently running at the time of this writing. All three have found their place in SRI Research Center's coveted top ten in the Adwatch Survey of *Advertising Awareness* (regularly published in *Advertising Age*), have reaped their share of awards, and have attracted new business to the agencies that brought them forth. But most important—from the advertiser's point of view—all three have generated a very substantial boost in sales.

E. Gallo's Bartles & Jaymes is one such success story. Only a few months after appearing on television, the two laconic, straight-faced, but compelling bucolics, Fred and Ed—dreamed up by Hal Riney's advertising agency—had pushed the brand into the number one position in the $700 million wine cooler market just as the industry was approaching its most competitive peak.

The story of "I Heard It Through the Grapevine" commercials is equally impressive. Scenes of shuffling raisins shown in claymationed dancing created by Will Vinton Productions first appeared in September. Sales went up 1 percent in October after 12 flat months. In November they jumped 5%; in December they went even higher than that. Sighed Bob Pinney, ad director of the Raisin Board: "Wow. Eat your heart out, Coca-Cola. We're beating the guys who're spending ten times more than we are." (Coke placed second on the "Top-of-the-Mind" list.)

Isuzu's "He's a Liar" campaign showed Joe Isuzu (David Leisure) as a bubbling archetypical car salesman espousing the cause. Sales raked up a 25% gain compared with the same period a year before, while during the same eight months total car import sales dropped 2%—and all this was accomplished on a relatively modest advertising budget (for a nationally sold automobile) of $28 million.

Production costs of these campaigns were not particularly high; some even below average. What caused them to produce such spectacular results was the "big idea" behind each of them and the excellence of execution—contributions of the clients' advertising agencies.

Selecting an Agency; Give It Some Thought

Because the choice of an agency is so important, allow yourself enough time for making the best possible decision. Meet the agency more than once, and talk to those who have taken their business there. Mistakes can be costly, both in human terms and in sales. In this chapter, we will discuss some of the factors that are part of the agency selection process. The one you choose will be your business partner, it is hoped, for a long time to come.

Agency Names — Where to Find Them

The easiest — and often the quickest — way to find the "right" agency is through its own creative display in print or on the air. If you like what you see or hear, the sponsor of the commercial will help you to identify the agency responsible for the campaign. Or the television station will tell you.

Word-of-mouth recommendations are another dependable source. As in any other business, customer — in this case, client — satisfaction is the best of all reassurances.

Not every advertising agency is able to take any account that comes its way, however. Account conflicts or other problems may stand in the way. In that case, the agency may well recommend another (or several others) of compatible philosophy; i.e. a "creative" shop will suggest an agency of like talent, a marketing-oriented agency will recommend one with marketing sophistication. It is said that in its heyday, Doyle Dane Bernbach was one of the major protagonists of the very organizations it helped to spawn. Clients looking for the "DDB touch" but too small for the now-large agency would be steered toward smaller shops founded by former students of the great William Bernbach.

A list of member agencies is also available from the American Association of Advertising Agencies (New York) and As-

sociation of National Advertisers (New York). While neither organization is willing to set itself up as an ex officio recommender of agencies, both are a source of a wealth of information about the business in general as well as the capabilities, records, and financial status of specific member agencies.

A comprehensive compilation of advertising agencies is published in the *Standard Directory of Advertising Agencies* — the "Agency Red Book." This nearly 1,000-page volume is available three times a year (about 25% of the information changes with every issue) from National Register Publishing Company, Skokie, Illinois. The names of over 4,000 agencies appear in these books, along with annual billings of every agency, accounts, association memberships, branch offices, and key personnel. Included also is a breakdown of gross billing by media (newspapers, magazines, transit, collateral, etc.).

AdWeek Agency Directory lists the names of 5000 ad agencies, 1,500 public relations firms, and 300 media buying services. It is available in six regional editions and a one volume national edition. Included are regional clubs and associations, as well as charts of the top-billing worldwide agencies. Also published by National Register Publishing Company is the *Standard Directory of Advertisers* — the "Advertiser's Red Book." The names of some 20,000 advertisers are listed in these volumes, along with their annual advertising appropriations, key personnel, and the agencies that service them. Supplements are issued monthly to keep the reader up to date.

Even more complete is AdWeek's up-to-date data base of more than 200,000 companies and names, on magnetic tape or printed mailing lists. For information call Adweek in New York City.

A checklist of agencies also appears in other books, if perhaps in less detail. Already mentioned is the *Creative Black Book*, published every year by Friendly Press, New York. Names of agencies —

accompanied by samples of their work (often in color)—are shown in *The One Show* (One Club for Art and Copy, Inc., New York); *Advertising Agency Register* (Association of National Advertisers, New York) which also issues a videotape presentation; *Source Directory: Direct Response Advertising Agencies* (Direct Marketing Association, New York); and *The Agency Book* (Gaving Brackenridge & Company). All of these books are avail-able in most large business libraries and in the New York Public Library.

Several times a year, *Advertising Age* issues a well-researched compilation of about 700 agencies, complete with their recent histories. In addition to its special East, Southeast, Midwest, Southwest, and West editions, *AdWeek* also publishes its own "Agency Report Card" covering six categories that assess agency trade records over the past year.

One of the most efficient ways to find an agency is by finding out about their work in print and television. Campaigns shown here were created by Hal Riney & Partners and Hill Holliday Connors Cosmopulos — not coincidentally, the two fastest-growing agencies in the business.

COCAINE

©1987 DDB Needham Worldwide Inc.

Public service campaigns often attract the finest talents in the field, eager to do their best for less exacting non-profit clients. Sponsored by the AAAA's and executed by various agencies — these by Needham Harper Worldwide — anti-drug ads have appeared in over 2,000 newspapers thus far. They speak eloquently of the ability of the agency — once the "creative" is let out of the closet.

Accounts in Review

BUDGET	CLIENT/BRAND	LOCATION	INCUMBENT	CONTENDERS	DECISION DATE

$100 million	**General Motors' Saturn Corp.**	Troy, Mich.	New account	Tatham-Laird & Kudner/Chicago
				Leo Burnett/Chicago
				D'Arcy Masius Benton &
				  Bowles/St. Louis, N.Y.
				N W Ayer/N.Y.
				Hill, Holliday, Connors,
				  Cosmopulos/Boston
				Dailey & Associates/L.A.
					May

$70 million	**E. & J. Gallo Winery**	Modesto, Calif.	Hal Riney & Partners/S.F.	Dailey & Associates/L.A. Levine, Huntley, Schmidt and Beaver/N.Y. Wieden & Kennedy/Portland, Ore.	Undetermined
$20 million	**Holiday Inns Inc.**	Memphis, Tenn.	BJK&E/N.Y.	Young & Rubicam/N.Y. Ogilvy & Mather/N.Y. N W Ayer/N.Y.	Undetermined
$20 million	**Revlon Inc.**	New York	BJK&E/N.Y.	Young & Rubicam/N.Y. BBDO/N.Y. Della Femina, Travisano & Partners/N.Y.	Undetermined
$17 million	**New York State Lottery**	New York	McCaffrey and McCall/N.Y.	McCaffrey and McCall/N.Y. J. Walter Thompson/N.Y. Grey Advertising/N.Y. BJK&E/N.Y. DMB&B/N.Y. DDB Needham New York	Late March

$16 million	**Uniroyal-Goodrich**	Akron, Ohio	Young & Rubicam/Detroit	Meldrum and
				  Fewsmith/Cleveland
				Griswold Advertising/Cleveland and
				  Ross Roy/Bloomfield Hills, Mich.
				Wyse Advertising/Cleveland
				Beaumont Bennett/N.Y.
					March

$15 million	**Pizza Hut creative**	Dallas	Ogilvy & Mather/Dallas	Undetermined	May
$12-15 million	**Scott Paper Co.**	Philadelphia	BBDO/N.Y. and J. Walter Thompson/N.Y.	Ally & Gargano/N.Y. The Bloom Cos./N.Y. HHCC/Boston Warwick Advertising/N.Y. Weightman Advertising/ Philadelphia	June
$10-12 million	**Montgomery Ward broadcast and print creative**	Chicago	Young & Rubicam/Chicago	Undetermined	March
$10 million	**New York State Department of Economic Development**	Albany, N.Y.	Wells, Rich, Greene/N.Y.	DMB&B/N.Y. Grey Advertising/N.Y. Lintas:New York J. Walter Thompson/N.Y. Wells, Rich, Greene/N.Y.	March
$10 million	**Ralston Purina's Rice, Wheat and Corn Chex**	St. Louis	Wells, Rich, Greene/N.Y.	Wells, Rich, Greene/N.Y. Ally & Gargano/N.Y. Scali, McCabe, Sloves/N.Y. HDM/N.Y. McKinney & Silver/Raleigh, N.C. Avrett, Free & Ginsberg/N.Y.	Spring
$7-10 million	**S.C. Johnson's Agree, L'Envie Parfum hair-care products**	Racine, Wis.	J. Walter Thompson/Chicago	Foote, Cone & Belding/Chicago Lotas Minard Patton McIver/N.Y.	March
$5 million	**Ralston Purina's Meow Mix**	St. Louis	Inactive	DDB Needham Chicago Gardner Advertising Co./St. Louis Martin Marshall Jaccoma Mitchell/N.Y.	Undetermined

Let it not be said that advertising is a dull business. Trade journals keep a close watch on accounts on the move — the slightest tremor may signal an earthquake. Published regularly are reports such as this appearing in ADWEEK.

The Art of Listening to a New Business Presentation

A new business presentation may consist of a single three- to four-hour session. More often than not, however, it takes more time than that to hire an agency with the new business presentation itself only the beginning of a long-drawn-out process. Clients may wish to interview all key people in the agency, sometimes only one or a few at a time. Elaborate questionnaires precede hiring the agency. The information gathered may cover a number of factors. The most important are:

Size of agency

Location (headquarters or branch office?)

International capabilities

Research expertise

Strength in depth

Ability to provide auxiliary services

Willingness to accept work a la carte

Method of problem solving

Work flow through the organization

Business gained and lost

Growth record

Number, size, and type of clients

Agency philosophy

Experience in certain product/service categories (but do not base your selection on this factor alone)

Management background

Record and reputation (media, creative)

Media mix

Financial stability (credit rating, prompt payment of bills, discounts passed on to clients, accounting practices followed)

Possible account conflicts

Compensation methods

The $100 million U. S. Army account presented more than 125 questions to the five agencies it invited to solicit the account, and that in addition to the 120 minutes it allowed each agency to make its presentation.

Some agencies are especially skilled in making new-business presentations. Among them are the more established ones, with long histories on a variety of accounts. Ogilvy & Mather, one of the best-known agencies in the world, has sample reels tailored for clients from different industries. Other agencies shape their portfolios to best meet clients' particular needs and temperament. A "creative" client would see the best creative work. Market-oriented clients would see well-thought-out market-oriented advertising campaigns.

Here are a few tips with generous helpings from Whit Hobbs, an advertising consultant with years of experience listening to agencies putting their best foot forward:

1. Keep your list down to three or four when looking for an agency. Maybe five. (Association of National Advertisers recommends a maximum of six to eight agencies narrowed down from a preliminary list of ten to fifteen.) Check client lists carefully; make sure at the outset there are no conflicts.

2. Keep your selection committee at a manageable number.

3. Have a pad in front of you to take notes.

4. Insist that the agency give you an agenda before the meeting.

5. Spend some time indoctrinating each agency. Be fair. Present a white paper, spelling out all the agency needs to know.

6. Give all candidates a month to prepare for the presentation.

7. Schedule meetings at the agency, not your offices. Your own conference room may not be the best place after all. Too many interruptions make concentration difficult.

8. Two or three presentations a day will probably be all you can handle if yours is a long attention span.

9. Discourage the agency from spending too much time on its past history. That's the easiest part of making a presentation. You are there to find out what the agency will do for *you*.

10. Between one and two hours should be sufficient for a meeting. Leave enough time for questions and answers.

11. Have a score sheet ready for use. Grade your agency's performance as well as its ability to work with people at your end.

12. A good rule: Do not discuss a presentation immediately after it is over. Thank the agency people for the good work and tell them when they can expect a decision.

And Now, a Few Caveats

1. Slickness in execution — graphic technique and writing style — is one thing. Substance — the presence of a solid concept — is quite another.

2. The larger the agency, the more it will have in the way of a track record. But remember that bigger does not always mean better.

3. Listen to sales success stories carefully. Was it the creative excellence that made it all happen? Or sheer media weight? Did distribution create demand for the product? An inspired client? Outside talent making contributions?

4. Top management present at the initial presentation may or may not actually serve the account. A client once told of Marion Harper (past president of McCann-Erickson and a legend in his time): "Yes, I did see the guy at our new business presentation. He was impressive as hell. I met him again in the bathroom of the agency about five years after. The only one in my company who saw him more than once."

5. Treat creative stars with respect, but not awe. Wait and see how they will do on *your* account. Only God is omniscient.

6. Did you sense the overwhelming presence of a "big idea" at the presentation? Or were you rather taken by polished execution? Sleep on it. Then the next day ask yourself what it is you still remember. Your product? Or the ad itself? Remember, it is a product you want to sell, not advertising.

7. Don't confuse the agency's encyclopedic knowledge of your product or your market with their genuine creative insights. Sometimes it is difficult to tell the difference between the two. Look at it this way: One can be acquired. The other one is much harder to come by. As we said earlier, you want your agency to supply you with advertising ideas. Not with information you already know. "Right brain, meet left brain."

Rules of Etiquette. Each agency should be told about the decision before any announcement is made to the press. Notify the winner only after you have told the others that you are sorry but they are no longer in the running. A follow-up letter may be the best way to handle this delicate issue.

The Association of National Advertisers suggests this example of a polite rejection letter:

We appreciate the very fine presentation made by *(name of agency)* to *(name of client)* management on *(date)* and regret to advise you that we have decided not to pursue the possibility of a client-agency relationship any further at this time.

Following our completion of the agency selection process, we will be available to discuss the reasoning behind this decision in detail, should you so desire. This is expected to be some time shortly after *(date)*. In the meantime, we would appreciate it if you would keep this matter confidential.

Thanks again for the opportunity to know you, your associates and your work.

Creative Presentations — Handle with Care

For the most part, advertisers do not ask for specific creative recommendations at new business presentations. Some agen-cies refuse to offer specific solutions to problems as a matter of company policy, but many — perhaps the majority — do it anyway. They may be against the practice on philosophical grounds but the chance of winning a new account can be a powerful incentive to break the rule. If you feel that the agency should make a creative recommendation, a fact sheet prepared for them may be helpful. It is difficult to build campaigns in a vacuum; no two clients have exactly the same problem. Lack of solid information is one of the major causes for campaigns that miss the mark. And don't forget: The longer you work with agency the better they understand you and your business.

Should you pay for specific creative recommendations made at a new business presentation? Sure — if you are in a generous mood. Some advertisers have done just that. Eastern Airlines once awarded $100,000 to every agency invited to make a presentation. Hyatt gave $10,000 toward repaying agencies for their expenditures in putting together a pitch.

It doesn't take much to bring out the troops. "New business" is the lifeblood of the advertising industry. Though making creative recommendations is often frowned upon as an unsound practice — lack of information, it is said, can lead to ill-conceived solutions — agencies have been known to do just that to stay in the fray. Speculative presentations can be an elaborate and costly affair, employing the best talent in the agency.

What's Love Got to Do with It?

There is a school of thought that says you'd better leave your emotions at the doorstep when choosing an agency. We are not so sure. Once again, it is the left hemisphere that offers this advice, and the fact is that decisions should not be made on that side of the brain alone. Likes and dislikes—call it "chemistry" if you wish—are also part of making a sound business judgment, and so it should be.

You have hired an organization, but you will be working with *people*—perhaps no more than a few of them. Ask yourself these questions: Do I see eye to eye with those I will share my problem with? Is the account executive whom you'll be working with most on a day-to-day basis the type who looks for positive solutions in crisis—or someone who simply plays back the problems to you? Is that person showing genuine interest in your business—or do you get the feeling that, in his eye at least, you will be only another profit center for the agency? Does he work well with the creatives in his office? What are his administrative skills? Will he represent your point of view as well to the agency as the agency's point of view to you? Is he a hard worker? Will he stay involved—or will his patience wear thin as soon as you become a client?

Small Agency? Big Agency?

Size of an agency is in the eye of the beholder—much depends on the location of its office. In New York, an agency billing less than $50 million would be considered "small"; in the rest of the country the figures are slightly less exalted. Even by Big Apple standards $100 to $200 million in billing passes as "large."

The number of agencies in the United States has exceeded 10,000, according to the Census Bureau, if you include the one-, two-, or three-person operations—the "mom and pop store" equivalent in the agency business. The figure indicates a better than 25% increase in the last five years, mergermania notwithstanding. Several other related enterprises go by a different appellation (studio, sales promotion, direct mail professionals, various advertising specialists, television stations) but create, prepare, and sometimes even place advertising just the same. There are over 2,000 advertising agencies and counselors listed in the Yellow Pages for New York City alone. The number of members in and out of New York in AAAA (American Association of Advertising Agencies, which carefully screens its members based on their work, track record with media, recognition in the advertising community, and financial viability) is over 750. Apparently, there is a wide choice of agencies from which to pick; a big pond filled with fish, small and large.

Some of these agencies specialize in certain fields (theatre, fashion, retail, travel, publishing) in which case there never is the type of "account conflict"—groups of people working on competitive businesses—that has become a source of concern with large, packaged goods agencies. Most agencies engage in a wide variety of activities but their focus remains advertising itself. Rare is the advertising agency that tries to grow by route of diversification into other areas (though megamergers may soon change that).

At least 100 agencies in the United States report gross income of around $10 million, if one takes all forms of advertising into account. At the time of this writing, the five largest United States-based agencies in terms of gross income are Young & Rubicam; the ever-expanding Saatchi & Saatchi (Compton actually had more income and billing at the time of its merger than the company it merged with); BBDO Worldwide; Ogilvy & Mather Worldwide; and McCann Erickson Worldwide. About half of the 130,000 Americans in advertising work in one of the top ten agencies.

Marketers in large companies turn to larger agencies for assistance, often as if by force of habit. In a survey taken by Video Storyboard Tests, Inc. for *AdWeek* of the "Agencies Marketers Would Consider Hiring" all those mentioned exceeded $300 million in billing. To wit:

J. Walter Thompson

Ogilvy & Mather

Young & Rubicam

BBDO

DDB Needham Worldwide

Leo Burnett

Chiat/Day

Size alone, however, does not guarantee clients' attention. Several very large agencies — among them such outstanding ones as Wells, Rich, Greene; Saatchi & Saatchi DFS Compton (now also including Ted Bates and Backer & Spielvogel); William Esty Company; SSC&B; Backer & Spielvogel; McCann-Erickson; and Campbell-Mithun — failed to make the list. Given the caprices of the business, this state of affairs of course has all the permanence of the weather.

Many large companies want — and need — the range of services large agencies have to offer. Among such services are direct mail, publicity, research facilities, marketing experience, and a network of global offices, all of which require considerable financial resources. Also important is the muscle that large-volume media buyers (found mostly in large agencies) have with media.

Other influences — some that are rarely spoken of — also play a part. Friends in high places are important to the upwardly mobile with an eye on networking. A large agency dealing with major corporate executives is more likely to be involved with the rich and famous, the influential, the tastemakers. Moving in its orbit are top law firms, important movie and tele-vision celebrities, politicians, athletes, and others worth cultivating.

This is not to suggest that smaller agencies remain second choice. Sophisticated clients are in constant search for new talent — it simply makes good business sense. There is always a generous sprinkling of less established agencies among the "hottest of the year." Six among the top ten in one such listing billed less than $100 million a year, easily outperforming — in growth at least — most other agencies, even those five to ten times their size. Increase in billings among the upstarts far outpaces industry averages in any given year. One could argue that their base was more modest to begin with, but a good look at the numbers, however, proves that this would be too simple an explanation of a trend that has long been with us.

There is some basis to the claim that an advertiser will get more — and probably avid — attention in a more humble environment. Here top management, usually the founders of the agency with much at stake, are apt to spend more time with their clients. In larger agencies, work tends to drift down into the lower and less experienced corporate tiers because of the volume of assignments, with expediency often overruling attention to quality. After all, even second-rate work is better than jobs incomplete, come deadline.

What's more, labor — and that can often mean top talent in the agency business — is considerably more costly in a larger company. An art director or writer at a large firm can easily make $1\frac{1}{2}$ to 2 times the income of his peer toiling in a smaller agency. And yet there may be little, if any, difference in the quality of work between the two.

The chances are also that a smaller agency responds more readily to the needs of the client — an important consideration in a fast-moving business. There are fewer layers of authority in the agency to oversee the work. In a larger agency, copy lines are often given to painstaking research before being presented to the client. Several art directors and copywriters may be assigned to tackle the same problem, like athletes trying out for the team; the "winners" are selected by members of the creative board only after lengthy and tedious deliberation.

The larger the organization, the more likely it is to have its own firmly ingrained bureaucracy, and the resulting corporate neuroses. As a result, as much energy—ultimately paid for by the client—may be spent on office politics as on the creation of advertising. In a smaller, more close-knit organization, this situation is less likely to develop.

Does all that mean that an advertiser had better vote in favor of a smaller agency? There is no easy answer to that question. Every case follows its own rules.

On occasion, smart advertisers try to get the best of both worlds. They may decide to assign certain projects to smaller agencies while keeping their accounts with a larger house. Or they may insist that even in the confines of a large agency they should have access to the free-spirited exuberance of several small autonomous creative satellite groups. Or they may suggest that the small join forces with the large—which is one of the main reasons why so many agencies have taken the merger route as a shortcut to success.

The Urge to Merge: What's in It for You?

There is nothing particularly new about the need—or the desire—for one agency to pool its resources with another. Still fresh are the memories of Harper's Interpublic Companies of the sixties—an umbrella holding company of agencies and communications resources getting together for the avowed purpose of providing improved in-depth service to its clients. The venture ran into some financial difficulties and mergermania came to a temporary halt until the eighties when Ogilvy & Mather and J. Walter Thompson were again feeling each other out for a possible combination called Operation Toto. The concept of corporate matchmaking was here to stay. Today, giant mergers between agencies are becoming commonplace. For added interest, non-agency investors, too, had entered the picture—among them such giants as Lorimar, American Express, and Shamrock Holdings (of Disney fame), to mention a few.

There is no shortage of rationale to "prove" that merging one agency with another is good for the agencies, their clients, and for consumers in general. Here are some of the arguments to show that being bigger is better:

1. *Improved international facilities* for clients with global marketing concerns.

2. *More clout in media buying.*

3. Opportunity to conduct *cross promotions* and other *sales incentive programs* among products handled by the same agency, and thus gain new powers among retailers.

4. *Broader-based services.* The agency has wider resources available.

Less often cited but nevertheless important from an advertiser's point of view are these two developments that may be part of a merger.

5. *Housecleaning.* Restructuring of the organization provides the agency with a once-in-a-lifetime opportunity to rid itself of some of the deadwood. Such people may be occupying highly paid managerial positions and have long since stopped making contributions to the day-to-day production of advertising. With the help of golden parachute clauses, equity options, and other sweeteners included in the contracts with the new partner, their exit now can be made less painful for all parties concerned. One top executive in recent years was "fired" from his newly absorbed agency and became over $100 million richer for it.

6. *Tighter control.* The advertiser can look forward to firmer financial control, trimmer staff, more accountability, and most likely, a more sophisticated management team fixed upon bringing new disciplines to bear.

The disadvantages are the by-now-familiar symptoms of giantism, chief among which is *loss of creative autonomy.* Not all good creative professionals thrive in a faceless corporate structure, and so they simply seek employment elsewhere. Mergermaniacs will passionately argue this point and call attention to the fact that the advantages of working for a larger corporation—better training methods, presence of fresh creative talent, more money available to find outside talent—far outweigh the disadvantages. But as we have said, advertising is a people business. Absence of compatible philosophy between teams creates tension. An executive at a top agency, who has been through it all himself, says: "Three to five years ago, everyone was driven by greed. They went into merger situations quickly and blindly, convincing themselves they could make it work. Now the money managers realize you're going to lose people and accounts and you'll be hit by a tremendous management trauma that comes with two companies that are labor intensive."

Perhaps the most telling question the advertiser should ask himself in the case of a merger situation is this: Has the agency joined forces with another in the interests of its clients or simply to provide its top management with a windfall profit? For it is a fact of business life that mergers provide opportunities for founders of companies at last to enjoy the fruits of their lifelong endeavor, and this is as true in advertising as in other fields. The nature of advertising is such that almost everyone—with a special talent or willing clients or both—can go into business with minimal capital; new business takes care of cash flow requirements. An offer to purchase an agency brings in a huge pay-out for those who started it all, and now perhaps are ready to retire.

Is There Life After New York?

New York is still the center of advertising —9 of the top 10 agencies are located in this city, and more than half of the top 100.

The reasons are many, some real, others imagined. For one thing, the largest concentration of talent by far works in this area. The New York Business to Business Yellow Pages alone lists over 2,100 commercial photographers and 700 illustrators.

New York is probably also the most fiercely competitive, and thus stimulating, of cities, and the advertising community is as much part of the scene here as is entertainment, publishing, or financial services. *New York Magazine*—a voice of the now-aging babyboom generation— regularly features a two- to three-page "On Madison Avenue" report. All the major newspapers, including the *New York Times*, the *New York Post*, and even the *New York Daily News,* devote space to the industry on a regular basis. In total agency billings, this city outpaces its nearest competitor (Chicago) almost fourfold. Total billings of agencies in the next 25 cities are still under those of New York.

This is also the place of museums, exhibits, conventions, theatres and movie houses, and a never-ending series of cocktail parties where peers gather, and talk. Nine out of the 15 most prestigious national and international award shows are held here. Everywhere one meets members of the advertising fraternity, as at the nearby suburbs and second-home summer places—the Hamptons, Fairfield County in Connecticut, and towns in Westchester.

"It's not so nice but I like to work there" has long become a familiar refrain. An interview conducted by Louis Harris Associates with over 400 leaders of industry shows that 23% of corporations plan to open offices in New York. Los Angeles came in a far second. Others mentioned were Chicago, San Francisco, Atlanta, and Washington, in that order. Emotions were more mixed as to quality of life. Most of them named Atlanta as "the best place to locate a business" with San Diego, Tampa, Los Angeles, Boston, Chicago in pursuit. New York came in number seven.

Still, New York is no longer the only city that feeds advertising agencies. Advertising talent now comes from all over the country; increasingly, large and important accounts sign up with regional advertising agencies. Nearly half of the "year's best" ads in the One Show Annual have been designed by agencies outside the New York area.

Nor is there a shortage of top talent among illustrators, photographers, designers, television directors and producers, and other creative services in cities west of the Hudson River. Photographer Wayne Massie (Guess print ads) works in Dallas; Bill Werts (Yamaha) in Los Angeles; Shelling (Perrier) in San Francisco. The finest of illustrators, too, can be found everywhere: Jared D. Lee is from Lebanon, Ohio; Bartels is from St. Louis; Ramsay from Honolulu; Fred Hilliard is from Seattle; Jackie Geyer is from Pittsburgh. Television director Joe Sedlemaier (Federal Express, Wendy's, Alaska Airlines, Nike, Subaru) calls Chicago his home (and office), while Will Vinton (creator of the dancing raisins on television) performs his magic in Portland, Oregon.

By and large, it costs less to produce advertising outside New York — an important consideration for budget-minded advertisers. As mentioned earlier, agency salaries are 20% to 30% lower on the average than those paid in New York. Suppliers too have lower overhead.

Interestingly enough, every other city generating advertising has developed its own creative style — distinct from that of New York. Like speech, ads too have their regional accents. Subtle as these differ-

ences may be, they do not escape the eye of experienced professionals. Said one well-known art director serving as a judge on many an exhibit: "Show me an ad and I'll tell you where it's from."

Here is a quick (albeit subjective) rundown as to how cities differ in their approach to advertising:

New York. All business. Account executives reign; research lives. Long hours, hard work (possibly at the expense of personal lives) are the norm. This is the place to play musical chairs; job opportunities are — or seem to be — plentiful. Salary levels (widely publicized by headhunters with a vested interest) are used as a yardstick to measure excellence.

Chicago. Second to New York in total advertising revenue. Glass and steel reaching for the sky, the rumble of traffic below — yet deep down a city intrinsically Main Street, U.S.A. Home of the Jolly Green Giant, Marlboro Man, the Pillsbury Doughboy, Charlie the Tuna, and McDonald's family commercials. Humor with emphasis on belly laughs and horseplay, with little tolerance for the acerbity of the likes of Woody Allen. Sophisticated graphics still cause raised eyebrows. "We're kind of basic around here," explains a Leo Burnett creative executive.

Los Angeles. Third in aggregate advertising spending. High in spirit; the sun is always shining, with outdoors and indoors merging into one. Thanks to a population that prefers driving to walking, radio is considered a major media here. Proximity to Hollywood makes for efficient (and economical) television production. The insularity of the ad community provides a fertile market for creative freelancers. Even the steadily employed find it hard to resist moonlighting. Says Richard Zien, a principal of his own agency: "We prefer to have the best people at any one time, rather than a full staff of mediocre ones." Not much hierarchy in agencies. Account executives wane, art directors and writers wax.

Over half of the recent entries at The One Show have originated outside New York. Examples here are by D'Arcy Masius Benton & Bowles (St. Louis), Chiat/Day (Los Angeles), and Sharp Hartig Advertising (Seattle).

AMAZING FEETS.

We bring the exciting world of dance to St. Louis.
For tickets - or other information on our '85- '86 season-call 968-3770.
Or stop by any Ticketmaster outlet.

Dance St.Louis

Keeping up with a Porsche 944 has just gone from difficult to impossible.

Experience life behind bars.

The aerospace industry has
So has the electronics industry. Automotive companies. Chemical firms. Even the Department of Defense.
And, judging from their response, they've loved every minute of it.
Bar code is speeding up their inventory process. Making their shipping/receiving departments actually ship and receive. And making their work-in-process tracking hardly any work at all.
Only one manufacturer can provide these companies with all the components needed to make a complete bar code system. That's INTERMEC.
And around here, only one distributor can

provide you with INTERMEC.
That's us.
So you won't have to deal with different vendors and different distributors for different products. Because we have everything you need to build a complete bar code system from the ground up.
Like printers. Readers. Laser scanners. Wands. PC interfaces. Port concentrators. Labels. Over a hundred separate components in all.
We'll help you through the entire process— from providing general information about bar code to providing full service after the sale.
Give us a call. And start putting yourself behind bars.

DISTRIBUTOR NAME AND INFORMATION HERE

You can't meet God's gift to women in a singles' bar.

If the singles life sometimes leaves you feeling alone and empty, remember that God's gift to all women and men is Jesus Christ. Come join us in worship this Sunday in the Episcopal Church.
The Episcopal Church

52

For fast, fast, fast relief take two tablets.

In the Episcopal Church, we believe that some of the oldest ideas are still the best.
Like the regular worship of God. Come join us as we celebrate this Sunday.
The Episcopal Church

Contrary to conventional wisdom, stress is not a 20th century phenomenon.

The Episcopal Church can't promise an end to stress. But we can promise to help you live better with
stress through the love, support and fellowship of Jesus Christ. Come join us this Sunday.
The Episcopal Church

This top award-winning series of ads for the Episcopal Church (used by hundreds of churches of different denominations) was created by Fallon McElligott in Minneapolis. Over a dozen creative luminaries in the agency had a hand in this campaign, and it shows.

Detroit. The fourth-largest advertising-producing city. Automobile clients are the rich uncles. Loyalties are long-lived. Campaign themes change as cautiously as next year's car model—a fender here, a new rooftop there. Don't get cute. On an average day of an average year, it's sunny five out of ten daylight hours in Detroit. That's less than in most other cities. Is Detroit advertising a reflection of its climate?

San Francisco. Not Los Angeles, by any stretch of the imagination, though both cities front the same ocean. Considers its much larger neighbor 400 miles south downright provincial. Many important innovations start here, be they in fashion, music, art, or theatre. Enjoys living on the edge. The mood of the sixties and seventies still lingers on. Oddballs are welcome. All of which makes this city one of the least reliable of all test markets; its psyche does not match the nation's.

Dallas and Houston. Two important cities in the world of advertising. Bold, masculine, and direct, their advertising reflects the Texas state of mind. Important market of the wealthy—though taste may be middle-brow. The rules are simple: If it glitters, it must be good. Home of Neiman-Marcus and all the store stands for.

Boston. Though steeped in tradition, the city bustles with born-again energy, thanks to the influx of the young. Some define Boston as a giant campus town. Advertising still bears the legacy of Norman Rockwell's Americana, but with New York only four hours' driving distance away, this is changing.

Atlanta. As in Boston, past, present, and future blend beautifully. Literally raised from the ashes at the end of the Civil War, Atlanta hasn't stopped growing since. Its skyline changes every year—architects make front-page news. The charm of the old South is still very much in the air. People are gracious, hospitable — but also ambitious, determined — *pushy* is the word Scarlett O'Hara used. Its advertising community is thriving; its advertising is aggressive. Some of the best graphics studios are located in this area.

Other cities of note: *Seattle:* Outdoor posters never had it so good. *Miami:* Plenty of ex–New Yorkers here, including some real talent. *Washington and Baltimore:* With politicians as clients, both cities have made image-building advertising campaigns their specialty. *Greenville, Winston-Salem, Richmond, Raleigh:* Powerful advertising had by all, especially in print. *Minneapolis:* Fallon McElligot is here.

But Will the Marriage Last?

Let's hope so. But if not — well, there can always be a parting of the ways.

The vows taken in the client/agency contract should not be taken too lightly, under any circumstances. The most successful partnerships are those that have lasted for many years, often for decades. Many large and important accounts — among them such stellar performers as Ford, Coca-Cola, Unilever, Noxell, AT&T (it worked with N.W. Ayer without a written contract its first seventy-five years), Texaco, Sunkist Growers, Mattel, Johnson & Johnson — have tried their best to give the word *partnership* more than lip service, and with resounding success.

Be that as it may, however, "account switches" among agencies are as much a part of life as changes in partners among babyboom marriages. At any given time there may be as much as $250 million in billing on the move. The trade press — and sometimes even major general publications — treat such news with all the insouciance of a bird-watcher watching a flock of geese routinely heading South. *AdWeek* — a lively trade publication that often succeeds in scooping the news — lists "accounts on the move" in its

issues 20 to 30 times a year. *Advertising Age*, no slouchy reporter either, is not far behind. Sometimes, account moves are perceived months before they happen; foreseers have a field day. The slightest hint of a restless client is enough to set a hungry agency in pursuit.

In any country except the United States, it is considered less than ethical to approach an advertiser already berthed at another agency. But ours is a free country, and that means every agency for itself. It could be argued such competitive spirit is healthy, and perhaps it is unless you're ulcer prone.

"New business" constitutes the lifeblood of many an agency. The average tenure of clients (large and small) in the industry is just a little over two years. As a rule, the larger the advertiser, the more stable his business, but not even this is certain. For every steady advertiser mentioned at the beginning of this chapter there is one who believes in frequent switching of partners. The chairman of Chock Full o' Nuts had gone through four agencies in five years, including J. Walter Thompson. His personal involvement with advertising was total. Other clients known for their fickle ways are Revlon, Lowe's, Gallo Wines, and a host of retailers — but then again, perhaps they have not found the right agency yet, the knight on the white horse.

Jim	David	Rocco	Kevin	Don	Chun Yung Lau
President	Chairman	Vice	Media	Creative	Delivery Boy
Moo Shu	*Shrimp*	Chairman	Director	Director	Wok 3rd Avenue
Beef	*with*	*Ta-Chin*	*Ginger*	*Sweet*	
	Lobster	*Beef*	*Chicken*	*and*	
	Sauce			*Sour Pork*	

Great advertising doesn't always happen 9 to 5.

The Agency's Self-Image: Reading Between the Lines

A good way to find out about the agency is by listening to its own self-description:

> We believe that images must translate into sales (Smith/Greenland)

> Brought to you by an agency that only does financial (Albert Frank— Guenther Law)

> Speaking powerfully to healthcare professionals (Barnum Communications)

> What is black, professional, worth over 50 million dollars, and not a basketball player? (Burrell Advertising)

> Great advertising doesn't always happen 9 to 5 (David Deutsch Associates)

The ad above, which appeared in the Agency Book, shows key executives hard at work.

There is nothing agencies enjoy more than formulating pithy one-liners about their own corporate philosophies. And why not? They are in the business of positioning products, so why not themselves? You can take these statements with a grain of salt or accept them at face value. Never should they be ignored altogether. These statements could constitute the most telling clue yet as to how the organization goes about solving its advertising and marketing problems.

Risk Not, Fear Not.

Risk is an ad campaign that makes your Board of Directors squirm. It's uncomfortable, like the wrong sized golf shoes. Safe advertising fits in like a good, long lunch. Give us a call. We've put "safety first" in advertising for over 50 years.

MAMMOTH PERVASIVE AND BLAND Inc.

Advertising • Public Relations • Lunch

(213) 477-5249

"Comfortable advertising by comfortable people."

As a matter of policy, does your advertising agency always argue with you? Question your decisions? All for the sake of so-called "fresh" advertising? Maybe what's "fresh" is their disrespectful attitude.
It's time you heard our Mammoth, Pervasive and Bland policy: "Never forget who pays the bills." Sound more comfortable? We think so, too.

MAMMOTH PERVASIVE AND BLAND Inc.

Advertising • Public Relations • Lunch

(213) 477-5249

With our exclusive "Same Day Service" you get the advertising you want when you want it. Guaranteed*

MAMMOTH PERVASIVE AND BLAND Inc.

Advertising • Public Relations • Lunch

*Available to clients with budgets of $10 million or more, and limited to official "Requests for Advertising" submitted to our office, by phone or in writing, no earlier than 9:00 a.m. but no later than Noon, PST, Monday through Friday, except for National and Religious holidays. All "Requests for Advertising" honored on "first come, first serve" basis. In the event of ties, we retain sole right to determine order of service. Excludes "Requests for Revisions" which are honored as soon as possible, normally within a week or so, depending on current work load. No other warranty, expressed or implied, is applicable. Subject to change without notice. Void when prohibitive. For complete details, call your Account Supervisor. Prospective clients please call William "Roy" Nestor, President, (213) 477-5249.

"Your Mammoth, Pervasive and Bland campaign is really stupid."

(One out of 1,252 phone calls ain't bad.)

keye/donna/pearlstein

11080 olympic boulevard, los angeles, ca 90064 (213) 477-0061

Campaign by keye/donna/pearlstein to attract new business in Los Angeles might have been intended to be tongue-in-cheek — but the message hits home with many an advertiser and advertising professional. Mammoth Pervasive And Bland, Inc. is a fictional agency that has put "safety first in advertising for 50 years." The organization excels in "advertising, public relations, and long lunches." Ads appeared in several publications, including the *New York Times*.

56

MP&B
Answering Machine Message #5

Hello, this is William "Roy" Nestor, president of Mammoth, Pervasive and Bland, answering your call personally. Our switchboard operator, Lorraine Berman, is at home today with another migraine headache, and I'm presently engaged in a lengthy business luncheon. So please leave your name, your title and your company name. If your advertising budget is $10 million or more please also leave as long a message as you like. If your budget is less than $10 million, please keep it short. And thanks for calling Mammoth, Pervasive and Bland, the comfortable people with comfortable clients.

This is the response that callers would receive. Hundreds took the bait, showing that advertisers, too, are people. After all, they still know how to smile.

MAMMOTH PERVASIVE AND BLAND
Media

"Numbers 'R Us"

What can you say about a Media Department that leaves "creative thinking" to creative thinkers, where it belongs? It's a department that knows there is safety in numbers. And safe numbers mean safe media buys.

Why? Numbers are numbers. Numbers don't lie. Numbers are facts, not fantasy. Truth, not fiction. Or as our media experts here on the 10th floor say, "Numbers 'R Us." So, it's a department that won't lose valuable sleep at night worrying about Reach vs. Frequency, or other time-wasting questions.

And you'll sleep better knowing that anyone who strays from our "safe-numbers" philosophy may not attend a free media lunch for a period of six months. A hard-nosed policy? Sure.

Research

Is the train coming or going?

"You can't tell which way the train is going by looking at the tracks." That's the kind of straight talk you can expect around our Research Department, here on the 11th floor, right next to our employee coffee room and vending machine area.

This is where science gets down to advertising. Or as our staff anthropologist, Dr. Bud Finch, puts it, "Advertising without research is like winking at a girl in the dark. She knows you're there, but she doesn't know what you're doing." And without our proven research techniques, you wouldn't know this important fact: "Singles win more games than home runs."

MAMMOTH PERVASIVE AND BLAND
Account Services

See new lunch policy

You heard "better safe than sorry" on the 6th floor. You'll hear it even louder on the 7th and 8th floors, our Account Services Department. Why? Because we don't hire an account services person only on the basis of his or her good grooming habits. We hire people with a healthy respect for authority. And around here that means the client's point of view. We may be "partners" in business, but we never forget who pays the bills.

If you don't like the color blue, we don't like the color blue. If you think Jerry Lewis is funny, you'll get no argument from us. If you want free tickets to the Superbowl, we'll see you on the 40 yard line, or the end zone, depending on your overall, annual expenditures. (Other restrictions may apply. Check with your Account Supervisor.)

OUR "V.P. SERVICE"™

To assure that "service" is not an empty promise, each and every member of this key department, above the rank of Jr. Account Executive, is an MP&B Vice President. That means, more often than not the person working on your business has the experience and clout to follow through on your important decisions.

For example, let's say an Account Services person brings you an ad that falls short of your expectations. It doesn't matter that it has passed the agency's creative approval system, which is 7-layers strong, including myself, with 30 years of experience. You may want another headline, a total copy rewrite, a bigger logo, or a completely new campaign with our good friend Jerry Lewis as your spokesman. Just tell your Account Services person, who will phone your "Requests for Changes" to the agency.

Most client "Requests for Changes" are honored on a "First Come, First Serve" basis. We also have "Same Day Service" available for clients whose changes are phoned-in before lunchtime.

NEW TAX LAWS AND YOU

The new tax laws concerning business-entertainment write-offs have forced us to revise our policy on the number of lunches and dinners we will invite clients to each week. A limit will be set for existing clients. However, no such limit will affect new clients for the first 12 months or 12 million dollars in billings, whichever comes first. Golf outings and tickets to ball games are excluded from this policy.

SAFE AT HOME

Some agencies will swing for the fences every time at bat. We'll settle for a clean hit up the middle. Especially when it brings a runner around third, sliding across home plate, and the ultimate umpire, Mr. or Ms. Consumer, cries "Safe!"

Safe at home. That's why you should make your next agency Mammoth, Pervasive and Bland.

Over 1,500 prospective clients received copies of the disguised k/p brochure. (Shown here are randomly selected pages describing the wide gamut of "services" offered by Mammoth Pervasive And Bland, Inc.

To Sum It Up

Upon entering into a relationship with an advertising agency — a serious commitment having far-reaching consequences — several factors should be taken into account. Among them are the talent and track record of the agency, client-agency "chemistry," dedication, and fiscal discipline.

The advertiser must set his own priorities; they could be uniquely his own. Is it in-depth marketing that he needs the most? Brilliant, breakthrough creativity? Taste in execution that reflects his product and services? A "take-charge" agency that requires minimum supervision and frees the advertiser to concentrate on refining his product? International capabilities? In-depth servicing? Experience in new-product introduction? Easy geographic access?

All agencies — just as their clients — do have their own distinct corporate "personalities." At their beginnings, this usually emanates from the founders who tend to clone themselves down the line. Larger agencies, however, rarely carry the stamp of a single or few individuals. They break into small units within the organization, many that exercise complete creative autonomy — an especially important feature to consider in today's merger-happy environment.

New business presentations serve as a major get-acquainted meeting between client and agency. They provide the advertiser with an opportunity not only to view the agency's work but also the people who produce it.

Not everything should be taken at face value at such a presentation. Some agencies are particularly skilled at making a "pitch" — only to reduce services to a routine once the account is "in the house." The advertiser should know at an early stage the names and experience of the key people assigned to his account. Watch for the agency's own self-image. It may be the most telling clue as to its approach to handling the account.

5

The Alternatives to an Advertising Agency: In-House and A La Carte

If an advertiser chooses not to employ the services of a full-service agency, a number of other services are available to him.

Why would an advertiser choose to take this route as opposed to hiring an agency offering a variety of services — and probably making his life easier? A number of reasons suggest themselves:

1. *Economy.* Working with service houses directly could prove to be less costly than working with a full-service agency. No markups, no commissions to pay.

2. *Control.* The advertiser is in the position to select whomever he wants, define his needs, and provide one-on-one creative contact. If the work is prepared by the in-house staff, his control is absolute.

3. *Inherent expertise.* The advertiser — or his in-house advertising department — may be just as capable of allocating and farming out work as is the advertising agency. In some areas, his expertise may even surpass that of his agency; i.e. preparation of point-of-sale material, special promotions, corporate literature, exhibits and dis-

plays, and other projects intrinsic to the company.

4. *Convenience.* Lines of communication are short, cutting down the possibility of misconstrued instructions.

5. *Confidentiality.* Privacy is more certain when the advertiser has direct control over a supplier. If the work is done in-house, it is less apt to catch the attention of a competitor.

In-House Advertising Department: Functions

Companies with on-premises facilities stress that they provide only those services that they feel can be more efficiently handled inside, and that only after careful analysis. Quite a few maintain both an outside and an inside advertising group, each with its own set of clearly defined responsibilities.

A study conducted by the Association of National Advertisers found that the most common in-house functions are:

Print advertising placement
Print production

Print creative
Sales promotion
Broadcast advertising placement
Audio-visual
Product publicity
Shows and exhibits
TV creative
TV commercial production

Other functions that may be performed in-house are:

Speech writing
Meeting staging
Training programs
Direct mail
Broadcast traffic
Network bill/pay
P-O-P production
Direct response
Trade advertising
Package design
Display materials
Magazines
Talent and residuals payments
Technical publications
Distribution and mailing lists
Brand budget control
Brand media planning
Network scheduling and costing
Creative for some brands
Radio creative and production
New product positioning
TV program production
New product assignments
Test marketing

In-House Advertising Department: Organization

Size of staff may vary from 3 to over 400 (at General Electric, for example), depending on the needs and structure of the company. In most cases, organization is based on type of advertising functions: sales promotion, print and television advertising, news publicity, media, research, exhibit and display—much as in an ad-

vertising agency. All of the subgroups report to the head of the in-house agency, usually an executive with an in-depth understanding of advertising and marketing. The agency may also be divided by product groups, each of which provides advertising support to one or several brands. Still another way of separating responsibilities is to do so by markets: agriculture, chemicals, overseas, and so on.

Companies differ as to making the use of their in-house services mandatory throughout their entire organization. Many leave the choice up to their brand managers or other heads of divisions, and encourage direct contact. Others are more rigidly organized, and are quite specific about assignments that should be done in-house.

The cost of running these departments either is considered company overhead (charged to the company) or the expenses are covered by: (1) media commissions, (2) fee or some percentage of operating cost to each product division user, (3) charges based on time and markups.

In-House Advertising Department: Disadvantages

To do all work in-house has its own set of problems:

1. *The peaks and valleys syndrome.* Fixed cost of employees and other overhead calls for a steady flow of work. Downtime can be expensive. Using agency services may be more efficient; they have a synergistic advantage.

2. *Buying vs. making.* It is easier to judge other people's work than do it yourself. There is probably a wider selection of talent at the agency or from the outside.

3. *Difficulties in attracting and holding top talent.* Agency salaries are higher, and creative life spicier when work-

ing on not one but a variety of accounts. The perception could be that an agency offers more growth opportunity.

4. *Too close to home.* Proximity to an inbred corporate management can be a psychologically inhibiting experience. The work is more apt to gravitate toward formula solutions. More so than in an agency, talent goes stale in the relative isolation of a company whose main business is not advertising.

5. *Lack of objectivity.* The fact that the heads of internal units often wear two hats — client's and agency's — eases the approval process but not always for the better. The result is a less challenging environment.

6. *Media recognition.* There could be some tarrying with media insisting on dealing with an agency or media-buying service. Credit history may need to be established first.

Special Problems of the Small and Medium-Sized Advertiser

The decision whether or not to employ an advertising agency as opposed to using services a la carte or an in-house group is a particularly difficult one for a thinly capitalized company. The choice cannot always be made on purely philosophical grounds; also to be considered is the bottom-line figure. Advertise the company must, but who in the organization has time enough to take the responsibility — and at what cost?

In such cases, advertising often falls into the lap of a junior or senior executive of the company, or even the owner himself. This ad hoc "advertising manager" may or may not have the proper background to make appropriate decisions. He must know when help is needed, and where he can get it expeditiously.

The following are examples of ingenious solutions to what appeared to be difficult problems at first:

A cabinetmaker was looking for ways to gain new customers. Having purchased names of tenants in newly erected co-op and condominium high-rises in his neighborhood from a list broker, he contacted the personnel director of a local art school, who recommended that a senior student photograph and design a four-page brochure for him. These were distributed door to door by — you guessed it — three junior students from the same institution willing to work for near-minimum wage.

A motion picture house manager wanted to know how he could best take advantage of the small-space newspaper mat ads he would regularly receive from the film production companies. The media representative of the city's newspaper suggested a twelve-month-long schedule in the entertainment section of the publication, supplemented by radio announcements at a station owned by his management. The disc jockey would deliver the message free of charge.

A used-car dealer was eager to get on television but production costs crimped his plans. The local television station offered to include the cost of taping three television commercials as part of the price of six 30-second spots he agreed to purchase. He wrote his own script, and acted as the spokesman for his dealership. When the hometown newspaper picked up the story, he gained additional exposure at no cost.

A young woman with her own recipe for making apricot preserves was encouraged by friends and relatives to go into business. A young agency agreed to handle the account for a small monthly fee, plus an option to purchase stock. The company made a public offering two years later, and both the advertiser and the advertising agency were delighted to see their investment paying off beyond their wildest dreams.

Advertisers like these are well advised to consider going a la carte and to try developing a comfortable ongoing business relationship with an art studio, free-lance copywriter, photographer, printer, engraver, offset house or even — as did the lady with the recipe for her apricot preserves — seek out a new agency willing to take a chance.

Plenty to Pick from

Never believe that an advertiser without an agency is like a captain without a ship. Advertising is a highly competitive business; not only is there a great abundance of agencies, eager to get business, but also suppliers offering a wide variety of specialized services.

Consultants

More and more businesses find that it is more economical to turn to an outside expert for help than go through long periods of experimentation in-house. Such an individual can open new horizons to those who have not yet made the journey.

Consultants come in many stripes, depending on their professional experience and personal inclinations. Some have business backgrounds, while others developed their specialty as teachers or researchers. Those from academia tend to have important theoretical insights, a large store of information, and a sense of perspective. Background in industry and commerce, on the other hand, tends to foster pragmatism, a can-do attitude, bottom-line thinking. Generally speaking,

our quick-fix culture tends to side with the pragmatist even though there is ample evidence that the so-called "practical approach" is not always the most practical for long-range planning. The problem should dictate your choice. If it is the type that calls for immediate solutions — say, to overcome retail resistance in distributing a new product — you may need the no-nonsense and adaptive leadership of someone from a corporate environment. For answers to more enigmatic questions — the effect of economic forecast on your future sales, for example — look to the professorate.

The consultant's specialty may be creativity, administration, marketing, advertising, public relations, media buying, research, or franchise operations. It is important to find out where his strength lies *prior* to engaging his services. Multifaceted talent — the so-called Renaissance person — still exists in our midst but as an endangered species.

Consultants may be hired to assist the company on any number of specific projects. They may be asked to make direct specific contributions (designing the interior of a store, for example), or they may act only as advisors to others in the company. Normally, they are to report to a board or, in some cases, to only a single company executive, often the very person who retained their services in the first place. (This can be risky at times. An agency president once called upon a consultant to help his organization produce better advertising. Looming high on the consultant's list was the recommendation that the president should retire.)

Most consultants work on a fee basis. A typical contract will stipulate time spent with the company, length of service, method of payment, and areas of responsibility. Contingent on performance, the consultant may be offered a bonus in addition to his fee. Few consultants negotiate terms for less than six months. Some stay with the company for many years, and become an integral part of top-level management.

Now you have a second opinion.

There are two sides to every story.

As of March 1st. Washington will be a two newspaper town again!

Start the day fully informed.

Consultants may supplement agency services — or even offer a viable alternative at times. The above project was assigned to a consultant for reasons of confidentiality. Shown here are proposed full page ads for a new major newspaper in Washington, D.C. A consultant proposed that the new newspaper best avoid open confrontation with the *The Washington Post,* and try to convince the public to buy both papers for a more complete point of view instead.

Media-Buying Services

Advertisers of all types can have an independent media-buying service, and for obvious reasons. These services often represent the best of media buying, the crème de la crème of the profession.

Their services can be contracted for by the advertiser or — in some cases — by advertising agencies. Their contributions can be especially helpful for small and medium-sized advertising agencies who do not have the leverage of a large ad budget. (No small thinkers are the buyers of media. One such service on the West Coast buys over $1 billion worth of spot TV every year.)

The disadvantage in using a media service is that such an organization does not offer any other type of service, and certainly not — with a very few exceptions — any that have to do with creative. Making ads would put the buying service in head-on competition with the client's advertising agency, an awkward situation at best. Media buying, in fact, is an art unto itself, enough so to encourage many clients to hire the service of both an adver-tising agency (creative) and a media-buying service (for placing ads in specific media). Quite a few maintain an in-house media-buying service.

Media services work usually on a commission basis, much like their agency counterparts. Since they offer no other services, they are able to work at a lower commission rate, usually between 7% and 12%. Their rates depend on the extent of negotiations with media (buying print from rate cards is less involved than negotiating for time with television stations) and size of the buy (large purchases generate larger profits, so they can be made at a lower commission rate).

Information needed. To implement your advertising strategy, the media buyer needs a wide range of information — including your goals. As described in detail later in this book, your marketing target (geographic, demographic, and psychographic), distribution areas, existing and projected marketshare, extent of competition, company history, and advertising appropriation — all come into play in the making of media recommendations.

RATIONALE FOR PLAN

The 'News' was selected as the primary vehicle for the

advertising for the following reasons:

1. While the Prime Time shows appealing to the target might have more audience individually they are more costly relative to the Late News and would limit the the frequency and continuity exposure.

2. The same can be said for using Weekend Sports as a base. However, when Sports are added, when you have already reached the target through another daypart, they can become more efficient as you are adding to the frequency.

Part of a preliminary corporate media plan compiled by AllScope Media Service. The 14-page presentation includes two alternative plans based on different budgets. Included are estimated weekly rating levels, (reach and frequence), schedules, markets, coverage, and time periods.

3. If you consider the life style of the executive, he is probably up early, may turn on the Early Moring News, or listen to the News in the car on the way to work and on the way home. At night he will probably watch his favorite Late News before going to bed.

Thereforeif we place advertising on all the Late News programs, as well as the Early Morning News programs, the chances are extremely high that we will reach the target you are looking for.

Bear in mind that no matter what prime time or sports program he is watching during the evening he will turn to his favorite News program before going to bed.

This plan has taken advantage of this by placing advertising in the News on all the stations he night turn to, both in the morning as well as the evening.

In addition to Road-Blocking the News programs in the top 10 markets on Television, we have added Radio in the morning and afternoon Drive Times on selected stations ie: News, Talk, Classical Music etc. Radio will add to the message frequency of the television as well as adding some of the executives we might have missed on television.

All in all, both of these Plans, will do an effective job. The $4.0 Million plan will do it a little faster.

Please bear in mind that this is a preliminary and rough look at what might be done. Once actual budgets are established as well as further marketing criteria, a plan can be developed to fine tune the advertising effort so that results can be maximized.

Art Services: Illustrators

There is a continuous need for graphics assistance by just about any type of organization, and advertisers without the expertise of an agency often have a difficult time in finding the right kind of help in this area. There are two basic types of art services, and while they seem similar, they are not the same. There are individual *artists* (who may or may not be represented by an agent) and there are *art studios*.

Artists usually work from their own homes or studios, pursuing what is essentially a solitary craft. On the other hand, art studios are organizations offering a wide range of graphics services (see next section).

It is important to remember that the work of any two artists is not exactly the same. Most artists strive to develop a style of their own—their "signature"—that sets their work apart.

There are many ways to find the artist you are looking for. The easiest is to simply go through books and various publications (as well as watch animated movie cartoons on television) to find what you want, and then contact the artist through the sponsor. A bookstore can be a treasure house of information, especially the children's books section. Art studios, art representatives, and art schools usually have a large stable of illustrators and portfolios.

A word about portfolios of people sent to advertisers for an interview: check authorship. Bent on impressing the interviewer, some free-lance artists and writers (and we emphasize the word *some*) assume a rather cavalier attitude toward taking credit for work they have at best been only partially responsible for. Remember that most advertising campaigns prepared by agencies are the result of team effort. Contributions come from all corners: account, art directors, copywriters, media buyers, research specialists, and, yes, even clients. Many employ-ment agencies, well intentioned but with less intimate knowledge about the field, tend to overlook this fact, taking the applicant's word at face value.

During the days of creative breakthroughs at Doyle Dane Bernbach not long ago, for example, the same award-winning Volkswagen proofs would show up in sample books over and over again. A senior art director at Young & Rubicam said: "In about ten years I had six art directors and eleven copywriters take responsibility for Volkswagen's 'Lemon' ad. A lot of people must have come up with the same idea in the same week."

The author of this book had a personal encounter with the curious peregrinations of a single idea. So far no fewer than six agencies have taken credit for his "Let Your Fingers Do the Walking" campaign for AT&T's Yellow Pages, and God only knows how many art directors and copywriters. No doubt, this number will in-

Advertising concepts usually originate with one person, but given the nature of the business, many others make contributions in time. It then becomes increasingly difficult to assign credit to the exact source.

crease as the walking fingers keep on limping along.

Award shows, art galleries, advertising workshops are another rich source for talent. Particularly helpful are art directors' and illustrators' exhibits, such as *The One Show* (over 10,000 entries with art and copy judged together), *National Exhibition of Illustration* (sponsored by the Society of Illustrators), *Creativity Show* (over 1,200 award winners), *Obie* (outdoor advertising), *New York Festivals* (among its 7,000 entries are included real estate and annual reports), *The Advertising Club of New York* (8,000 entries from all over the world), *Art Directors Club* (the granddaddy of award shows with close to 15,000 entries), *Arena* (outstanding newspaper advertising with about 5,000 entries), *Pro-Comm* (business-to-business advertising with over 2,000 entries), *New York Type Director's Club Competition, Communication Arts* (about 35,000 entries that appear in the *Advertising Annual of Commercial Art Magazine*), *International Advertising Film Festival at Cannes* (over 300 entries), *Magazine Publishers Association Kelly Award* (winners of best magazine campaigns are featured in national magazines, such as *Fortune*), and *Clio* (over 20,000 entries). Art schools, too, exhibit the wares of their students; new talent can be discovered on the spot and for less cost. *Art Direction* (Advertising Trade Publications, New York) offers comprehensive calendars of shows about to be held in New York and throughout the country in its monthly issues, as well as profiles of "Upcoming Illustrators." Listings of artists and illustrators appear in various Yellow Pages, (national data bases on all Yellow Pages are available), *The One Show Annuals* (Art Directors Club, New York), *Madison Avenue Handbook* (New York), *Illustrator's Annuals* (Madison Square Press, New York), *Art Directors' Index to Illustration, Graphics & Design* and *Art Directors' Index to Photographers* (Rotovision, Geneva), *The Creative Black Book* (Friendly Press, New York), *Commercial Art Magazine* (Palo Alto), *Graphic Design USA* (Watson Guptill, New York), *Creative Source* (Wilcord Publications, Toronto), *American Showcase Photography* and *American Showcase Illustrations*, (American Showcase, New York), *American Illustration* and *American Photography* (Abrams, New York), *AdWeek/Art Directors Index* (ASM Communications), *Literary Market Place* (R. R. Bowker, New York), N.Y. Gold (Watson-Guptil), and the *Graphics Annuals* (Graphis Press, Zürich) classified by media (publications, posters, packages, TV, etc.). All of these books are available through regular book and major art supply stores or can be ordered through the publisher. Major sources are the Art Direction Book Company (New York), Hastings House (New York), Abrams (New York), Craig Publications (Chicago), Watson-Guptil (New York), Van Nostrand Reinhold (New York), and Rotovision (Geneva, Switzerland). Ask for their latest catalogues. Many other books and TV reels are available through Art Direction Book Company (New York). A friendly chat with an agency, art studio, or local art supply store will go a long way to put you on track.

Cost of finished art varies greatly, depending on the nature of the work (quick fashion drawings are less expensive than a complex full-color magazine illustration), the experience and status of the artist (a "name" illustrator may charge up to 10 to 25 times as much for the "same" drawing), end-use (one-time use costs less than multi-use — appearance in a national publication costs more than in a local newspaper or an advertiser in-house brochure), color (the more colors, the more expensive), size (the bigger, the more it costs), type of assignment (an original concept is worth more than rendition of someone else's), schedule (the artist may charge extra for a rush assignment), indirect benefits (prestige, wide exposure, accompanying publicity, permission to sign the illustration), and the advertiser's ability to pay. This last factor, referred to by some as the "deep pocket theory," may come as a surprise — *shock* is perhaps a better word — to some clients, but setting aside ethical consideration, it has long become a fact of life in advertising, just as it has in most other businesses. Work done for a large company or through a large agency (whose clients, it is presumed, are accustomed to pay for the best) comes higher. Conversely, a small retail store or new enterprise in financial straits is likely to get work at a lower price — provided it can engage the artist's services at all.

Information needed. Most commercial illustrators work from rough layouts, but not all. Some will sketch out their own concept (usually in a "comprehensive" form), or perhaps several. Smart is the advertiser who invites early contributions from his artist.

It is important that the buyer insist on estimates. Art is subjective, and if you do not like the end result, you still have to pay as long as the artist can prove he has followed your instructions; the assumption is that you have bought his particular style. Best way to settle differences of opinion (and there can be many) is through arbitration at The Joint Ethics Committee (New York), an organization with in-depth experience in solving problems in the graphics field. Its excellent booklet on *Code of Fair Practice* can be obtained by writing to Box 179, Grand Central Station, New York, NY 10163.

The work of illustrators, photographers, designers, and other graphic services appear in many books, both black and white, and in color. This page is culled from the *Corporate & Communications Design Annual.*

The Annuals of American Illustrators have long been an excellent display of available talent. Over 500 illustrations appear in these volumes, the bible of the industry. The originals are hung at the Society of Illustrators' annual exhibitions.

Pat Nagel

Jackie Geyer

Ed Lindlof

Ed Renfro

Comprehensive lists of illustrators, photographers, retouchers, typographers, printers, engravers, models, stylists, pre- and post-TV production houses, music and sound studios, advertising agencies, and other creative services are published in *The Creative Black Books*, at the beginning of every year. Additional samples of an artist's work are available on request. Part of Jackie Geyer's 8-page sample brochure, containing 31 inspiring illustrations, is shown here. Comparative fees paid for illustrations are listed on the following two pages. Costs may vary with the artist's talent and experience, location, and other factors. These general guidelines are based on information compiled by the Graphic Artists Guild from various practitioners in the field.

Comparative fees for magazine and newspaper advertising illustration*

	Black & White	Color
National magazines		
Spread	$4,000	$5,500
Full page	3,000	4,250
Half page	2,250	3,000
Quarter page	1,700	2,000
Spot	1,250	1,500
Regional and mass trade magazines		
Spread	2,700	4,000
Full page	2,200	3,000
Half page	1,700	2,200
Quarter page	1,300	1,700
Spot	1,000	1,300
Specific trade and limited audience magazines		
Spread	2,000	2,500
Full page	1,700	2,200
Half page	1,500	2,000
Quarter page	1,250	1,500
Spot	850	1,100
Newspaper advertising, national campaign†		
Spread	3,500	—
Full page	3,000	—
Half page	2,000	—
Two column (quarter page)	1,500	—
Full color newspaper supplement		
Spread	—	4,000
Full page	—	3,500
Half page	—	2,500
Two column (quarter page)	—	1,250

* Add 25 percent for each color overlay.
† No specific prices are available for smalltown local newspapers. A broad range of fees are negotiable depending on budgets and the artist's reputation.

Comparative fees for brochure, catalogue, and mailer illustrations

	Black & White*	Color
Fortune double-500 and major companies		
Spread	2,500	4,000
Full page	2,000	3,000
Half page	1,500	2,000
Quarter page	1,200	1,500
Spot†	850–950	1,000–1,200
Smaller and regional companies		
Spread	1,700	2,000
Full page	1,500	1,700
Half page	1,100	1,250
Quarter page	900	1,000
Spot†	700–800	750–850

* Add 25 percent for each color overlay.
† Fee depends on size and complexity.

Comparative fees for point-of-purchase illustration (counter card, display, in-store promotion)

	Black & White*	Color
Complex	$2,500	$3,000
Simple	1,700	2,000

* Add 25 percent for each color overlay)

Comparative fees for packaging illustration*

	Black & White†	Color
Major company with national distribution		
Complex	$3,000+*	$4,500+
Simple	2,300	3,000
Smaller company with regional distribution		
Complex	2,500+	3,000+
Simple	1,700	2,500

* In this category, the size of the print order is the best method of determining the fee. Illustrations for packages produced for test marketing only should be priced accordingly; 100 percent payment should be specified for the eventuality of full production.
† Add 25 percent for each color overlay.

Comparative fees for major city transit-car card iilustration

	Black & White	Color
Major corporation	$2,500	$3,500
Smaller corporation	2,000	2,500

Comparative fees for 24-sheet outdoor billboard advertising illustration

National campaign in major cities	$5,000+
Regional campaign in large cities	3,500+
Local campaign in one small city	1,700

Comparative fees for corporate identity and logo design

	Research and Presentation*	Development of Approved Logo†
Fortune double-500 company	$6,000–11,000	$3,500–5,000
Other major corporation	3,500– 8,000	2,500–3,500
Smaller company	2,500– 3,500	1,500–2,000
Nonprofit organization	1,500– 2,000	1,000–1,250

* From one to three logos.
† Approved logo is applied to letterhead, envelope, and business card; additional applications are billed separately. Two to three sketches average.

Comparative fees for counter card design

National use	$1,000– 1,500
Regional use	900– 1,250

Comparative fees for poster design

Corporate	$2,000– 3,500
Motion picture, major studio	6,000–11,000
Motion picture, minor studio	4,000– 6,000
Theatrical	1,700– 3,000
Nonprofit organization and institutional	1,000– 1,750

Art Services Continued: The Studio

An art studio usually employs a staff, each person assigned to his or her specialty. There is nothing new about the "studio" concept; it is said that many of Rubens's "original" canvases were painted with the able assistance of several of his pupils — some who would specialize in painting, say, wild beasts. Such division of labor bears a striking resemblance to the structure of today's commercial art studios.

Commercial art studios are more than just a source for finished illustrations and design. As mentioned earlier, today's graphics problems demand a wide spectrum of human and technological skills. Here is just a quick sampling:

- mechanicals
  (pasting all the elements — type, illustration, borders, etc. — on a single board, in preparation for photoengraving)
- air brushing
- color matching
- preparation of mock-up packaging, displays, presentation board, model making, and props
- designing
  (logos, stationery, type layouts)
- layouts
  (both rough and comprehensive)
- storyboards and TV animatics
  (the latter for consumer testing)
- slides, charts, and other material for audio visual presentation
- embossing
- hand lettering
- hot stamping
- silk screen printing
- compugraphic typesetting
- blow-ups
- photography
- retouching
  (color or black and white)
- dimensional illustrations
  (sculpturing)
- offset printing
- desktop publishing
- computer graphics

The studio may also have access to writing, advertising, and media talent. Large full-service studios, in fact, often stand in for advertising agencies, in many cases becoming agencies themselves.

Then again, the "studio" may be nothing more than a collection of talent that, whether under one roof or not, is represented by the same management. To avoid internal competition, the chances are that the individuals' styles will be different enough for an agent to represent them by name. His portfolio may include the work of as many as ten to twenty artists; one "studio" in New York includes black-and-white and color reproductions of over forty illustrators in its folders mailed to art directors. The organization has no headquarters, save for the agent's secretary who answers the telephone.

Still other studios specialize in retouching, or design, or "hand lettering," or — a specialty much in demand — the rendering of tight, comprehensive storyboards.

No doubt, the advertiser pays extra for the luxury of having someone stand between him and the individual free lance. Only he can tell if this expense is warranted. It may well be. Competent art studios and agents run their offices on a strict businesslike basis. They furnish estimates, see that deadlines are met, make deliveries, correct mistakes, keep in touch, act as negotiators, and, last but not least, function as peacemakers par excellence between artists and clients.

Payments are based on hourly rates ($25 to $35 per hour) or a set fee, depending on the complexity of the work, the cost of talent required, the studio's overhead, and its location. Agents get between 20% to 40% commission on the work they sell. This is payable by the artist. Payments are usually made at the completion of the assignment, but by agreement, they can also be made in two or three parts.

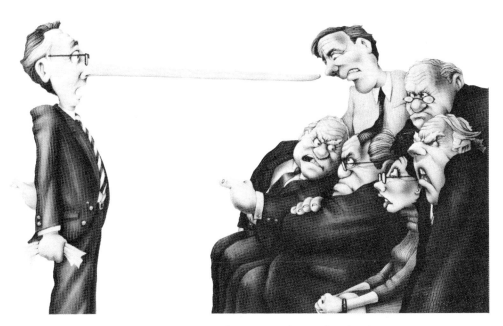

Art studios (representatives or even the artists themselves) often maintain easy-to-file sample reprints of their work for handy reference.

CHARLES SANTORE

EXQUISITE CHARACTER ILLUSTRATION.

ELWYN MEHLMAN

CONCEPTUAL ADVERTISING AND EDITORIAL
ILLUSTRATION.

LOUMYERS

TAKE ONE LOU MYERS CARTOON
AND CALL ME IN THE MORNING.

The experience you seek   KENT

Illustrated By:
Michael David Brown

Both artists and photographers strive to develop their own distinctive style. The work of artists shown here are very different from one another. Yet they are represented by the same agent, along with several dozens of others.

Photographers

To say that photographers "take pictures" is a gross oversimplification. Few would consider their art to be only transferring images to film. They too develop a style of their own, just as do their colleagues in the illustrative arts.

Looking for just the right photographer could be time-consuming, but it may well be worth the extra effort. Photographers' names are listed in the books and publications mentioned earlier. Almost all award shows include their work.

Remember that your commercial photographer, particularly if he works out of a studio, not only shoots but "arranges" a picture. His is a multitude of tasks. Among them are casting, selection of props and clothes, the hiring of a makeup artist and hairdresser, "accessorizing" the model, type of take (close, medium, or long shot, wild shot, etc.), lighting the scene, choice of camera (hand, reflex, still, tripod, precision, flash, stroboscopic, telephoto), size of prints (35 mm, 120 mm, $2\frac{1}{2}'' \times 3\frac{1}{2}''$, $9'' \times 5''$, $5'' \times 7''$, $8'' \times 10''$, $10'' \times 12''$).

All this, in addition to administrative chores, such as bookkeeping, legal (negotiations with the modeling agency), and getting food, lodging and transportation. Usually, he has a staff at hand to assist him in setting up a shot.

For black-and-white reproduction, the photographer first submits "contact prints" — sheets of several dozen photographs, showing the model in different poses, with different expressions, and perhaps from different angles. The client is asked to select the pictures he likes, along with recommendations made by the photographer.

The selections are then enlarged and refined in the darkroom. Not surprisingly, the final choice — the one to be used for reproduction — is given particular attention in the developing. The client (usually his print production experts) may prefer a "hard" or "soft" contrast print depending where and on what kind of stock the picture is going to appear.

For color photographs, transparencies or prints are submitted as explained in the next section of this chapter.

Costs are based on the complexity of the assignment, the photographer's proven track record, and again, the client's ability to pay. Photographic sessions may take from one day to weeks. Average daily fees run between $1,000 and $2,500. Well-established, "name" photographers charge more than that. On the other hand, it is possible to buy, or assign, photographs to lesser known photographers, and get high quality results for a few hundred dollars.

Information needed. Rough layout, purpose, budget, schedule, use, product features you wish to emphasize.

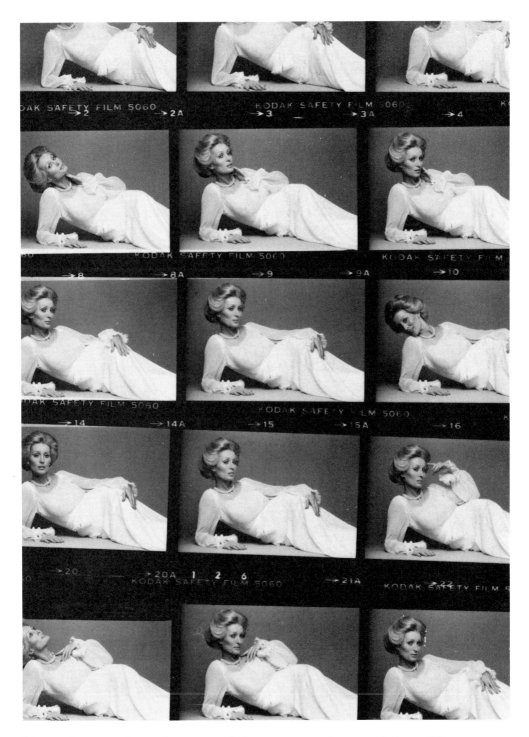

Many photographs — often several dozen — are taken, each in a different pose, different lighting, different shutter speed, and so on before arriving at a final choice. The shots appear on so-called contact sheets such as this. Blow-ups are made from the ones selected for a closer look; several more are eliminated at this point. The final print is carefully developed and retouched for reproduction. Barry Evans has taken these photos of Oleda Baker, a beauty and health expert.

Shown here is the art director's rough sketch for a 30-second NYNEX Yellow Pages commercial. Using a minimalist approach, a clean seamless background, and no fancy camerawork (no transitions) this wordplay on product and service categories appearing in the directory — in this instance a dozen uniformed cadets doing the funky chicken, windmill, James Brown, and other lockstep maneuvers to act out "Rock Drills" — won a Gold Pencil Award for Robin Raj and Marty Weiss of Chiat Day, the highest form of compliment for creative accomplishment in advertising.

Prints, Chromes, Retouching

More often than not, the advertiser wants to "see" the photograph exactly as it will appear on the magazine page, display, postcard, or brochure. As pointed out earlier, with a black-and-white photograph, this is not much of a problem. But when the photograph is taken in color and submitted as a transparency, that is altogether a different matter.

Projecting the transparency on a white surface (screen or wall) is one way to view the results; making quick, inexpensive prints — such as Kodachromes, Ektachromes, or Polaroid shots — is another. But neither provides the fidelity needed to make a selection. A transparency projected against white affects added brilliancy, more than it would in print form. Mass-produced, inexpensive prints, the kind the average photohobbyist receives, usually fail to bring out the highest potential in a photograph.

The advertiser looking for more-exacting information may insist on high-quality "professional" prints. They may also be used for reproduction purposes, depending on the type of print. They can be ordered in quantities at considerable discounts. The names of organizations specializing in custom reproduction are listed in the Yellow Pages under "Photographic Color Prints and Transparencies," in the *Black Book*, and in various trade publications. Ask the supplier to send you a price catalogue, or better still, meet you in person.

These are the questions the advertiser must ask himself before deciding on what type of print he should order:

Use. To what use will the print be put? Will the final version appear as a magazine ad, catalogue, brochure, poster, illustration, exhibition print, or slide transparency? For purposes of high-quality reproduction, the print must be "repro quality." For lectures and workshops, photocomps, press kits, sales presentations, binders, prints of less than repro quality may be perfectly adequate (and less costly).

"First-generation" transparencies (i.e. not photos of photos), where the engraver shoots directly from the chromes, will give you the best results. Color prints offer the next best choice. In this category, color-corrected dye transfers offer the highest fidelity. They are followed in quality by C-prints, laser and other high-pixel-resolution computer impact prints, color stats, and color machine photocopies, in that order.

Time. Making prints — black-and-white prints, Ektachrome slides, Kodachrome and Ektachrome processing, C-prints, presentation proofs — can take from 24 hours to 48 hours. "Repro quality" transparencies require additional time for delivery.

Additional Laboratory Services Available. In addition to providing prints, most labs also offer mounting, large blowups, retouching, for an extra charge. Some make slides, and a few even build complete exhibit mounts. Thanks to the new analog and digital reproduction methods, many houses are also able to print murals on such nonpaper stock as canvas, vinyl, cloth, and polyester.

Writers

Free-lance writers are generally hard to locate. In fact it often seems to take the services of a private investigator to ferret them out. But they are around. Most of them work in advertising agencies, in-house departments, public relations firms, or at a publication house during office hours and come out of hiding after sundown like so many nocturnal creatures.

Advertisers often complain that it is hard to find a writer who understands their particular problem. This is often true, but it is generally the advertiser who is at fault. It is not easy for a writer to sing the praises of a product or service that he is less than intimately familiar with. Give a free lance enough background material to work with.

Like artists and photographers (and generally speaking, all creative talent), writers too come from a variety of backgrounds. Some are strong on food or detergents but weak when writing business to business. Others are fluent in fashion speak. Still others are capable of waxing eloquent about the features of an electric drill in the piquant words of an accomplished poet. To recognize the exact talent you need requires consummate expertise — coupled with no small amount of luck.

Most free-lance copywriters charge on a project-by-project basis. End-use (print, television, publicity release, mailing piece) will affect costs, as always. Some may agree to get paid by the hour (or even the number of words) but are the exception. A writer's ability to come up with a basic advertising concept — the "big idea" (see Chapter 13) — adds to his worth, and payments should reflect the importance of his contributions. Hiring a wordsmith is one thing. Hiring an "idea person" is quite another.

Names of advertising writers appear in the *Standard Directory of Advertising Agencies and Madison Avenue Handbook*. Various professional clubs such as the One Club for Art and Copy, American Society of Journalists and Authors, local and regional writers' clubs (over 40 states have at least one), or such national organizations as Associated Business Writers of America, Direct Marketing Writers Guild, Writers Guild of America issue directories of their member writers. Advertising workshops provide a chance to meet writing talent in person, working for an agency or self-employed, like the one held annually by *Advertising Age*.

Information Needed. A writer is a glutton for information; he eats and sleeps research. So tell him about your product, your consumers, your advertising strategy, your competition, your taste, your personal hopes and aspirations. If the information should be kept in strict confidence, say so. And if you're really apprehensive about this point, get his commitment in writing, have it signed by a notary public, and send a copy to the writer.

Modeling and Talent Agencies

Nearly all models and "talent" (the distinction between the two can often be a blurred one) are listed either with an agency or an individual agent. Representatives charge between 10% and 50% for arranging appointments, taking care of legal and financial details, administering "bookings."

A large part of their promotion comprises periodical distribution of "headsheets" or "composites" complete with brief background data. This form of resume includes such essential information as the model's height, size, weight, shoe size, color of hair and eyes, age range, hat size, and glove size. If the model has "good" hands (i.e. long, slender, and photogenic), that is duly noted, too. Mentioned are his or her educational background, film and print (particularly on magazine covers) experience, and any skills that may be helpful in getting a photographic or television assignment; i.e. the model's ability to play tennis, act, play a musical instrument, dance or sing.

Once the selections are made from these pictures, the model (or talent) is asked to come in for a personal interview (referred to in less complimentary trade jargon as "cattle call" or "go-see"). The candidate may be auditioned on camera with the picture transmitted to other areas in the agency (or even the client's office). Needless to say, these rehearsals put enormous pressure on the interviewee who may be asked to read or recite the lines on relatively short notice. Every effort should be made to make the performer feel at ease, and give him or her more than one try, if necessary.

If the picture is used only in a printed advertisement, appearance is of prime importance. What counts is the model's ability to "move" in front of a camera, act out emotion, look the part, and be able to "wear" the clothes. Beauty, however, is not always a prime factor in the selection process — either for television or print. The advertiser may be more interested in finding the "type" of individual who best conveys his message: housewife, girl-next-door, businessman, athlete, or steel worker.

In print, skilled makeup artists working with the photographer can turn an ugly duckling into a princess, a frog into a prince in less time than it takes to tell the fairy tale. Years can be added to or subtracted from the model's face. A model can be made to look shorter, taller, fat or skinny, well or unwell.

Television tolerates less tinkering with Nature. A movie camera can be a cruel instrument indeed, telling tales out of school. It will bring to the screen a poorly executed golf swing, the stage fright of an actor, and crow's feet at the corner of the eye.

That is why casting directors spend days, and sometimes weeks, searching for just the right face, the right body, the right personality for the part. They insist on auditions on stage or the camera. If you are an advertiser electing to be your own talent scout, you would be well advised to follow the same procedure. The eyes of the camera are not the same as those of a human.

Babies and animals in particular need long and careful consideration. Babies will cry just when their faces are supposed to break into a smile. Dogs will sit when they are told to stand, cats will go to sleep, birds will fly away. Your chances for success will improve when you deal with seasoned professionals. Do not ever rely

Sean Smith

Professional models develop a strong sense of style, reflecting or even dictating trends. This is J.J. Kinnersley, one of the Ford Agency's "Today's Woman".

on your neighbor's kid to come through his first time in front of the camera; he never does. Or the cat who, his owner swears, represents the Second Coming of Morris. If you need animals, try a professional animal trainer who has established lines of communication with his beast, as if by osmosis.

Models usually charge by the hour, by the day, or by the session. Their traveling time and "above-the-line" expenses are built into the estimate, as is the usual contingency fee. Location shots do not require the stage setting of a studio shot but the cost of air fare, hotel accommodations, and other overhead may add up to more than the cost of shooting on home turf.

Most models (for print work) have a set charge based on working hours. Hourly charges range from $50 to $10,000 a day. Modeling agencies keep a close eye on what the market can bear. A cover shot, prime-time appearance in an award-winning commercial, publicity (or even notoriety) can put an end to the model's fixed hourly rate schedule ever after.

Performers usually charge by the day. The "initial payment" is regulated by SAG (Screen Actors Guild) if the shot is made in a film studio on film or tape, or AFTRA (American Federation of Television and Radio Artists) if it's taken on videotape outside a film studio or used as a wild commercial.

It is important to know whether or not the performer is a "player" (or "principal"). A player does not have to be on-camera to qualify as such. Anyone who speaks a line identified with product, performs a stunt, appears in certain types of stills or stop action may be called a player or a principal. He or she need not be a professional. The definition of a player is complex, and it is best to get that information from the respective talent union.

Minimum payment to a principal at the time of this writing is $379 for an eight-hour day, time-and-a-half for the next two hours, and double after that. The weekly (five days) payment is $1,319. An extra receives $91 daily. Continuous re-

payments must be made to principals if the commercial is used more than once. Consider your media schedule before the shoot to avoid surprises later as you receive the bills for residual payments. Generally speaking, future payments depend on the number of times the commercial is aired (13-week cycles are common), the cities in which it is shown, and whether the spot is used "wild" or for a program. New residual payments are due at every additional 13-week cycle.

Cities are ranked by units according to their "marketing weight" as defined by marketing and television exposure data supplied by Nielsen. All cities except New York, Chicago, and Los Angeles are computed this way. For example, Philadelphia is given 5 units; Boston and San Francisco, 3; Atlanta and Pittsburgh, 2; and so on. All but the 18 largest cities in the United States receive only a single unit. Predictably, running a television campaign in New York can be three to four times as costly as in a city only one or two units strong.

Celebrities — or more accurately, their agents — write their own ticket commanding an especially high price for their performance. According to *Forbes Magazine*'s annual report on the highest-paid people in the United States, entertainers make more than major executives and athletes. Some advertisers — Pepsi-Cola, for one — have paid over $10 million for star performers in their television commercials.

This has been just a quick overview of payment schedules. Agencies, unions, and television stations can provide more detailed information on this important subject.

Information needed. Print layout or storyboard, or at least a script or outline, defining the purpose of the advertisement. Tell the talent what he or she should wear, what additional clothes to bring, whether to appear already made-up. The shoot should be scheduled to the hour. Payments should be discussed with the talent agency.

PARIS VOGUE

40

Renee Simonsen

Height 5'9"
Size 8-10
Bust 34
Waist 24
Hips 35
Shoe 7
Hair Blonde
Eyes Blue

THE FORDS
753-6500
688-8628 T.V.

As do illustrators and photographers, models also have "samples" of their work — photographs displaying a variety of poses and attitudes, and other information important to the advertiser that must choose from among them.

Male, female, mothers and grandmothers, sophisticated, happy-go-lucky . . . all types of models are available. Ford model Elle brings youth to the camera, Paul Fordsman an image of a successful male, and Kaylan Pickford a sense of maturity. Jan Leighton (freelance talent) has that just-your-average-guy look.

More and more "models" turn into performers in every sense of the word. Shown here again is Jan Leighton metamorphosing into whatever role the assignment calls for.

Photographers, too, are a fractionalized lot, both in style and use of peripheral services. Selection of models and talent, locations, fashion, accessory, and props all fall within the province of "photography." At top of the page is a 4-foot long facade built for Michelin Tires by miniature-set specialists McConnel and Borrow. Pictures taken by Lawrence Robins show his sure control over animals. Only babies require that kind of supervision.

Television Producers, Directors, Studios

Unlike in feature-length movies where the producer is the king, in a television commercial that role is given to the director. His "style" will manifest itself at every turn; he oversees a television commercial from beginning to end. No director can be expected to turn a poor concept into an outstanding one, no more than a cook can be hoped to whip up an outstanding dish using the wrong ingredients. But even if the director does not succeed at omniscience, he can at least try. With a viable script in hand, he has a chance.

Experienced art directors and copywriters know only too well the importance of the director's role in the making of a commercial. Not infrequently they decide on a director before they even conceive the storyboard. They know that the likes of Joe Sedelmaiers, Steve Horns, Bob Giraldis, Joe Pytkas, and many others are known for shooting award-winning commercials; it makes good business sense to take advantage of their creative talent.

Directors in a position to pick and choose their raw material — the basic concept of a commercial — will almost always do so since they are judged by the standard of their work. If faced with a storyboard that is thin on the creative, they have but two choices: suggest improvements (difficult with an already approved storyboard), or politely turn it down, perhaps claiming lack of time. It is for that reason that so many directors show interest in getting involved in the creative process beginning inception. Others insist on discussing the storyboard with the advertiser or the advertising agency and provide input along the way.

Star television directors often have a long queue of clients with assignments. Your assignment may or may not get immediate attention; in fact days, weeks, or even months of waiting are not unusual. Some directors average as many as 100 commercials a year.

It is important that the advertiser or his agency view the director's sample reel carefully before making a commitment. Mistakes in judgment can be costly. When in the screening room, concentrate on the show, not the glowing commentary of the director's agent sitting next to you. Don't be overwhelmed by the dimension of the silver screen in front of the room. Imagine it the same picture as it will play on the home television screen. Many clients, in fact, insist that they view sample reels on a regular 19" television set, so as not to be misled by the sheer magnitude of the image.

These are the things to look for in a sample reel:

1. *Casting.* This is, or should be, wholly a director's province. While it is true that the advertiser usually has veto power over casting, the director should *never* be asked to direct a performer he does not have full confidence in.

2. *Cinematography.* The director is also solely in charge of the photography. His is the choice of the cameraman and probably the production crew. He is responsible for approving each and every shot, controlling lighting, optical effects, camera angles, camera movements, color, temperature, and other technical details that will govern the way the final print will appear in its final form.

3. *Acting.* The director coaches, develops interaction between actors, and controls the rhythm of their performance. Every good director has rapport with his performers; many have studied acting themselves.

4. *Sound.* It is the director's responsibility, with his innate ability, to blend audio and video. It is important that these two ingredients blend in perfectly with one another. He selects voice-over, music, sound effects, and directs the performers. He is at recordings in the sound studio and supervises the mixes.

Acting skill is becoming increasingly important, what with the demands created by the electronic media. Commercials can provide valuable exposure for even well-established celebrities. Casting ranks high on the priority list of agency producers and television directors. The father/son relation is beautifully acted out (left column) in this People's Bank of Connecticut message (David Deutsch Associates). Director Steve Steigman (right column) has made a reputation in bringing the best out of relatively inexperienced talent.

5. *Pacing.* The director participates every step of the way in the editing process, from rushes to the final answer print. He works with the editor in the cutting room, decides on the sequence, creates the right transitions between scenes, moves the commercial toward its climax.

6. *Editing.* Every film or tape goes through an editing process after its being shot. Many changes can be effected at this stage. Good directors follow through on their work to the very end; the results show it.

7. *Creativity.* Sample reels do not accurately tell of the director's creative contributions, so it's best to find out who was responsible for what. Was the storyboard so powerful a concept as to allow no room for improvement? What contribution has the performer made to the commercial? Do spokepersons Brooke Shields (Levi's), Lee Iacocca (Chrysler), Yogi Berra (Miller Lite) need coaching to be themselves?

8. *Attention to detail.* Decisions about use of props, locations, makeup, hairstyle, wardrobe, and sometimes even selection of the manicurist, all rest with the director.

Still, the director's personal touch should be in evidence throughout the commercial. Sophisticated critics will readily sense his presence in every scene. Does the camera stay too long on a face? Are the transitions too quick—or slow? Are performers looking into the camera when they should really be looking at each other? Do the testimonials given by "real" people have a disturbingly phony ring? Is the commercial too loud for its own good? Or too quiet to be noticed? All of these decisions are but a reflection of the director's personal taste.

While the director's chief concern is to strive for artistic excellence, the *producer* makes sure production comes in within budget, schedules are met, the adminis-

trative details are all taken care of. He is the left brain of the operation. He works hand in hand with the director, and helps him to do his best. Unlike in theatrical movies where it is possible for producers to fire "their" directors, or film studios to fire "their" producers, in the world of television there is no time for family squabbles. Clients simply wouldn't stand for it; too much of their investment is at stake.

Some commercial film studios maintain a full stable of directors. That, however, does not mean they control "their" directors' every action. Star directors are a notoriously independent lot. They often insist on working with their own production crew, with whom they have developed a working relationship. Almost always, they choose their "own" camera operator, an important contributor to a commercial. It can be said that for all practical purposes, most established directors both produce *and* direct their commercials.

Both the director and producer must be acutely conscious of costs throughout the commercial, lest they get out of hand. As in the movie business, there are horror stories about commercials that cost two or three times as much as specified in the budget. The fault lies in planning as often as it does in execution.

The majority of commercials are shot on film stock, usually 35 mm or—in some instances—less expensive and technically inferior 16 mm. Many moviemakers like film for its editing capabilities. Picture quality can easily be manipulated, sound interlocks can be changed, and a great variety of opticals and special effects lend themselves for use in film.

However, there are some advantages to videotape. Videotape offers the "you-are-there" immediacy, making the commercial more believable. Video editing is "instant." The tape can be viewed in the control room as it is being shot, recorded in one piece, and put on the air in a short time. On the average, videotapes appear on home TV sets four or five days after shooting—ten to twenty times faster than a color film commercial. The editor plays back the tape at once and edits it hands-on and electronically. Dupes can be made overnight at low rates.

On the other hand, video offers only limited editing opportunities; for instance, animation and subtle transitions can be created only by digital manipulation. Moreover, color resolution is better with film stock, though advances in technology are narrowing the differences between the two media. Most video commercials are shot on $\frac{3}{4}$" videotape, with $\frac{1}{2}$" steadily gaining in popularity. Almost all television stations accept both filmed and taped commercials.

From start to finish, the production of a television commercial on film may take anywhere from a month to three months, depending on the time required for preparation, casting, set construction, shooting days, travel, editing, development, animation, shipping, and, of course, the time out for client's approvals.

One way to have the cake and eat it too is to transfer tape to 16 mm for editing and final reproduction — a common budget-saving device.

These are the checkpoints in film production:

Dailies (or "Rushes"). They represent all that has been put on film a day or two before. On the average, a 30-second commercial requires four to five hours of consistent shooting.

Work Print. The film has gone through rough editing and been cut to the length of the final commercial. The scenes are now spliced together for continuity. There is still a chance to make changes. The sound mix may now include music, voice-over, lip-sync, sound effects. Artwork or animation also may be included at this stage.

Answer Prints. This represents an assembly of the final prints, with opticals, artwork, and other elements inserted in place.

Release Prints. These are made from the master print and the "dupes" (now usually on tape and checked for quality by the advertiser) are sent out to various stations throughout the country. Overnight services are available.

The majority of commercials last for 30 seconds, with the second most popular lengths being 15 seconds and, more recently, 10 seconds. One-minute commercials are becoming rare though they can still be seen during "off-hours" like late at night. They are also particularly effective in direct-response advertising where it is important to convey precise information, even if this means repeating the same message within the same commercial.

Names of television production studios (film and video), animation, post-production, music and sound, radio, and recording studios can be found in the Yellow Pages, *Black Book, Madison Avenue Handbook,* art directors' annuals, trade magazines such as *Art Direction, Advertising Age, Backstage, Millimeter* (Penton Publishers). The last two publications (both in New York) also publish directories annually that list various television production services (production houses, editing facilities, etc.) broken down by type and geographical area. Semiannual brochures issued by Motion Pictures Enterprises (Tarrytown, New York) called *Motion Picture, Television & Theatre Directory* are also available. The most comprehensive guide is the *Audio Video Market Place,* or *AVMP,* published annually as a reference source for suppliers by the R. R. Bowker Company (New York). This nearly 800-page long book includes names and numbers of over 4500 producers and distributors or services, as well as names of associations, awards, festivals, media-oriented periodicals (over 160), reference books (over 250), and a calendar of events.

Information needed. Storyboard (rough or finished), or other explanation of the general concept (verbal or written). It isn't always necessary to come up with the exact scenario. Leave room for improvisation. Important are the selling points of the product for general guidance.

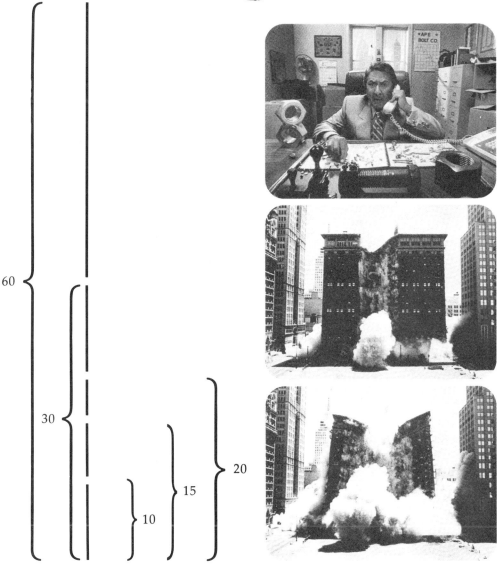

60

30

20

15

10

In print, the size of an ad is defined in inches — on television and radio, the "space" turns into "time" with seconds as the unit of measurement. The most popular time frames for commercials are (in that order) 30, 15, 10, 20, and 60 seconds. Each length calls for different pacing, camera work, and in most cases, basic concept. A single, strong statement usually works best in a 10-second spot such as the one created by Ally & Gargano for Federal Express. Says the man on the telephone: "Listen, if I don't have that package by 10:30 a.m. tomorrow, my whole business will collapse."

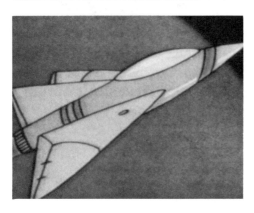

A wide variety of techniques are available today for use in television commercials. Limited cel animation, sophisticated application of camera movement, and computer-generated imagery, offer new creative—and cost-cutting—options. This ID for a Disney Channel uses flipbook drawings to quickly lead the viewer through the evolution of flight—making one aircraft turn into another. Colossal Pictures produced it.

The rubbery red figure of "Noid", created by Will Vinto Productions for Pizza Hut, has a life all its own. This is "claymation" at its best. The illusion of motion is achieved by manipulating the figure by hand, and taking a different shot for each and every movement.

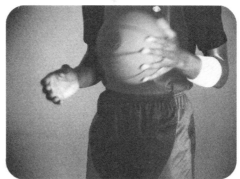

SUBARU.
Inexpensive. And built to stay that way.

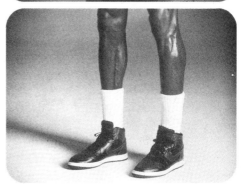

No hard-and-fast rules can be made about the pacing of a commercial. Director Steve Horn boldly cut from one scene to another in this commercial for Subaru. The camera slowly sweeps down to reveal a pair of Nikes. Director Pytka choose to have the camera stay fixed on spokesman Jaymes.

The camera is the eye of the viewer. Experienced directors are able to completely empathize with their audience—that is, they see the scenes exactly as they will appear on the screen.

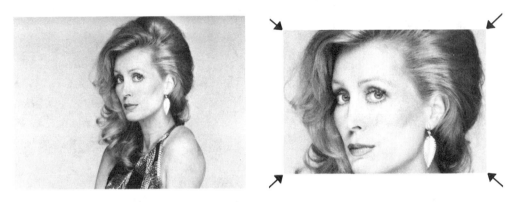

Quick cuts from scene to scene hurry the commercial along, creating a sense of excitement. This may or may not be desirable.

A camera moving in on a scene to a close-up (CU) slows down the pace and invites the viewer to take a better look. Curiosity and suspense are built up.

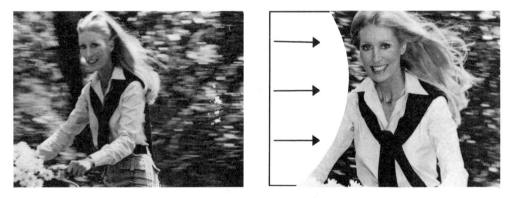

A wide variety of transitions are available today. Fast cutting, fading, and dissolving are optical effects, each of which establishes a different mood.

Direct Mail Services

In using direct mail, the advertiser will be looking for three types of services:

1. List managers

2. Creators and producers of direct mailing pieces

3. Follow-through

List managers comprise brokers, compilers, and suppliers. There are over 15,000 different mailing lists available (a broker can have the names of as many as 100 million prospects) today, and their number is growing. State-of-the-art computer technology and the vast amount of information available make it possible to focus in on market segments in ways never before thought possible. Through new market data and juxtapositioning, new lists are being created continually. Lists can be broken down geographically, demographically, and psychographically; i.e. lists by earned income, ethnic backgrounds, age, hobbies, locations, lifestyles. There is no end to the possible combinations. Cost of names can run from $10/M (Bible publishers) and $50/M (toastmasters) all the way to $1,000/M (cardiologists) and $1,500/M (collectors of impressionistic paintings).

Creators and producers of mailing pieces are computer services, data service bureaus, photo finishers, printers, envelope manufacturers, lettershops, typesetters, art studios and graphics designers, consultants, copywriters, and full-service direct mail companies. All may perform a single service or combination of services. Following through on orders are the product fulfillment houses, mailing services, telemarketing agencies, subscription agencies, and distribution centers.

Mailing houses usually specialize in products and services sold to consumers and industry. Many will have their own updated, "active" mailing lists, which include customers who have previously responded to offers. These organizations continually "merge and purge" their lists —i.e. use the computer to remove inactive or duplicate names, or those who have proven to be deadbeats.

Names of brokers appear in the Yellow Pages under "Advertising—Direct Mail" and "Mailing Lists." Valuable sources for services are also *Magazine Industry Marketplace* (R. R. Bowker) and *DDMP Fact Book on Direct Response* and *DDMA Catalogue Directory List* (lists about 500 catalogues), both published by Hillary House, Hewlett Harbor, New York. About 50 direct marketing associations, clubs, and organizations are listed in the *Direct Marketing Market Place* (Hillary House), a veritable wealth of information on the subject. Direct Mail Marketing Association (New York) also maintains a comprehensive reference library of direct mail advertising.

Creators of mailing pieces usually work on a fee basis. The cost of writing and designing a complete package (pieces fit into the same envelope) can be anywhere from $1,000 to $10,000 depending on the skill and reputation of the professionals involved.

Information needed. The more information about the product and prospects, the better. Direct mail advertising is always aimed at a well-defined target. The offer you make should be complete; your customers want to know exactly what they are paying for.

Telemarketing

This method of selling—telephone calls made to prospective buyers, usually by a trained operator—is among the fastest growing in today's marketplace. It has proven itself as a relatively simple and cost-effective method to develop a customer base, conduct special promotions, create company and product awareness, and perform research. It can be used as a form of "hot line"—a way to establish and maintain one-to-one contact with your consumers.

The simplest way of compiling a list of prospects to call is to use "secondary" sources such as phone books, memberships of target organizations, chambers of commerce, street-by-street directories, and various buyer's guides. Governmental regulatory agencies also keep up-to-date records on the names of companies they regulate. Still another source may be The Standard Industrial Classification Code (SIC) which gives annual sales, annual volume and potential volume of sales, credit rating and history, size of the last sale, and average sale size, in addition to name and location.

By far the most viable lists are those that are of customers who have already responded to offers of similar kind by whatever method. You can use your own company's list — a good yet often overlooked source — or established lists purchasable through lists brokers.

You can train your own staff to handle phone calls, or rely on professional telemarketing sales representatives (TSRs) as do most companies. Most calls last from 2.5 minutes to 5 minutes, so it is obviously possible to "visit" more prospects by means of telephone than in person. An experienced TSR can establish 30 to 50 contacts a day, in contrast to a peripatetic field representative's 4 or 5. He or she can also take orders, and give out information about the product.

Figure $3 for a 3-minute complaint-answering conversation. Expensive as this may sound, the payoff comes back in the form of repeat customers.

Telephone sales representatives usually work at two to three times the current minimum hourly rate. Based on about 30 hours of calling per week, such a person earns between $15,000 and $20,000 a year, plus a 25% to 50% incentive package. A TSR should not be asked to be on the phone more than 6 hours a day, five days a week. "Overtime" work should not be encouraged; a tired voice suggests a tired salesperson.

Information needed. Compile a written reference guide about the company, the product, the needs for the product, and the guarantees offered by the company. Explain the selling procedures in detail, including questions most often asked by the prospect.

Stock Houses: Photography, Art, Sound

Use of existing illustrative material — whose copyright may or may not have already expired — offers substantial savings to the budget-conscious advertiser, and at no sacrifice in quality. Often, the work is outstanding, having passed the most stringent criterion of all, the test of time.

Stock photos can be purchased outright or rented for one-time use from numerous sources, most of which are located in New York City and other centers of commercial activity. The major ones are these:

Photographers often have a large collection of photos at hand, some that they have taken experimentally, some that have been rejected for one reason or another, and some that were taken by other than themselves. Over 1,500 photographers in the United States have a supply of such pictures, sometimes as many as 10,000.

Stock photo/news agencies maintain huge libraries of black-and-white and color pictures, up to several million in some cases. There are over 250 such houses in the United States, and many more abroad. Some specialize in "commercial" shots (subjects used in advertising), others lean toward collecting "editorial" shots (news events, candid pictures). Most have both on file. (Some agencies will also accept assignments.)

Picture quality varies greatly, both in concept and execution. Conventional shots are exactly what the name implies; choice of models, situation, composition all follow established patterns (i.e.

mother, father, two kids, and a dog, having a picnic). Some agencies, however, offer a large selection of more unusual photographs taken by top creatively oriented photographers in the field. These agencies will mail their catalogues to you on request.

Costs are based on nature of shot, authorship, the agency, end use of material, and exclusivity (is the picture made available to others, perhaps one of your competitors?) There may be a holding or research charge for the picture, whether or not it is selected for use. It is best to call in advance to find out if the picture you want is in fact available. Most houses honor phone and mail requests. Many encourage walk-in browsing at no extra charge.

Work is almost always classified according to subject matter, as for example:

Advertising
Aerial
Agriculture and Rural Life
Animals
Armed Forces
Art and Architecture
Business and Industry
Children
Disasters
Editorial
Education
Entertainment
Environment
Fashion
Futuristic
Geography
High Technology
History (foreign)
History (U.S.)
Inventions
Medicine
Movies
Nature
Nudes
Occult Sciences
Oceanography
People and Life-Styles
Personalities
Photojournalism/Reportage
Pornography
Scenics and Views
Science
Space
Sports and Recreation
Still Life
Symbols
Transportation

Individual photographers and **agencies** are not alone in supplying stock art. *Business sources* may also provide free photos and drawings and their public relations offices will respond to your call. *Historical sources* (historical societies, public libraries, educational institutions, museums, and picture archives) are another rich repository of material. The New York Public Library's collection, for example, consists of more than 8 million pictures, organized by subject matter and period — and loaned to card-holding members free of charge. *Official sources* (local and federal governmental agencies, public information services, chambers of commerce) are accustomed to dealing with the public. *Film, television, and newspaper sources* provide news film footage as well as still photos for a nominal charge.

Names of photographers and their representatives are listed in the Yellow Pages, *The Black Book, Madison Avenue Handbook,* various annuals, photo publications (over 35 in the United States), membership lists of advertising, publications, art directors, and photographers associations, *Stock Photo & Assignment Source Book, Photography Market Place, Literary Market Place* (all published by R. R. Bowker).

Illustrations. Sources for existing artwork also abound. Some "clipboard art" services issue monthly collections of black-and-white drawings on an individual or subscription basis for both paste-up and computer graphics use. Numerous books (many published by the Dover Pictorial Archive Series) include thousands of copyright-free illustrations, letters and borders, and antique specimens, with reproduction privileges.

It is possible to obtain stock photographs for just about any purpose. Purchases can be made on an exclusive or non-exclusive basis — the former usually limited to a given time period. Not all houses offer the same type of photographs; some specialize in certain subject areas. Others sell the use of black and white prints, and still others only of color transparencies. On the left are samples from one of Galloway's catalogues; the house has an enormous library aimed at satisfying mainstream demand. Pictures from Four By Five (right column) represent the work of top photographers looking for clients willing to pay a little extra for quality.

Old-fashioned steel and wood engravings are available through pictorial archives who collect and publish these renderings copyright-free, (usually up to ten items at a time). A diversity of subjects, crisp black and white lines, and adaptability to typography make these drawings favorites with artists, designers, illustrators, and art directors. To the budget-conscious advertiser, they offer substantial savings. Shown here are pages from Dover's Pictorial Archive Series, whose publishers have put out about 200 books thus far, some of which contain over 400 illustrations.

Ready-to-use copyright-free art is also available through the brochures of various clip art services. Black and white illustrations are printed on glossy stock and can be cut out for immediate use, thus eliminating the need for statting. They can be purchased directly from the publisher or through art stores.

FROM THE BETTMAN ARCHIVES
AND BETTMAN NEWSPHOTOS

FROM ENCYCLOPEDIA OF
SOURCE ILLUSTRATIONS

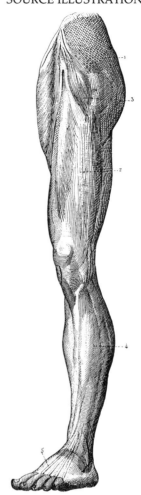

FROM WOODCUTS BY THOMAS BEWICK

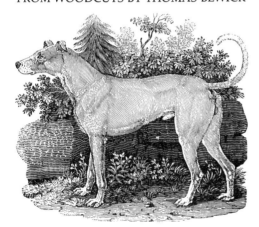

FROM THE RUBBER STAMP ALBUM OF LOWRY THOMPSON

Other sources of illustrations, decorations, and sundry inspirations.

B5275

PT074 42 lines per inch	**PT058** 48 lines per inch	**PT051** 50 lines per inch	**PT121** 55 lines per inch	**PT122** 65 lines per inch	**PT061** 8 lines per inch
PT065 10 lines per inch	**PT062** 16 lines per inch	**PT069** 19 lines per inch	**PT063** 32 lines per inch	**PT071** 34 lines per inch	**PT064** 48 lines per inch
PT123 10 lines per inch	**PT066** 16 lines per inch	**PT067** 32 lines per inch	**PT068** 48 lines per inch	**PT124** Wavy Line	**PT059** 26 lines per inch
PT060 16 lines per inch	**PT070** 30 lines per inch Roofing Tile	**PT072** 13 lines per in./Slate	**PT126** Double Line	**PT127** Triple Line	**PT202**
PT125 Cross Hatch	**PT164** Radiating Lines	**PT165** Radiating Lines	**PT012** Textile Pattern	**PT013** Undulating Lines	**PT078** Wide Undulating Lines

Black and white, and color, cut-out graphic aids represent a wide range of often-used illustrations, graphic symbols, patterns and shadings, type, or other art. Printed on opaque, microthin acetate film, these can be purchased in most art stores. Adhesive coating on the underside allows transfer of the image to paper or other surfaces and screens.

We Have Specialists For Organs You Didn't Even Know You Had.

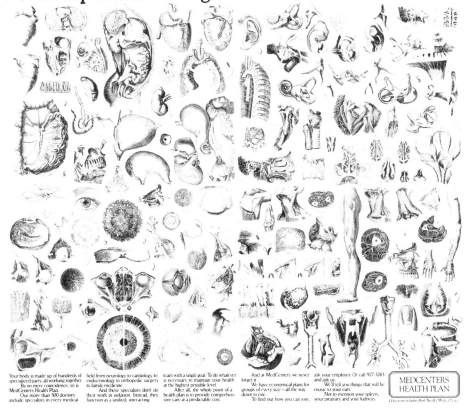

Your body is made up of hundreds of specialized parts, all working together.

By mere coincidence, so is MedCenters Health Plan.

Our more than 500 doctors include specialists in every medical field from neurology to cardiology to endocrinology to orthopedic surgery to family medicine.

And these specialists don't do their work in isolation. Instead, they function as a unified, interacting team with a single goal: To do whatever is necessary to maintain your health at the highest possible level.

After all, the whole point of a health plan is to provide comprehensive care at a predictable cost.

And at MedCenters we never forget it.

We have economical plans for groups of every size – all the way down to one.

To find out how you can join, ask your employer. Or call 927-3263 and ask us.

We'll tell you things that will be music to your ears.

Not to mention your spleen, your pituitary and your kidneys.

MEDCENTERS HEALTH PLAN

HOWEVER POWERFUL A MESSAGE IS, SOME PEOPLE MAY NOT BUY IT.

People have an overwhelming tendency to question what they're told. Even when it's cast in stone.

That's what makes us human. We make our own decisions. Sometimes right. Sometimes wrong. But always our own.

So it's hard to believe when people claim that advertising made them buy something they didn't want.

Sure, we'd like to think that the advertising we create has a powerful impact on you.

But the truth is we simply present facts. Try to make them interesting and entertaining. Then sit back and hope we get through.

As for having some kind of power over people's actions, greater forces than the advertising industry have tried.

And God only knows, no one does everything they're told.

ADVERTISING
ANOTHER WORD FOR FREEDOM OF CHOICE.
American Association of Advertising Agencies

If this resembles your agency's organizational chart, give us a call.

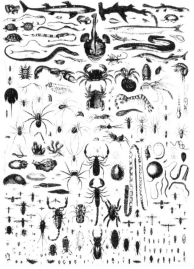

Fallon McElligott Rice, 701 Fourth Avenue South, Minneapolis, Minnesota 55415, Telephone 612-332-2445

Old fashioned drawings have been put to excellent use by Fallon McElligott.

WAITING FOR A TAX BILL COULD PUT A LOT OF AMERICANS TO SLEEP.

There's only one thing worse than tax reform.

And that's waiting for it.

Because while the country waits for the arduous process to be finished, the country suffers.

Investors become wary investors. Industries stop making decisions to wait for the outcome. It's no wonder it drags on. For a

plan that aims for simplification, it's mighty complex.

And there's certainly enough to quibble about.

But any good piece of legislation has both supporters and opponents. Without them, the system wouldn't be working the way it was designed to.

No one would argue that tax

reform has to be done right. Because down the road, no one wants to go through tax reform reform. But one thing is certain.

It must also be done quickly. Because if we put our economy

to sleep, we may have to shake it hard to wake it up again.

For a copy of *Tax Reform and Corporate America: A Preliminary Analysis*, call 1-800-237-8000, Ext. 55.

Drexel Burnham

Drexel Burnham Lambert Incorporated

Art director Sal DeVito has combined yesterday with today in this newspaper ad for Drexel Burnham Lambert. Old steel engravings have been smartly altered by the touch of a modern pen.

TELEVISION COMMERCIALS
(Approximate Working Days)*

FILMED COMMERCIALS	Approximate Working Days
Concept, script/storyboard	14
Internal OK	4
Client OK	2
Bids/Estimates	7
Pre-Production (castings, sets, etc.)	11
Shooting	3
Processing of dailies (editing, rough-cut, fine-cut)	7
Voice-over recording	1
Musical scoring, sound mix, recording	6
Opticals	3
Answer print/tape, for Agency/Client OK	3
Agency OK	1
Client OK	1
Quantity Tapes	2
Shipping	5
Total	**70**

VIDEO-TAPE COMMERCIALS	
Concept, script/storyboard	14
Agency OK	4
Client OK	2
Bids/Estimates	5
Casting and Pre-Production	10
Shooting	3
Tape Editing	2
Agency OK	1
Client OK	2
Quantity tapes	3
Shipping	5
Total	**51**

NOTE: Above does not provide for special considerations such as : (a) required pre-air testing; (b) pre-air use dates; (c) required legal and Network clearances; (d) unusual original music requirements; (e) unusual talent search/negotiation; (f) shooting at difficult locales.

* Animated commercials not included

PRINT MEDIA
(Approximate Working Days)

		Newspaper or Magazines		
		Black & White	2 Color	4 Color
1.	Concept, headline & copy	5	5	5
2.	Layout	4	5	5
3.	Agency OK's	2	2	2
4.	Production cost est. (if needed)	1	2	2
5.	Client OK's	3	3	3
6.	Finished Art	5	6	8
7.	Typesetting and mechanical	3	3	3
8.	Agency OK's	2	2	2
9.	Client OK's	2	2	2
10.	Publication materials/proofs:			
	Letterpress			
	Original letterpress engravings	2 - 5	2 - 5	15 - 20
	Duplicate plates (Cronars)			
	from originals (incl. proofs)	2	3	5
	Offset			
	Original offset film	2 - 5	2 - 5	15
	Duplicate film	1	1	1
	Gravure			
	Original gravure film	8	10	20
	Preprints/Reprints	2	3	5
11.	Forwarding	3	3	3
	Total			
	Letterpress	36 - 39	41 - 44	60 - 65
	Offset	35 - 38	39 - 42	56
	Gravure	40	46	60

NOTE: Above does not provide for special considerations such as: (a) required copy testing at various stages; (b) pre-publication uses (sales meetings, etc.); (c) required legal clearances; (d) special photography locations/situations.

Stock Music. It is as easy to find stock music as it is to obtain "used" pictures. If the piece is copyrighted, permissions may be available from the owner of the rights for an appropriate fee. The National Music Publishers Association (New York) is probably the quickest way to find out if the music is copyrighted, and if so, in what countries. Copyrights are not always all inclusive. Sometimes they apply to only a certain arrangement (folk songs, for example) or to one set of lyrics. Nor do all copyrights cover the work worldwide.

Obviously, stock music costs much less than an original score. If a new score is needed, this can be done relatively quickly. Instant selections of melodies can be made in a sound studio, recorded or played live.

An enormous quantity of music is available at reasonable cost, most of which has been rescored over and over again to fit changing musical tastes. Stock music is listed in library catalogues, classified and cross-indexed by subject matter, mood, national origin, instrumentation, time periods, composers, titles.

Engravers and Printers

Engravers. Engravers prepare photoelectrotypes from which to run off copies in small or large quantities; with letterpress, offset, and gravure being the three commercially most popular methods. Prices vary depending on the method used, size, number of colors, line or halftone reproduction. Of all, offset is the least expensive but also the least brilliant in color.

It is up to the advertiser to select the method that best suits his particular needs, and at an affordable cost. For many purposes, offset is perfectly adequate. For work where quality of color illustration is of prime importance (financial reports or a museum catalogue) you may want to explore other reproduction methods. It makes poor business sense, however, to strive for the best (and most expensive) reproduction method where high quality would be wasted, as for example in black-and-white newsprint or a monthly bill.

Photoengraving is a highly competitive business. Overhead expenses vary from shop to shop. With the differences in wages from location to location, it is often good economy to turn to an "out-of-town" shop to get the job done—or even turn to a service in some other part of the world.

Other ways to save: use leftover paper stock, be flexible on time (during "downtime," prices dip), look for "gang-run" programs, stay with standard sizes and signatures, cut down on the number of colors, and supply color-separated artwork.

Printers. Printers take over where engravers leave off. The selection of the printer should be entirely contingent on the type of job you wish to print. Small runs should be assigned to small-platen presses (even hand-fed, if the quantity is only a few hundred or so), larger runs to larger presses. Giant web-fed machines can process an enormous amount of work in a relatively short time, sometimes folding, inserting, perforating, envelope-inserting the work all through a single continuous run, in addition to putting through routinely four- to seven-color printed matter.

To stay competitive, many printers have added a wide variety of services to simply duplicating original copy. All under the same roof may be art studios, photographers, computerized typography, printers, and even mini advertising agencies, direct mail services, and publishing companies. They create material as well as see it through completion: bind, emboss, die cut, engrave, mount, laminate, photocopy (Xeroxes, Kodachromes), personalize letters, typeset, electronically interconnect, spot deliver, and warehouse—all this in addition to what is traditionally construed as "printing."

There are several times during the process that proofs can be inspected. Engravers' proofs allow the advertiser to compare the results with the original. Corrections can still be made at this point. An approved version of the engraver's proof should always be sent to the printer for point of reference. The client should be invited to see the first proof as it comes off the press. Since mailing a proof to and waiting for a decision at the office may mean downtime at the plant, it is often more practical to pay a persona grata visit to the printer at the beginning of the run.

Names of engravers and printers appear in the Yellow Pages, the *Black Book*, and various graphic publications.

Typographers

Typographers set type by hand (rarely), on a machine, photographically, or by modern digital and laser technology. Most typesetting houses have a large selection of fonts at or nearby the premises. There are over 5,000 different typefaces available today—a bewildering variety to hold in mind even for a seasoned art director. And this does not include the infinite variety of additional possibilities that photographic and digital equipment can generate.

All typehouses have free catalogues of their selection of typefaces. Such a guide shows thousands of specimens, often set up in blocks to help the reader visualize the effect *en masse*. Mentioned also are the point sizes obtainable through the shop.

Choosing the "proper" typeface is a mysterious process, and one that can easily intimidate the uninitiated. Suffice to say, it is not so complicated a process as some mythmakers in the profession would like others to believe. It is not necessary to learn by rote all the typefaces available, unless one wishes to make the *Guinness Book of Records* on eidetic memory. Knowledge of a few dozen typefaces is sufficient to accomplish most jobs. David Ogilvy, for one, a man never short of strong personal opinions, advocated

the use of Caslon in all his ads. He liked this typeface for its timeless beauty, readability, and authority. Simplistic as his approach to type selection may appear in hindsight, there is a ring of truth to his belief; readers read, they do not examine typefaces.

Shown on page 109 are most commonly used specimens. Some are new; others more than a century old and still as young as ever. Chances are they cover almost everyone's needs, and then some.

Once the type is set, the client usually receives one or several typeproofs. This is his chance, possibly his only chance, to look for "typos" (typographical errors by the compositor) and use aesthetic judgment as to line and letter spacing and the placing of emphasis. Graphic tomfoolery that looked all right on the sketching pad can now appear an invitation to visual chaos. Now is the time to make corrections.

For exact copy fitting, most advertising art directors insist on film or electronic typesetting, both of which automatically "justify" lines, eliminate each "widow" (an overly short line of type that falls at the end of a paragraph), and even out spacing between letters. With the advent of computers, electronic typesetting has gained wisespread use, virtually eliminating error prone human typesetters. Most newspaper and magazine copy is now set this way. The computer stores the type; the results are displayed on the screen, and then relayed elsewhere by satellite or other means of telecommunication. Complete page layouts can be made on the spot, visualized on the screen. Elements are moved into position, fitted to size, cropped, enlarged or reduced in a matter of seconds. Desktop publishing (see page 114) never had it so good.

Costs depend on a number of factors. One is the skill and taste of the typographer. The others are the variety of available typefaces and ready technology. Some photocompositors represent investments running into millions of dollars.

The typeproofs are pulled and sent to

the advertiser for checking purposes. Sophisticated — and rich — clients insist on glassine proofs — type printed in black or color on a transparent, resilient sheet of paper that can be laid over the original layout for position. Less meticulous — and more budget-minded — clients use opaque galleys to see if the type fits.

Desktop Publishing: Type and Graphics All in One

This is a relatively new field, and one that is growing fast. Its advantages lie in its speed, shortcuts, flexibility, and up to 50 percent saving on production costs. All that is required is a personal computer (at the time of this writing, the magic names are the icon-laden McIntosh and the more businesslike IBM), software for word processing, charts and drawings (clipboard art is available) if desired, printer (laser preferred but not absolutely necessary — if high-resolution hard copy is required, laser and linotron printers can be rented economically to produce reproduction quantity), and publishing applications such as a layout. The computer operator mixes graphics and text on the page — selecting typefaces, designing a page layout, justifying text material — and becomes both a typesetter and the designer. Illustrations can be dropped into position either directly or by the printer (the human kind). The great advantages of this method are that the operator can make his changes instantly and that the computer screen displays the page exactly as it is going to appear — what you see is what you get. For small runs (say, under 2,500), all that is required is a photocopier. Consider desktop publishing for your training and technical manuals, brochures, forms, newsletters, maps, charts, diagrams, drawings, and more. But make sure that the computer operator is artistically inclined. Computers do not design. People do.

Century Schoolbook

One of the most readable of faces is Century. Designed over a hundred years ago, this type shows no intention of making an exit.

Helvetica

Helvetica is one of the most popular sans serif typefaces available today. Clean, contemporary and authoritative, it is a favorite with contemporary designers.

Primer Italic

Cursive typefaces are used mostly for special decorative purposes. Graceful, decorative, and unique in appearance, they are most resplendent in display.

Hobo

Many other typefaces are available for the artistically adventurous.

Every typeface (more about this in Chapter 13) has its own distinctive "feel", affecting not only readership but the mood of the message. Typographers usually have a wide variety of fonts available, either in-house or through outside sources.

PRINK SHADED

PRINK SOLID

QUADRANT CAPS LIGHT

QUILL SHADED

RADIUS Extra Light

RADIUS Light

RADIUS

RADIUS Moditalic

RADIUS outline

Bold Radius Outline

RADIUS Contour

RADIUS shadow

RECLAIM reclaim

REGINA TITLING

REGINA SHADOW

REKA REKA

REKLA rekla

ROBUST Robust

ROMAN no. 1

ROMAN ornate

ROYAL ornate

SANDERS black

SANDS sands

SAXON saxon

SACKET
Sacket

SCHAFT schaft

SEA CROW CAPS

SEIG seig

serendipity

SEVEN STAR seven star

Silverwood

SLIMBOY CAPS

SLIMSHANK slimshank

Most typographers have their own specimen books available for distribution. These provide the user with a working tool for text and display type selection. Such catalogues are often divided into several sections as in M.J. Baumwell's Typography Book, shown here. A large selection of typefaces is available.

All sizes below were keyboard-set using a special font, then camera-enlarged. Such 'enlarger' fonts retain the unique design

jklmnopqrstuvwxyz 18 **ABCDEFGHIJKLMN**

lmnopqrstuvwxyz 20 **ABCDEFGHIJKLM**

nopqrstuvwxyz 24S **ABCDEFGHIJK**

pqrstuvwxyz 24L **ABCDEFGHIJ**

rstuvwxyz 30 **ABCDEFG**

stuvwxyz 36 **ABCDEF**

tuvwxyz 42 **ABCDEF**

vwxyz 48 **ABCD**

wxyz 60 **ABC**

wxyz 72 **ABC**

Even within the same font, a user has the choice of many sizes to fit his or her layout exactly. All designs can be further modified for extended or condensed versions, or "in-between" size requirements. Shown here is Helvetica Bold, from 14 pt. to 72 pt.

Garamond Bold

Fine typography is the result of nothing more than an
attitude. Its appeal comes from the understanding us
ed in its planning; the designer must care. In contem
porary advertising the perfect integration of design e
lements often demands unorthodox typography. It m
ay require using wrong fonts, cutting hyphens in hal
f, using smaller than normal punctuation marks; in f
act, doing anything that is needed to improve appear

FILM SIZE: 14   METAL SIZES: 6, 7, 8, 9, 10, 11, 12, 14, 18

Garamond Bold Italic

*Fine typography is the result of nothing more than an
attitude. Its appeal comes from the understanding us
ed in its planning; the designer must care. In contem
porary advertising the perfect integration of design e
lements often demands unorthodox typography. It m
ay require using wrong fonts, cutting hyphens in hal
f, using smaller than normal punctuation marks; in f
act, doing anything that is needed to improve appear*

FILM SIZE: 14   METAL SIZES: 6, 7, 8, 9, 10, 11, 12, 14

Goudy Old Style

Fine typography is the result of nothing more tha
n an attitude. Its appeal comes from the understa
nding used in its planning; the designer must car
e. In contemporary advertising the perfect integr
ation of design elements often demands unortho
dox typography. It may require using wrong font
s, cutting hyphens in half, using smaller than nor
mal punctuation marks; in fact, doing anything t

FILM SIZES: 6, 7, 8, 9, 10, 11, 12, 14, 16

**Every style of type set in a block has its own distinctive "color", texture, and weight.
Garamond Bold (14 pt.), Garamond Bold Italic (14 pt.) metal composed, and Goudy
Old Style (14 pt.) film composed, both set in block, show how the type would appear
on the page.**

6505n

5503s

Special effects (curved type, vertical setting, open typeface, shadings, three dimensional, reverse, type joined, etc.) can be created by state-of-the art photographic techniques. This is one of many shown in Photo-Lettering, Inc., a catalogue designed to "stimulate the imagination and creativity of the user".

Advertisers — and their agencies — usually pay close attention to the way their message is typeset. Most prefer phototypography to fit the space perfectly. This invites readership and is also pleasing to the eye, as these two full-page newspaper ads, prepared by Fallon McElligott and Chiat/Day, so beautifully demonstrate.

Bit & Bridle

The Newsletter of the T. L. Pierce Riding Academy   Vol XXI

Sunset Saddle-up

Your adventure will start when the day ends. Next Saturday at 6:00 p.m., ride in the twilight over Madigan Hills to Dan's River, where there will be a cookout and songfest. An experienced wrangler (with excellent night vision) will lead you into a peaceful world of near darkness, the silence pierced only by the steady clip-clop of horses' hooves and the voices of the riders. Together, you'll ride over rolling fields under the soft moonlight and gaze at the sparkling lights of nearby towns. But it will be more than a feast for the eyes; our cook will prepare a meal barbequed to perfection. A warm campfire and sing-a-long will make you think you've discovered the wild, wild west. Ride 'em, cowboy!

Horse of a Different Color

If your horse harbors a secret desire to look like Rapunzel, dress her up, let down her mane and bring her to the Annual Costume Show, Friday at 3:00 p.m. in the Center Ring. Be sure to indulge your own wish to be a fireman, because both you and your horse must be in costume.

A parade will follow across Mairs Meadow, up Seiffer Street, across the bridge and into town.

It's an Open and Shut Case

Fine leather saddlebags will be awarded to the winners and ribbons to the runners-up. A colorful panel of experts will judge each of the participants on the basis of creativity, originality and good horsemanship. Jumping, singing and dancing are all optional. The judges might think they have seen it all, but we know that you can show them otherwise.

DAY CAMP FOR FUTURE COWBOYS

Rustle up the young 'uns. For the next three months, we'll be offering instruction in the fundamentals of good horsemanship; grooming and caring for the animal, saddling and bridling, and walking and trotting, all with an experienced leader. The class will teach students the skills they need to handle a horse in a show ring and out on the range. And it will give you time for a siesta. Morning or afternoon classes. Ages 5 through 12.

Rodeo Films Scheduled

Watch some of the Academy's greatest cowboys and cowgirls. Films of last week's grand rodeo held in Reilly Ring will be shown this Thursday at 8:00 p.m. in the Groom Room. So come Thursday night and watch the rodeo. After all, you never know when you may have to rope a calf.

Desktop computers offer an ever-increasing variety of typefaces and page make-up flexibility to the accomplished user. They represent one of the most economical — and certainly the fastest — ways of getting the type on paper. This newsletter was composed on an IBM PS/2.

Assistance Provided by Media

Magazines will often publish articles tying in with a major advertiser's basic product or service category. (For example, several magazines agreed to use color telephones for prop in their editorial photographs when AT&T first issued its basic instrument in other than black or white.) Special sections bound in the magazine are initiated in the hope of attracting advertisers looking for a targeted audience: summer sections, for swimsuits; travel sections to entice readers to visit faraway places; financial sections to introduce new financial strategies to sophisticated investors.

Available too are complete free-standing magazine issues or supplements, up to several dozens of pages, produced conjointly with one or several advertisers. The publisher will supply part or all of the text and illustrations on a specified subject, then produce and distribute the issue in exchange for space sold to advertisers; the advertising/editorial page ratio is usually about half and half. In effect, the advertiser "sponsors" the piece, much as he would a television program.

Many publications offer a variety of "merchandising aids" to their clients. These may be anything from reproductions of the advertisement mounted on cardboard and tagged "as advertised in . . ." (for purposes of a counter display) to tie-ins with other (say, radio or television) media programs. At times, publications will take it upon themselves to promote advertising success stories. The *New York Times,* for example, mailed out two oversized brochures of advertisements prepared by an agency to celebrate the first appearance of a full-page ad campaign sponsored by a bank in New York City. The mailing piece was paid for by the newspaper to invite similar financial institutions to follow suit; media, agency, and client all shared the limelight.

Publications may also make their in-house facilities available to the advertiser. Included among their services are graphics, copywriting, mechanical preparation, typesetting, and final reproduction. The charges usually fall far below those charged by commercial studios or advertising agencies.

Almost all newspapers and some of the magazines will "pub-set" headlines and text at the client's request. Working at their normal stepped-up pace, newspapers will have proofs ready for approval in a matter of hours. The client can call in his corrections by phone. He then will see his ad in finished form in the newspaper on the following day. While selection of typefaces may be limited, and the quality of work may not come up to that of a top — and more expensive — typehouse, savings in time and cost may justify the difference. All editorial matter is set in this manner, as well as small-space and classified advertisements.

On request, publications will gladly supply reprints of ads to the advertiser free or at a slight charge. These can be sent to distributors or special customers. (IBM has ordered 500,000 reprints of its multi-paged insert in the *Wall Street Journal.*) It is important that requests be made before or shortly after the ad has appeared. Newspapers are quick to cast aside yesterday's news.

Radio and television stations may also provide in-house facilities to the advertiser. The disc jockey is often made available to read announcements. If he has a loyal audience, his words could border on a testimonial. To take full advantage of such a talent, some advertisers send only a rough outline draft of their spot announcement to the station, encouraging the announcer to deliver the message in his own personal style.

Some publications (a few) also make their subscription list available to advertisers — at a discount. These lists can be quite valuable. What better way to reach millionaires than to mail to subscribers of a magazine called *Millionaires*?

Local television stations have expert

staff and readily available technical equipment on the premises. This makes it possible for budget- and time-conscious advertisers to tape their spots at the station's studio or in an easily accessible outdoor setting. What the resulting footage may lack in slick execution is made up by the sense of you-are-there spontaneity — and the credibility that goes with it. Also,

costs are substantially lower than those for a comparable spot produced in a commercial studio.

Information needed. Tell the media representative what it is you are after. Media representatives are a creative bunch — and they want your business. They know their business, and have the resources to give you what you want.

FIGURE 1. U.S. FERTILITY RATE has been declining for 200 years, with minor fluctuations. The exception was the baby boom, which peaked in 1957. Current fertility patterns represent a return to previous historic trends.

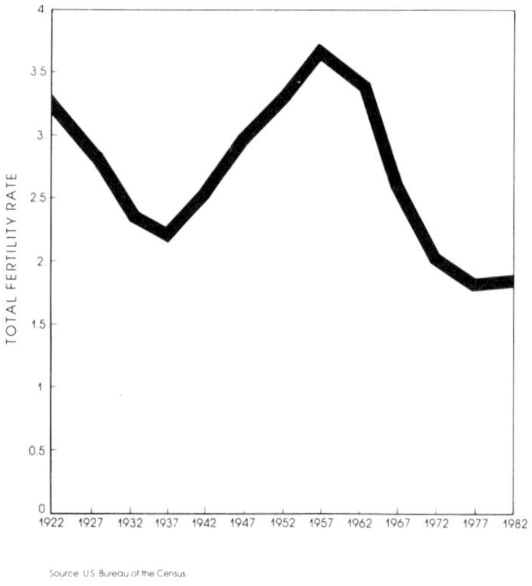

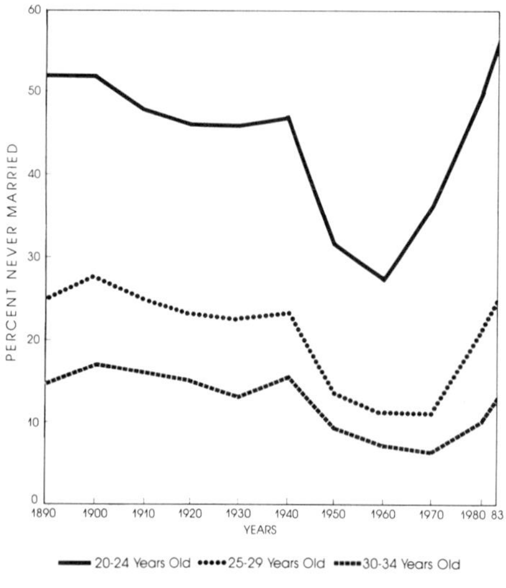

FIGURE 3. DEGREES EARNED BY WOMEN between 1955 and 1980 in the fields of medicine, law, engineering, architecture, and business administration advanced sharply from 1970 on as women pursued higher education to advance their careers.

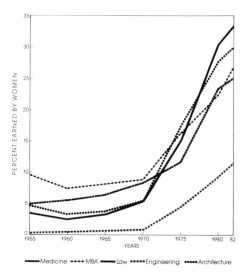

FIGURE 2. POSTPONEMENT OF MARRIAGE is shown in the percent of women never married between the ages of 20 and 35. The upswing in this number signals a return to marital patterns common before 1940. The dip marks the baby-boom era.

FIGURE 4. LABOR-FORCE COMMITMENT is underscored by the steady increase in married women with children taking jobs between 1950 and 1984. Two-thirds of all married women with a child over 6 and half of all married women with a child under 6 were in the labor force by 1984.

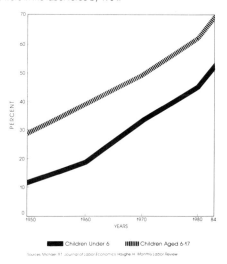

One of the best sources of marketing information is the media itself. Not surprisingly, they keep close track of their audience, and will gladly share their information with advertisers. This page is from a comprehensive report issued by *Cosmopolitan* on the profile of women customers — the result of a thorough survey.

Time Magazine advertises its own advertisers on its striking posters.

This 12-page two-color oversized brochure printed by the *New York Times* on
a full newspaper page was a campaign
for a large investment bank, mailed to
over 50,000 top business executives. A
picture of agency principals was shown
on the back page.

The oval-shaped Good Housekeeping
seal has long been associated with product excellence—and no wonder. The
magazine maintains 12 different laboratories, centers, and departments to test
the products of its advertisers, spending
over $2 million to check claims.

Public Relations

As pointed out before, public relations and advertising call for different orientations. They are not the same discipline, even if it may appear that at times. A public relations release gains currency for its newsworthiness; advertising for its profitability to the publisher.

Nevertheless, public relations and advertising often cross paths, like a couple of race cars tearing along the same track. Writers, photographers, and artists are important players in both fields.

Who really should be responsible for your next financial, recruiting or franchise ad, or the writing of a fund-raising campaign? And who is best qualified to put together a financial report, an employees' manual, a brochure about the product? It could be your Public Relations. Considering the fact that salaries and overhead are lower, you may be in for a substantial saving — and at no sacrifice in quality.

One thing is certain. The success of a public relations firm depends very much on its intimate contacts with media and the "movers and shakers" of the world. Experienced public relations firms keep a close watch on changes in the field, and make it their business to cultivate those in position to bring about these changes.

A public relations firm's function may begin with sending out press releases. But it certainly does not end there. Here is a quick overview of some of the other tasks a public relations firm may undertake:

Monitoring. This may involve getting clippings of ads or editorials appearing in the United States and abroad; arranging for kinescopes and tapes from television stations, and off-the-radio recordings from radio stations.

Through their large network of sources, public relations firms may also take it upon themselves to keep track of your print and broadcast ads on a day-to-day basis. A fee is usually charged for this service, plus extra payment for clipping each announcement.

There are at least 100 clipping services in the United States that are active; some send out as many as 20,000 clippings every day. Checking services help to audit advertising.

Research. This research is not the esoteric kind you get from agencies (pretesting, focus interviewing, screenings), but research that emanates from sources such as published material, governmental and local agencies, data bases, libraries.

Distribution. Your public relations firm has a long list of names on file, many that represent personal contacts built up through the years.

Scheduling. Your firm is probably familiar with a calendar of conferences and other newsworthy events, and can see that your presentation will not conflict with those of other organizations.

Information needed. Your general message, company history, pertinent facts that you feel will help dramatize your story. Look for newsworthiness from the point of view of your audience, not of the company.

Audio/Video Facilities

This may cover anything from putting together a modest one-man slide presentation to creating complex multimedia spectaculars. Modern technology allows reproduction on tape, film, disc, and slide of almost anything the eye can see or the ear can hear — and transmit the message anywhere in the world instantly.

Some of the organizations specializing in audio/video are:

- Software producers and distributors
- Production companies
- Video services
- Laboratories
- Cable programming

- Sound recording
- Music and sound effects libraries
- Film and TV commissions

Almost all offer not one but a wide range of services and equipment. A production house, for example, may have available both skilled manpower (scriptwriters, musicians, camera crew, photographers, artists, retouchers, editors, researchers) and the equipment needed to carry out the assignment. Equipment can be purchased outright or rented separately, depending on the nature and location of the assignment.

Duplication and transfer services are also available either through production houses or distributor services. It is possible to transfer just about any image from one medium to another.

FROM	TO
Print	Slide
Slide	Print
Slide	Videotape
Videotape	Slide
Film	Videotape
Videotape	Film
Slide	Filmstrip
Filmstrip	Slide
Artwork and color negative	Slide, videotape, film
Slide, videotape, film	Artwork and color negative
Computer graphic	Slide, videotape, film
Slide, videotape, film	Computer graphic

Digital technology also makes it possible to convert conventional signals into computerized zeros and ones.

FROM	TO
Film, tape, slide	Television screen
Television screen	Film, tape, slide
Single image	Videotex terminals
Laser printer	Transparency film

Specific programs can be produced on assignment or purchased through available stock. They are available on 8 mm, 16 mm, and 35 mm film (it is possible to "blow up" or reduce film sizes), tape, or slide. Programs are usually classified by subject, with some companies specializing in one or two fields: business, children's programs, documentaries, full-length features, industrial, medical, sports, scientific, radio and television commercials, sales promotion and training, and so on. Rentals are also available. Some of the best programs are originated by companies (airlines, health agencies), associations, or governments looking for exposure; such films or tape are often available free of charge.

The best directories for names and numbers are the Yellow Pages, *AVMP* ("Audio Video Market Place,") and the *Equipment Directory*. County and city agencies also provide information, mostly of local nature, about permits, local casting, and location shooting. Associations and audio/video publications are also there to answer the advertiser's questions.

Employment Agencies and Other Recruitment Sources

Many employment agencies in large cities handle communications personnel, such as copywriters, art directors, graphics designers, bullpen artists, media buyers, production and traffic managers, research specialists, and so on. The chances of finding more-accomplished creative talent, however, improve greatly in going through agencies whose specialty is the advertising field. The two best known are Jerry Fields & Associates and Judy Wald Agency, both headquartered in New York. Both work with clients coast to coast and overseas. Fees usually range from 15% to 30% of first year's salary depending on the position.

Executive placement agencies do not like to be confused with employment agencies, though they essentially perform the same functions even if in a more sophisticated fashion. For positions paying six-digit salaries your chances will improve if you look for them here. Generally, the fee is one-third of annual salary offered, payable by the employer.

And Still More Services

It is impossible to make a complete list of all the services available to the advertiser, lest this book become the thickest and most voluminous Yellow Pages yet published. Suffice to say that there are thousands upon thousands of highly specialized services available. Here are a few more you may find useful:

Premium Items. Specialists in this field offer a wide range of products available for premium use — from calendars to luxury cars. Most have annual or biannual catalogues illustrating and describing the selection. To find state-of-the-art items, visit premium conventions, or other types of meetings that feature volume products. Almost anything lends itself to premium use, and you can always get a discount on quantity purchases.

Sales Promotion Specialists. They have expertise in putting together special events, expositions, demonstrations, programs. Get public relations involved at the planning stage.

Point-of-Sale Material. Store displays, dummy packages, shelf-talkers, streamers can be produced by almost anyone, including graphics studios, advertising agencies, printers and lithographers. Certain organizations specialize in this area. For their experience, you may have to pay a little extra, but it may be worth it. For one thing, they know what kind of material has the best chance for being used by retailers.

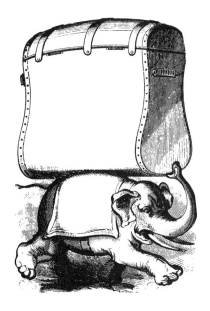

Brokers and Sales Representatives. In distributing a product (particularly a new product) independent sales organizations with established contacts may yet be your most efficient means. They specialize by industry, type of product, or geographic area. Some serve supermarkets; others visit only drugstores, bookstores, medical offices, business establishments. They may take your product on exclusive or non-exclusive basis.

Exhibits. These are the houses that make, sell, or rent ready-made or custom-made display systems, including panel and modular sections, headers, panel inserts, lighting systems, furniture. Many

problems — letters and symbols painted, raised, neon lit, silk screened, engraved, illuminated, or otherwise reproduced in kind. The place could be the side of a building, an outdoor poster, a truck panel, a marquee, a convention identification badge. You name it; the sign people will leave your name on it.

have the capabilities to put the whole package together, providing lettering, charts, photography, packing, shipping, installation. They are well aware of the space problems and house regulations set forth by exhibition halls.

Signage. Professional parlance for the advertiser's indoor and outdoor sign

Shipping Supply Companies. These houses make boxes, cartons, bubble paks, Jiffy Bags, corrugated boxes. The company may or may not have your package in stock. No problem; it will design and make it for you.

Putting Yourself in the Shoes of the Vendor

Getting the most out of a vendor is both an art and a science. Sometimes you get exactly what you had in mind—quality on time and in budget. Other times, things may get out of hand. Rare is the advertiser who claims to have received exactly what he had in mind *every time*. Communication—or the lack of it—lies at the root of the problem most of the time. While it is generally a matter of giving a vendor too little information, it is sometimes a matter of giving him too much. Listed here are things you should *not* tell your vendor in order to avoid confusion and uncertainty:

Company Politics. "Joe will approve it, Bob will not. Bob is that kind of guy. He is a royal pain in the neck. Too bad, since he is the one who has the final say."

We Can Talk About the Money Later. "I don't really know what the job is worth unless you show me a tight sketch—or the finished piece exactly as it is going to appear."

He Is an Old Friend of the President. "I am anxious to get you aboard. Frankly, we need some fresh blood around here, but your competitor, he knows the CEO's mother-in-law, so we may have a bit of a personal problem there, if you follow what I'm trying to say."

Who Knows Where I'll Be when You Finish the Assignment. "I told you before, and I say it again, I'll hate my job. With a passion. Why, I may not even be here when you get back with the finished job."

It is human to let go of one's inner emotions but to a vendor looking for clear directions, it can sound discouraging.

Remember, these people can make or break you. Keep them on your side for the long haul. Never has the phrase "friends in need" rung so true.

To Sum It Up

The most popular alternative to having a full-service agency is to have all or part of advertising done through in-house facilities. These can be organized to fit exactly the needs of the parent company. Speed, flexibility, and economy are some of the advantages of taking this route. Lack of objectivity, corporate office politics, less exposure to the advertising field, and difficulties in attracting top talent are some of the disadvantages.

Almost all advertisers farm out work a la carte to vendors or consultants, either through their agencies or on their own. Specialized services are offered by media buyers, art studios, artists, photographers, writers, television directors and producers, talent and modeling agencies, direct mail houses, engravers, printers, typographers, employment agencies, and many others. The advertiser has an enormous pool of talent from which to pick, and regardless of the location of his office, none is further away than the reach of his telephone.

6

Know Thy Corporation

Corporations are as individual as fingerprints. Each one has its own personality, its own character, its "psyche." The character of the organization of which you are part dictates the type of advertising it will do; moreover, in the final analysis, the corporate psyche as much as the agency shapes the advertising.

Clients: The Way Agencies See Them

To an agency, the "client" is a bicorporal being, made up of the executive as an individual representing the company and the company itself. If the two parts do not act in unison, dealing with it can be a troublesome experience. Two heads are not necessarily better than one, in this case.

Agencies evaluate clients from a perspective that is uniquely their own; this may or may not correspond with the client's self-image. Here are the points most likely to be taken into account:

Billing. For the most part, the larger the client, the more attractive his business. As in any other service business, demands made by smaller clients may not be that different from those with the larger pocketbooks.

Prestige. Size is not the only criterion here. High-ticket, high-quality product lines (luxury cars, perfume, jewelry, fashion, travel) give the agency an opportunity to showcase its artistic flair. Such clients are perceived to be more graphically sophisticated, more responsive to new ideas, even slightly offbeat ideas. Agencies large and small vie for them, regardless of billing.

Creative Freedom. Clients who are likely to give the agency its head are also much sought after. Art directors and copywriters are especially keen to work for them, as are young agencies eager to establish a creative reputation. Public service campaigns (against drunken driving, drug addiction, illiteracy) fall into this category; over 50 public service campaigns make the widely acclaimed "The One Show" year after year. News gets around fast about open-minded, fair clients. A good thing to keep in mind for a business that does not yet have a large advertising budget but is looking for top-quality work.

Some Product Categories Offer More Creative Opportunities than Others. Advertisers of soft drinks, perfumes, beauty products, fashion, media, beer, high technology, air delivery services, and travel seem to be able to maintain consistently high drama in their campaigns, at the time of this writing. Others are less fortunate. Food, soap, and household item makers show less ingenuity in their advertising. The same holds true of discount stores, movie and theatrical productions, hospitals, cruise ships, realtors, lawyers, schools, and publishing houses. (Our apologies to the brave who succeeded in breaking through the clutter.) Car manufacturers, insurance firms, tobacco companies, retail stores, and brokerage houses run the gamut between the two extremes.

Why this should be so may be something of a mystery to the average television viewer, but those in advertising know the reasons. It is a fact of life in the business that once a competitor manages to break away from the pack, the others will follow. In absence of leadership, the industry turns to formula solutions in its advertising.

Levi Strauss, perhaps because it is headquartered in the inspired environs of San Francisco, first set the tone for blue jeans advertising with his "mood commercials." His rivals saw the light. The industry has been collecting the largest share of creative advertising awards (in proportion to number of ads produced) of any ever since.

Putting Your Corporation on the Couch

As suggested earlier, corporations are in many ways live entities. Like people, they may bear the legacy of their beginnings. They may even have developed a few corporate neuroses along the way: adventurous or cautious, competitive or complacent, flexible or unflexible. Their "personality" often changes with new management, as it did at Apple Computer, Chrysler, NBC, and Macy's (New York).

The notion that a business organization is less an abstraction than a tangible being with almost-human qualities is shared by some of the keenest observers of the scene. Peter F. Drucker, professor of management at the New York University Graduate Business School of Manage-

ment, refers to business enterprises as "living organisms." Thomas Peters and Robert Waterman in their widely read treatises on the *Search For Excellence* examine their corporate subjects not only in terms of profit and performance but also make much of their benevolence, conviviality, intelligence, courage, and even sense of humor — human traits all. And in their nationwide best-seller *The 100 Best Companies to Work for in America,* authors Robert Levering, Milton Moskowitz, and Michael Katz also speak about their selections much the way one would about a friend or neighbor.

Advertising agencies tend to perceive their clients in human terms, too, as this author soon found out in his admittedly informal survey among acquaintances in the business and through his own personal experience. Clear-cut profiles of companies (such as those capsulated here) emerged:

AT&T. Ability to look far ahead. Typically, its business plans try to encompass five- to ten-year periods — a rare phenomenon in this country accustomed to quarterly earnings reports. Originality is encouraged as long as it is backed by reason. AT&T is used to delegating, to farming out work. But like many companies its size, while experimentation is encouraged, so is thorough research. Its agencies must learn to blend the two successfully.

Calvin Klein. A designer and prime mover, with an innate understanding of marketing. His company has created a place for itself in blue jeans, sportswear, coats, fragrances, underwear, and more recently in high fashion. Unlike AT&T, much depends on the taste — and occasionally whims — of the one man on top of the hierarchy. His unique talents are felt throughout the corporation, and certainly in its advertising department. Working with Calvin Klein gives art directors, writers, television directors, photographers, stylists, hairdressers, and fabric manufacturers a creative high.

Barney's. Founded by immigrant Barney

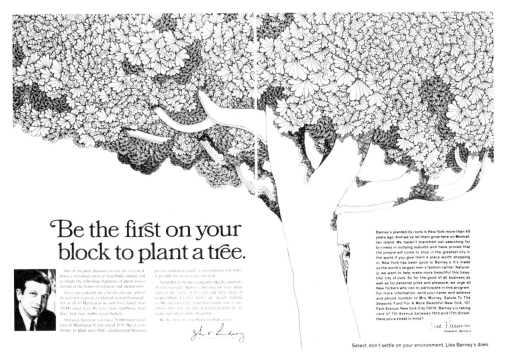

Be the first on your block to plant a tree.

Once of the great pleasures in our city is to walk down a tree-lined street, to hear birds singing and to inhale the refreshing fragrance of green leaves instead of the fumes of exhausts and incinerators.

Trees can certainly do a lot for our city and in the past few years we've planted several thousand. Yet in all of Manhattan we still have fewer than 30,000 street trees. We have more mailboxes than that. And more public waste baskets.

Our goal therefore is to have 30,000 more street trees in Manhattan by the end of 1970. But it costs money to plant trees. Only a partnership between private enterprises and City government will make it possible for us to reach our goal.

A number of major concerns, like the sponsors of this message, Barney's, because of their deep faith in the future of this city and their sense of responsibility for it, are already helping. We are especially grateful to them and to any others who will go into partnership with us to make our streets more beautiful.

Be the first on your block to plant a tree.

John V. Lindsay

Barney's planted its roots in New York more than 45 years ago. And we've let them grow here on Manhattan Island. We haven't branched out searching for business in outlying suburbs and have proved that the people will come to shop in the greatest city in the world if you give them a place worth shopping in. New York has been good to Barney's. It's made us the world's largest men's fashion center. Naturally, we want to help make more beautiful this beautiful city of ours. So for the good of all business as well as for personal pride and pleasure, we urge all New Yorkers who can to participate in this program. For more information, send your name and address and phone number to Mrs. Murray, Salute To The Seasons Fund For A More Beautiful New York, 101 Park Avenue, New York City 10016. Barney's is taking care of 7th Avenue between 16th and 17th Street. Have you a street in mind?

Fred Pressman
President, Barney's

Select, don't settle on your environment. Like Barney's does.

Some clients — such as Barney's in New York — maintain high standards in their advertising, even as they switch agencies. Other advertisers are never able to achieve success, no matter who the supplier. Obviously, creativity inspires creativity. This ad was prepared in 1970; the client hasn't faltered since.

Pressman as a tiny hole-in-the-wall store less than two generations ago (with him reputedly stationed in front with a long cane in his hand to pull prospects through the door), this store grew into the world's largest men's and now women's clothing center. This advertiser is a fine example of an alert management changing the image of a retail establishment to go with the times.

Mass media advertising has always played an important part in defining the store's image. Spending up to five times the A/S ratio (advertising costs based on sales volume) prevalent in retailing, Barney's made its presence felt in the most competitive marketplace in the world: New York City. Full-page ads in the *New York Times* and full-length and beautifully executed commercials in prime time on major networks suggested a large and important retail establishment.

Procter & Gamble. The account that agencies love to hate. One of the largest advertisers in the world, P&G has over a dozen major domestic agencies on its roster. These agencies are often referred to tongue in cheek as "P&G agencies," and for good reason. This client uses its clout. In the last few years, it has made a strong case against account conflicts caused by megamergers, rising cost of network television, fixed print media rate cards, indiscriminate across-the-board use of the 15% agency commission, and overly centralized management. The company has its own philosophy — and policy — on just about every aspect of business, including the type of creativity that works. Every ad must make a product claim, loud and clear, and the sponsor must be identified early. Subtlety has only recently entered the company's vocabulary. Few ads see daylight unless researched first. All

125

Don't let your kids get bad marks.

To make sure your kids do as well as they can at the dentist's office, you've got to make sure they do their homework. And that means brushing with Crest. Because, when it comes to toothpaste, Crest is the most cavity protection they can get. *More dentists' families use Crest than any other toothpaste. Shouldn't yours?*

Crest

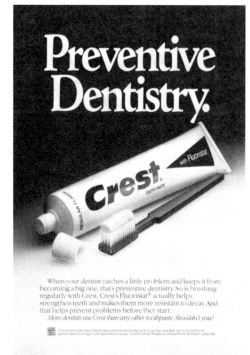

Preventive Dentistry.

When your dentist catches a little problem and keeps it from becoming a big one, that's preventive dentistry. So is brushing regularly with Crest. Crest's Fluoristat® actually helps strengthen teeth and makes them more resistant to decay. And that helps prevent problems before they start. *More dentists use Crest than any other toothpaste. Shouldn't you?*

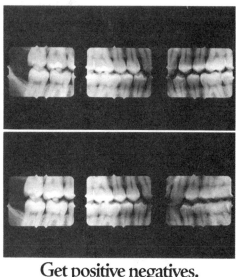

Get positive negatives.

When your X-rays come back, you want good news. And you can help make that happen. By brushing with Crest. Because, when it comes to toothpaste, Crest is the most cavity protection you can get. *More dentists use Crest than any other toothpaste. Shouldn't you?*

Crest

We do not recommend trying this demonstration with any other detergent.

In the past, Procter & Gamble, one of the largest advertisers in the U.S. used as many formulas in its advertising as in its detergents. That has changed with the public's increasingly sophisticated taste. The era of ''slice-of-life'' commercials with house-wives enraptured by the brilliance of flatware has given way to more genuine human reactions.

important decisions are made in writing. Within these parameters, however, there is room for plenty of creativity. Says Gordon Wale, an ex-employee of the company, now a consultant: "When I first arrived at P&G, fresh from Harvard, I kept wanting to say 'In my judgment.' I can still hear the response, 'Your judgment's no better than the drunk at Lytle Park.'" *Fortune* puts it this way: "P&G resembles an Oriental juggernaut—careful, thorough, convinced of the utter righteousness of its cause."

McDonald's. This $14 billion plus company is structured around its franchisees —it has almost 10,000 restaurants—but here, management rather than members of the chain sets direction.

Campaigns (originated at its "main" agency or any of the regional organizations) are usually presented in completed form to franchisees, even though these entrepreneurs carry most of the burden of paying for the effort. Yet satisfaction with the parent company's advertising runs high among its licensees. And with the public, too. McDonald's has succeeded in establishing a distinctive image, one that far transcends its Big Macs and Chicken McNuggets. Mention McDonald's and words like *family*, *warmth*, and *fun* spring to mind. Few companies, and certainly not McDonald's competitors, have succeeded in achieving this.

Pepsi-Cola. This advertiser has a clear idea where it wants its advertising to take it. Chasing at the heels of its nearest competitor, Coca-Cola, the company has positioned itself as the forerunner of each succeeding generation. Management understands the psyche of the young, taking advantage of every turn in fashion, music, and even vocabulary.

Working on this account is a heady experience. With its vast resources and willingness to try anything once, Pepsi-Cola is an art director's and writer's dream account. Its commercials are theatre at its best. Except for its marketing theme, "The Choice of a New Generation," Pepsi-Cola does not confine itself to any given campaign format, at least not in the traditional sense. Lack of strong continuity may weaken the impact of its advertising, but then again, in these fast-moving times, it may not.

Marketing and Advertising Make Strange Bedfellows

As many corporate advertising managers can testify, the relationship between the marketing and advertising departments in an organization is often on rather tenuous ground; the rules can be elusive. Since both deal with the same fundamental problem, selling a product or service, there is a tendency by top management to think of the two disciplines as much the same—if not in actual everyday practice, then at least in philosophy. This assumption seems to make sense at first glance but unfortunately it doesn't always.

The fact is that—though their responsibilities may overlap—each of the two departments operates within its own orbit. Their day-to-day working relationship can be at best confusing—or, at worst, can be unpredictable.

A close look at the activities of each highlights the basic differences between the two disciplines. Marketing's primary concerns are:

1. *Research.* Size and scope of the market. Future trends.

2. *Engineering.* Manufacturing equipment and costs.

3. *Quality control.* Responsibility to maintain it. Storage and handling capabilities.

4. *Purchasing.* Ability to economically obtain raw materials, new machinery, new vehicles, new manpower needed in manufacturing and distributing a new product.

5. *Sales.* All marketing decisions are made based on past, present, and future (projected) sales.

6. *Distribution.* Warehouse capacity. Efficient distribution. Franchise opportunities. Trade relations.

7. *Customer services.* How to best respond to inquiries and complaints. Getting the product to the customer fast enough.

8. *Employee relations.* Sales force. Union negotiations. Employee benefits. Management-employee information.

9. *Legal services.* Legal expertise needed to distribute and sell the product. Preview of advertising for compliance with legal requirements. Product liability. Warranties. Copyrights and patents.

10. *Financial analysis.* Keeping records of transactions, budgets, accounts, billing, cash flow, net and gross income, profitability. Translating marketing, sales, and production into numbers.

11. *Marketing and sales goals.* Long term and short term.

Advertising, on the other hand, involves:

1. *Media planning.* Selection of media to carry the message cost effectively. Definition of the target audience. Schedule.

2. *Advertising budget.* Setting annual budgets. Sales projections. Choosing the method to arrive at the figure. Breaking it down: media, creative, production, overhead (including agency compensation).

3. *Advertising strategy.* Creative recommendations, copy and layout. Technique of execution. Positioning the product. Evaluation of past, present, and future advertising. New opportu-

nities. Evaluation of competitor's advertising.

4. *Research.* Pretesting and posttesting advertising effectiveness. Use of primary and secondary research. Putting the information to practical use.

5. *Periodical agency evaluation.* Performance. Need for other services.

6. *Evaluation of other services.* Performance. Cost-effectiveness. The elimination of services or addition of new ones to fit the need.

Some functions are of vital interest to both marketing and advertising, and so they tend to overlap one another:

1. *Change in the product itself.* Call for a revision in the product or its packaging because of shifts in taste, new competition, retail attitudes, favorable or unfavorable publicity.

2. *The industry.* Current and future trends.

3. *The company.* Policies. Procedures. Past, present, and future performance criteria. In-house advertising, marketing, and sales services.

4. *Market share.* The company's and that of competition. Changes.

5. *Global sales potential.* Acceptance of the product or service outside the United States on a country-to-country basis. Effectiveness of global vs. local advertising.

Differences in marketing and advertising functions may be subtle—and sometimes even confusing—but they exist just the same.

Public Relations and Advertising

The relationship between the corporate public relations and the advertising departments may also be uneven, despite the fact that the talents of one usually complement the other. To corporations more concerned about their image than their products, public relations can be a vital function, and one that takes priority with top management, who often become personally involved in releases distributed to media. Here again, the advertising department may find itself playing a subordinate role to public relations, a curious circumstance since each performs a different function.

Sales Promotion and Advertising

Even more akin to advertising is the sales promotion department. After all, sales promotions too are based on the professional use of words and pictures. There are important differences between the two departments, however. While it is true that both are involved in moving the company's product off the shelf, sales promotion by its very nature is more focused on short-term results. Premiums, incentives, point of purchase, displays are usually designed to generate immediate store activity. Rarely do the people in sales promotion have patience for the tedious process of changing the consumer's attitudes and buying patterns — one of the goals of an advertising campaign.

It is important, however, that both departments be kept informed of each other's activities. For maximum effectiveness both sales promotion and advertising should be based on a common theme, reenforcing the message both in mass media and point of sale.

The Importance of Advertising to Top Management

Advertising plays a very different role in different corporations. It is important that those involved in the day-to-day execution of advertising be able to realistically evaluate the degree of attention their activities get from top management.

Nature of the business. All large consumer-driven companies *must* promote their products, whether they like it or not. Other companies are less dependent on advertising; here the advertising manager (if there is one at all in the organization) would be hard put persuading management to heavily invest in getting exposure. The decision whether or not to advertise is more likely to be based on finances than philosophy.

According to Pansophic Systems (Park Ridge, Illinois) which regularly issues competitive budget analyses, industries that have the lowest A/S ratio are manufacturers of such products as sugar, textiles, meat, paper, machinery, aircraft, and scientific instruments.

The most active advertisers are tobacco, beverages (alcohol, soft drinks, and malted liquors), watches and clocks, photographic equipment and supplies, computers, household appliances, food (packaged goods), drugs, and soap.

The sales ratio of course reflects only percentages, not dollar amount of advertising budget. Companies selling automobiles, communications, oil, computers, and chemical products are all giant advertisers. So is the U.S. government. But their overall budgets dwarf their advertising spending.

Not all companies even in the same industry follow the same spending patterns. For reasons of its own, a company may choose to far outspend its competitors. Columbia Pictures spends about four times as much based on A/S ratio as

American Broadcasting—though both are in the entertainment industry. Nabisco outspends Borden five to one. In the highly competitive wine coolers industry, most advertisers spent five to six times as much as an average vineyard, ignoring sales records. The average retailer spends three to four percent of his gross on advertising but there are many who better this figure and with good results—including a store already mentioned, Barney's.

Advertising is often dictated by the corporation's basic selling approach. Generally, there are two ways to generate activity. The first is "push selling," where the product is "pushed" on the distributor, so as to entice purchasers. "Pull selling" on the other hand creates a consumer demand, bringing people into distributors to look for the product. Needless to say, the latter requires a far greater up-front investment. Most companies use both methods. They try to get the consumer to pull the product through the distribution chain by asking for it and at the same time they make sure their product is in the store.

Top spenders at the time of this writing are Procter & Gamble, Philip Morris, Sears Roebuck, RJR/Nabisco, General Motors, Ford Motor, Anheuser Bush, Beatrice, McDonald's, K-Mart, Pepsi-Cola, and Coca-Cola. Not far from the top of the list are the U.S. government and individually sponsored public service campaigns run pro bono by media (a donation estimated to be worth over $1 billion annually, about four times that of similar efforts made by the federal government). The list does change through the years but not by much; generally, once a spender, always a spender.

The richest companies in the United States are not necessarily the most generous of advertising clients. The names of only two (General Motors and Ford Motor) of the top 25 companies in the Fortune 500 appear among the top 25 leading national advertisers.

Personal Whims and Predilections. Advertising is often evaluated on a purely subjective basis. Reactions vary. To quite a few corporate types, advertising is simply a parlor game adults play with pictures and words—on television. Personal likes and dislikes come into the open. If that is the case, it is the advertising manager who must demonstrate that advertising is both an art *and* a science.

APPROVAL	DATE

Selling Advertising to Management

Overcoming management resistance to advertising can be a trying experience. The few pointers offered here are to help the advertising manager to present advertising to corporate decision-makers:

130

1. *Document the efficacy of advertising.* The best sources for information on advertising success stories are *Advertising Age, Fortune, Inc. Magazine,* the *New York Times,* the *Wall Street Journal, U.S. Today, AdWeek, Media Decisions, New York Magazine, Time, Newsweek, Business Week, Forbes,* and *Barron's* and books aplenty. There are also a number of television programs that cover corporate success stories in which advertising has played an important part. Record them on videotape and use them when you have to.

2. *Competitor's advertising spending.* The prospect of being outspent — and outdone — by a competitor can be a warning to heads of the company. Sizes and breakdowns of various advertising budgets appear in the *Standard Directory of Advertisers* ("Redbook") and in *Advertising Age.*

3. *Show how sales will respond to increase in advertising budget.* Admittedly a risky proposition but one that may force management to reevaluate their advertising program. There is no shortage of case histories to substantiate your claim.

4. *Emphasize better dealer relations.* Retailers appreciate advertising and promotional support. Co-op ads, point-of-sale displays, and sales promotions all make an impact on sales. This is particularly true in the case of a new product; advertising may yet be the greatest incentive for stores to put the product on their shelves. Get written testimonials from retailers and show them to top management. It can prove to be your best argument.

5. *Look for someone in the company to help you in championing your cause.* Brand managers and sales and marketing directors have a vested interest in improving sales, just as you do.

6. *Back your arguments with facts.* Take advantage of the tools marketing and advertising research has to offer. Pretest your advertising themes, copy and art. Use syndicated market and consumer information, trade and associations studies, census data, library and university information, existing company intelligence, or other secondary research. This kind of information comes at affordable prices. Or go a step further and try your hand at original research, such as focus group interviews, laboratory tests, sampling, selected mailings, telephone interviews, and similar data gathering. Pilot studies involving no more than 200 to 300 interviews (on the street, shopping centers, or other high-traffic areas) can be done for a few hundred dollars, and only take a day or so.

7. *Use your advertising agency for all it is worth.* Your agency could be your greatest ally, since its success hinges on yours. Ask your agency to help you put together a professionally polished presentation, complete with visuals, slides, sketches, samples of ads, charts, back-up research.

8. *Play on corporate weaknesses, as well as strengths.* Sales have gone down; morale has reached bottom among the sales force; retailers complain about packaging and lack of advertising support. Your company is losing marketshare. Advertising may be the answer.

If your company shows strength, use the momentum to your advantage. Are product differences finally sinking into public consciousness? Let's rub it in a bit more. Does fragmentation of the marketplace offer new opportunities? Are profits so promising they warrant an increase in advertising?

Defining the Functions of a Corporate Advertising Manager

Having to report to this department or that, to this brand manager or that (the trend is to increase brand manager's power), the advertising department could end up implementing other people's ideas more than inventing its own.

The corporate advertising manager should:

1. *Participate in the advertising budget approval process.* In some companies, this has become a responsibility of top management, the marketing or sales department, or brand managers. The advertising manager's contributions should be a welcome addition.

2. *Work on advertising strategy planning.* If need be, he should work with the agency and other departments in the company. Never should advertising plans be developed in a vacuum, as if they had a life of their own.

3. *Deal with the agency on a day-to-day basis.* In many areas — certainly in creative — the advertising manager should be the agency's prime, and sometimes only, contact.

4. *Take charge of the in-house advertising department.* He should be responsible for the staff, flow of work, organization.

5. *Select the agency.* In some companies, this is done by top management at headquarters, often the CEO. Others rely on the judgment of the brand manager, marketing director, or sales manager. Be that as it may, the advertising manager should be invited to participate in the decision-making process.

Paving the Way to Getting Approvals

It is important that the "what" (marketing strategy, sales projections, corporate policies) be kept separate from the "how" (creative recommendations to solve specific problems, techniques used in executing ideas, assignment of personnel to perform various tasks, use of outside resources). The former involves directives from top management. The latter deals more with aspects of implementation, the follow-up on the creative.

Getting approvals on the "what" first will prevent sudden and unexpected changes in advertising from others in the company as the work progresses. For example, an agreement might have been reached with Marketing, Sales, Promotion, Public Relations on what product difference should be stressed in the forthcoming year. The advertising agency has been cued in; a campaign is built around that theme. It should now become easier to reach consensus on individual ads.

Once the advertising theme is approved and adhered to, there will be less confusion, duplication of effort, the start-from-scratch reworking of projects along the way — some of the major reasons for advertising campaigns not finished on time and then over budget.

How Much Money Is Enough?

It can safely be said that no two companies decide on the size of their annual advertising appropriations exactly the same way. As mentioned earlier, not only do marketing realities play an important part, but also the company's basic perceptions about the value of advertising — the orientation and personal predilections of those in position to approve campaigns.

With the ever-increased emphasis on marketing, however, CEOs are increasingly aware of the role advertising plays in the overall corporate sales strategy. Many chief executives today, in fact, have arrived at their front offices through marketing, sales, or advertising. Lee Iacocca (Chrysler), Bruce Atwater (General Mills), Dick Gelb (Bristol Myers), Victor Kiam (Remington), John Sculley (Apple Computer) all started their careers here. Others became founders of their own successful enterprises precisely for their exceptional marketing instincts. Such people are more receptive to advertising largesse, even when this seems out of proportion to the spending of others in similar industries. Not surprisingly, those with business administration, financial, accounting, or legal background are less inclined to commit money to advertising.

Deciding advertising budgets can be a complex issue. Here are the methods used most frequently:

1. *Advertising/Sales ratio.* This is the method used by most companies. Past or projected sales are used. Comparisons with other companies in the same industry are made. The problem with this approach is that it turns cause and effect on its head. It pushes advertising spending up with sales and vice versa. It ignores the fact that decrease in sales may signal more vigorous advertising.

2. *Allocation per unit, unit of sales, or retail outlet.* In this method, money is assessed on the basis of units produced, distributed, or sold during the previous budgetary period. Through projection, the advertiser is able to set his advertising budget. For example, an automobile manufacturer may decide to spend $100 on advertising for each car that sits in the showroom. A perfume maker may plan on allocating 30% of his selling costs to advertising. The inherent weakness of this method is that until the product is actually sold, no money is forthcoming for purposes of advertising. The advertising budget is contingent on projected sales.

3. *Plow-back method.* At the end of the year, the advertiser puts back all his net profits into advertising. This method works particularly well in advertising-rich new-product introductions.

4. *The scientific way.* Not surprisingly there are a number of mathematical formulas available on which to base a "reasonable" advertising budget. Most often these models are extremely complex and require sophisticated use of computers. Future projections are based on historical data. Analogous to this method are calculations used by "chartist" predicting of stock market performance based on past events. Unfortunately, as any

133

sophisticated investor knows, there is no guarantee that history repeats itself on any of the financial markets. The same holds true in advertising and marketing.

5. *Subjective evaluation.* Most companies rely heavily on the judgment and experience of individuals in the corporation, usually at high-level positions, in setting advertising appropriations. Whether they use formulas or not, these forms of divination appear to be about as accurate as other methods. Does that mean that advertising budgets are a hit-or-miss proposition, that no one should ever be held accountable for the outcome? Not in the least. But intuition does play a large part in their success.

EFFECTIVE CAMPAIGNS

AIRLINES
Eastern
TWA
Delta
United

CEREALS
Life
Fruit & Fibre
Wheaties
Total

BATH SOAPS
Ivory
Dial
Coast
Dove

LAUNDRY DETERGENT
Tide
Cheer
Bold

FAST FOODS
Wendy's
Burger King
Pizza Hut
McDonald's

BEER
Bud Light
Miller Lite
Budweiser
Coors/Light

COLD REMEDIES
Nyquil
Robitussin
Contac
Vicks

SOFT DRINKS
Coca-Cola
Pepsi-Cola
RC Cola
7-Up

ANTACIDS
Tums
Rolaids
Pepto Bismol
Maalox

ANALGESICS
Bayer
Excedrin
Tylenol
Anacin

Spuds Mackenzie, Bud Light's popular bon vivant spokespooch, went to the heads of millions of Americans.

JEANS
Levi's
Lee
Wrangler
Chic

DEODORANTS
Secret
Sure
Mennen/Real
Ban/Ultra Ban

Advertising budgets of competitors give the advertiser an opportunity to compare the rate of spending; creative awards suggest critical acclaim. Neither piece of information tells the whole story. One of the most accurate measures of effectiveness is the Cost Per Thousand Retained Impressions, or "CPMRI", a barometer of the relationship between media spending and recall of advertising. New York-based Video Storyboard Test polls 4,000 television viewers throughout the year to determine these figures, with *ADWEEK* publishing them every year. Shown here are advertisers that made the top of the lists.

A Few Words About Goal-Specific Advertising

Companies—and their advertising agencies—are often quite specific about the results advertising will bring. This may be expressed in terms of marketshare (the amount of money spent on advertising is aimed to generate, say, a 2% improvement in the coming year), sales (sales are projected to rise, say, 10% due to advertising), or even profits (corporate profits should grow, say, 3%). Such forecasts help to justify advertising spending, especially where management would be reluctant to spend money otherwise. But while it is true that there is comfort in numbers—and the more precise, the better—no projection guarantees success. Agreeing on the goal is one thing; knowing how to get there is something altogether different.

Why Advertising Budgets Should Never Be Carved in Stone

In most organizations, particularly the larger ones, it is customary practice to determine advertising budgets about a year in advance. Since advertising has a profound effect on corporate performance, and advertising expenditures may run into millions of dollars, it would be difficult indeed to plan ahead without taking this important outlay into account.

Advertising realities, however, are rarely so predictable. Room must be given for increasing (or decreasing) the advertising budget should circumstances so dictate. Lack of retail enthusiasm, for example, may necessitate tilting the budget in the way of special sales promotion. The company's falling from grace in the eyes of the public could justify a larger allowance set aside for public relations.

It is incumbent on the advertising manager, his agency, and his colleagues in other departments to monitor advertising closely, not once or twice a year, but constantly. Quick, unpredictable events may call for changes in the creative approach, media selection, and advertising spending within a month, a week, or a day. Perhaps Shakespeare put it best: ". . . a divinity that shapes our ends, rough-hew them how we will."

Consider these influences:

Changing Trends. Salad bars find their way into supermarkets. Sneaker manufacturers discover that over 55 million United States citizens walk for exercise and introduce "walking shoes." A major tool manufacturer advertises to women for the first time. A magazine called *Divorce* hits the newsstands with circulation of 100,000 to fill a niche in the marketplace.

Fickle Tastes. Rise in skirt lengths creates demand for remodeled kneecaps. The Monkees make a comeback after 25 years' near-silence. The President's decision to wear a tiny hearing aid gives the industry a boost.

Sign of the Times. The Bicentennial Anniversary of the nation makes Chevrolet sing "Heartbeat of America." Helena Personal Introduction Service promises its clients they will meet "that special someone . . . without risk to your health" in the midst of the AIDS epidemic.

Volatile Economy. A single day's drop of 508 points in the Dow Jones Average (in 1987) temporarily slowed down home buying and apartment hunting. Japanese imports cut deeply into the domestic car market.

New Distribution Opportunities. Levi's shows its full line of pants on video displays in retail stores to enable customers to order their selections from a "Jean Screen" electronically; delivery is within two weeks. McDonald's opens a restaurant in Moscow. "Anti-AIDS" condoms in cigarette-sized packages are sold via vending machines.

Bad News. Johnson & Johnson finds cyanide-poisoned capsules in some of its Tylenol packages; it introduces "caplets." Chrysler finds its executives took new cars on test drives with odometers disconnected; the public demands an explanation. Challenger explodes; NASA's image suffers.

New Competition. Polaroid introduces instant color photography. NYNEX Manhattan Yellow Pages finds it must fight an upcoming entry by Southwestern Bell. IBM cuts dealer prices to compete with leading clone models. Coke becomes a "breakfast drink," like orange and grapefruit juice.

Fluctuating Media Costs. Television network costs go up 45% in five years. Then suddenly they drop for the first time—for a few months. Direct mail manages to hold down price increases for six years. Economy makes 15-second "short spots" increasingly popular. A 30-second "avail" in the New York market presents itself on CBS's Superbowl a day before the playoff; it is up for grabs at a steep discount to the highest—and probably first—bidder.

Headquarters Sends the Word. Perhaps arbitrarily, perhaps not. In any case, those are the orders.

An overly rigid approach—with fixed media schedules and unalterable creative approaches—discourages this kind of experimentation.

Have Your Agency Report on Trends

Especially significant are the nearly unpredictable shifts in consumer-buying habits. The organization best qualified to watch them is none other than the advertising agency. Keeping a close watch on the market is one of its important activities or should be. If the advertising manager finds that his agency is lax in this area, he should immediately bring attention to the fact.

One Step at a Time

Changes in advertising approaches do not have to be made all at one time, necessitating large investments. Forget about jumping into the pool; test the waters first. Thanks to state-of-the-art technology, it is possible today to cut the market into small, manageable slices. New products, new marketing techniques, and new advertising campaigns can all be tried out at only a fraction of cost. Direct mail professionals, for example, are able to identify detailed profiles of millions of prospects and customers at a glance at the computer screen. Special products and services can then be tailored to predetermined market segments. Cost of accessing such data has fallen significantly—about a hundredfold in the last ten years.

Another way to find out about demand is to take one market at a time. In the past, this used to be called test marketing. The technique has come a long way since. It is now possible to carve out a marketplace not only geographically but also demographically and psychographically (on the basis of life-style). All can be cross-indexed. Specific, part-way experiments can save substantial sums of money for the company in the long haul. "We all make mistakes," one marketing executive said "but now they don't have to be big ones."

WHY

ADVERTISE

Courtesy of Pensions & Investment Age

1. Position your company, your services and your products.
2. Reposition your competition, their services, their products.
3. Create, enhance or maintain image, prestige and leadership position.
4. Introduce new company/new company name.
5. Change perception/remove prejudice.
6. Stand above/apart from competition.
7. Eliminate "me-too" image.
8. Secure and maintain professional acceptance.
9. Initiate, stimulate, or maintain momentum.
10. Direct "word-of-mouth" in the market.
11. Maintain consistent and controlled customer communications.
12. Reinforce personal sales calls, letters and direct mail.
13. Open doors for personal sales calls.
14. Free sales time for face-to-face contact.
15. Reduce sales costs.
16. Penetrate communication "static" in the marketplace.
17. Reach top management without disrupting current relationships.
18. Reach unknown but powerful influences.
19. Generate and pre-qualify leads and prospects.
20. Produce sales.
21. Make more sales calls.
22. Smooth cyclicality.
23. Retain existing customers.
24. Introduce new services and products.
25. Test new services and products.
26. Enter new markets.
27. Discourage, intimidate competition.
28. Promote multi service/product sales.
29. Promote new use for existing service/product.
30. Enhance employee pride, loyalty and morale.
31. Reduce employee turnover.
32. Minimize problems of employee turnover at your company.
33. Minimize problems of employee turnover at your client's company.
34. Improve quality of new job applicants.
35. Reduce hiring expense.
36. Announce hirings, promotions, acquisitions.
37. Disseminate important data and information quickly.
38. Provide useful data and information on trends.
39. Clarify company philosophy/position.
40. Report performance.
41. Promote technical benefits/data/features.
42. Exploit positive publicity and trends.
43. Mollify unfavorable publicity and trends.
44. Resell lost customers.
45. Attract new customer interest.
46. Educate prospects on needs/benefits/features.
47. Develop product or service acceptance.
48. Build audience for sales calls, direct mail and advertising.
49. Conduct research.
50. Offer brochures, reports and other data.

New Product: A Call for New Corporate Attitudes

During introductory periods, advertising/sales ratios tend to favor the former. It is estimated that it can take as much as two to five times as much to introduce a new product as to advertise an established brand. Once the product is established in the public consciousness, advertising spending usually levels off, if not in actual dollar amount then in proportion to sales. To put it another way: It costs a great deal less to *maintain* marketshare than to build one up — on the average, about twice as much.

Here is what a typical two-year projection for a new product would look like:

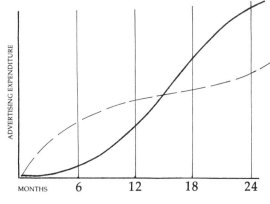

Breakeven (no loss, no profit) can occur anywhere from one year to five, depending on a variety of factors. Profits should then begin to show up on the balance sheet.

Here is a quick rundown (based on estimates made by four top media-buying services) of what it costs to advertise a new consumer product in its *first six months* — the launching period. Taken into account are major media costs — newspaper, radio, television, billboard — but not discounts to distributors, retailers ("slotting allowances," free advertising), and brokers. Neither is the cost of distribution, sales promotion, publicity, administrative overhead, warehousing, transportation, sales commissions, and other expenses that normally accompany new-product introductions.

New York	$800,000
Chicago	$500,000
Los Angeles	$550,000
Washington	$250,000
San Francisco	$200,000
Boston	$250,000
Philadelphia	$300,000

Large, established corporations — Procter & Gamble, General Foods, Lever Brothers, among others — can easily absorb investments of this, or much more sizeable, magnitude. Smaller companies may have a more difficult time of it. It should be kept in mind, of course, that the cities listed here represent major Standard Metropolitan Statistical Areas (SMSAs). They are not necessarily the best test markets. The cost of penetration in other markets and areas, including such mainstream cities as Peoria, Columbus, Phoenix, Milwaukee, Minneapolis, and Denver, could be substantially lower.

Don't Have Your Corporation Ask the Computer About Matters Creative

Computers have revolutionized the way we do business, making it possible to keep track of many corporate activities all at a single glance. It is tempting therefore to turn to electronic data processing to swiftly and neatly solve advertising problems.

Unfortunately, when it comes to creative, the computers are lost for both words and figures. You could just as well discuss your problems with your toaster or microwave oven.

There are those who will take issue with this statement. Computers, they insist, can be made to play chess, design cars, analyze golf swings, and tell you if you make a good pet owner. Why not break down creativity into components and use computer "artificial intelligence" to arrive at logical solutions to familiar problems? It simply cannot be done, not in this century and probably not in the next. The complexity that goes into writing a one-liner or designing a layout — not to mention a viable advertising campaign — defies even the largest of mainframes.

Advertising Problems Unique to a Franchise Operation

Approvals on an advertising campaign — creative and financial — are even harder to get when a company distributes its product via a network of dealers, each a more or less autonomous unit. Franchising is one of the fastest expanding segments of U.S. business; it is estimated that almost half of all retail in the United States is done by this method, selling about $500 billion worth of products and services every year.

As pointed out before, approaches differ among franchisers as to the advertising support provided by headquarters. With a few exceptions — McDonald's is one — management rarely assumes absolute powers over advertising.

Usually, the company offers a two-pronged advertising program to its franchisees. One is an "umbrella" campaign, possibly on a wide national scale. Media may include local or network television, radio, newspaper, outdoor, magazine, and direct mail. The other is more localized advertising and promotion. Here, the company provides a packaged co-op advertising program ("kit") along with a Grand Opening Package, ad mats, radio scripts, sample media and direct mail programs, publicity releases, and photographs, and in some instances even television commercials with room left for local sponsor identification. Costs of using the material are divided between the com-

pany and its franchisees, usually by way of a percentage of gross sales — 2% to 10% — of the latter.

Advertising and promotion are the two disciplines with which most franchisees feel least at home. They appreciate not only the advertising material provided by headquarters, but the instructions as to using it, including the advertising schedule together with dates — and cost estimates.

Advertising Problems Unique to Retail Stores

Retail approach to advertising differs from that of most other businesses. Department stores and other retail outlets do not depend on others to get their merchandise out into the field. They *are* the distributors. Most retail advertising is oriented to get quick results. The pressure is great; inventory *must* be moved swiftly to allow room for the next shipment.

While most companies have to deal with overly rigid advertising budgets, in retailing the opposite holds true. Rarely are budgets set a year or even three months in advance. Advertising is designed to respond to specific needs.

Not every advertising agency is set up to deal with "retail mentality" which amounts to — in the words of one agency executive — a "state of perpetual panic." This is why the majority of establishments have in-house facilities. Here, material can be produced overnight, and under considerable pressure.

Long-term planning can hardly be expected to be a major preoccupation with one whose job it is to move merchandise tomorrow, yet that sort of plannning may also be needed for the store to succeed. Customers today are not only looking for value but for good service, pleasant surroundings, and customer-friendly store policies. Selling items is one thing; building an image is quite another.

Supermarkets should wait on people, not vice versa.

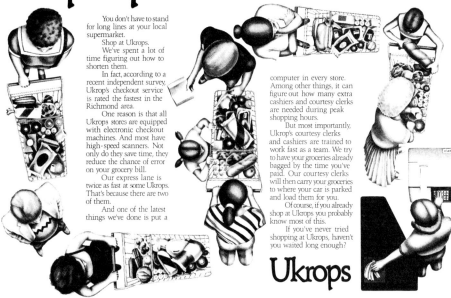

You don't have to stand for long lines at your local supermarket.

Shop at Ukrops.

We've spent a lot of time figuring out how to shorten them.

In fact, according to a recent independent survey, Ukrop's checkout service is rated the fastest in the Richmond area.

One reason is that all Ukrops stores are equipped with electronic checkout machines. And most have high-speed scanners. Not only do they save time, they reduce the chance of error on your grocery bill.

Our express lane is twice as fast at some Ukrops. That's because there are two of them.

And one of the latest things we've done is put a computer in every store. Among other things, it can figure out how many extra cashiers and courtesy clerks are needed during peak shopping hours.

But most importantly, Ukrop's courtesy clerks and cashiers are trained to work fast as a team. We try to have your groceries already bagged by the time you've paid. Our courtesy clerks will then carry your groceries to where your car is parked and load them for you.

Of course, if you already shop at Ukrops you probably know most of this.

If you've never tried shopping at Ukrops, haven't you waited long enough?

Ukrops

Don't buy cakes old enough to have birthdays.

When you blow out the candles and make a wish, it shouldn't be for a different cake.

Your cake should look fresh and moist. If it doesn't, it's past its prime.

At Dot's Pastry Shops in Ukrops, if we don't sell our cakes while they're fresh, we don't sell them.

The same goes for our pies, cookies, Danish, tarts and cupcakes.

In fact, the only thing that's old are our recipes. We use the same quality ingredients that Dot began using forty-four years ago.

Like rich fudge and pecans in our brownies. Fresh lemon juice in our famous lemon chess pies.

And you haven't lived until you've tasted one of Dot's delicious chocolate eclairs with creamy vanilla custard inside.

Another reason our desserts are so moist and fresh is because we don't overcook them. Actually, our cakes are taken out of the oven before they're quite done. (The heat that's still inside finishes baking them while they cool.)

In total, we bake 80 different desserts a day, five days a week. From scratch.

We'll even design, bake and decorate special order cakes for anniversaries, weddings, graduations, and, of course, birthdays.

And Dot's pastry chefs are fanatics. Each dessert has to look just as good as it tastes.

Our cakes are always decorated by hand, not machines. Our cookies have to be just the right size and shape. And if one of our gingerbread men loses his head, he's out the door.

Oh, there's one more thing. We don't add any preservatives to our desserts.

After all, they're never around long enough to need them.

Ukrops

Year End Clearance

Storewide Bargains

Halloween Savings

Sensational Values

Once-a-Year Event

Come In Today! *Now!*

Don't Miss It! *Win!*

Sweepstakes *Hurry!*

Enter Today *At Last!*

Free Delivery! *New!*

Easy Payments! *! !!*

CATCH OUR SEAFOOD ON FRIDAY NIGHTS.

The Greenhouse proudly reintroduces our popular Seafood Buffet on Friday nights from 6-11 P.M. Hook onto everything from Snow Crab Legs and Poached Shrimp to the Catch of the Day. Dine and Dance under the stars to live entertainment. Just $26.50 per person. For reservations call (212) 938-9100.

the Greenhouse
RESTAURANT and WINE BAR

THE VISTA
INTERNATIONAL HOTEL
AT NY'S WORLD
TRADE CENTER

SATURDAY NIGHTS BELONG TO YOU.

Enjoy dinner and dancing— to live entertainment and under the stars—in Old New York's most romantic setting. Join us on Saturday nights from 6-11 PM for an elegant 4-course dinner. Just $26.50 per person. For reservations phone (212) 938-9100.

the Greenhouse
RESTAURANT and WINE BAR

THE VISTA INTERNATIONAL HOTEL
AT NY'S WORLD TRADE CENTER

Few advertisers depend as heavily on the results of their advertising as do retailers. Next day's sales are used as no-nonsense criteria, with the emphasis placed on product and price. Some stores go further than that, however, in that they are also building up a long-term image. Ads created by Westbrook for Ukrops Supermarket (facing page) sell products and the store both at the same time.

Volvo's New York and New Jersey dealerships broke all the rules by putting its simple, stark ad in the midst of an ocean of hodge-podge, claim-laden small space automobile ads. The result is this stand-out-from-the-crowd advertisement.

The Greenhouse Restaurant and Wine Bar uses bold sillhouettes to lend its campaign a special flavor. The message changes, but art technique stays the same.

We're with you for the long run.

A difficult problem solved with imagination and creative verve. Hair styling products by John Paul Mitchell Services are distributed mainly through hair stylists. The copy makes much of the trust developed between stylists and their clientele. Two-page spread (top of page) is followed by four more in the magazine, listing salons using the product. This kind of advertising is usually produced by top advertising professionals. More and more retailers choose to take this route to gain control over their advertising.

142

What Are You Selling? Your Brand or Your Company?

Good products suggest good companies and vice versa. But there are vast differences between management philosophies as to whether to stress the product or the company that makes it. Some feel the name of the company is their greatest single asset, deserving prime emphasis. Others are content allowing the product to upstage the company.

Who is "right"? It depends on the circumstances. Companies that sell gasoline, for example, are probably just as important as — or possibly more so than — the brand of gasoline itself. Here, the product is considered a generic one. Companies where the maker is at least as important as the product are the airlines, insurance carriers, banks, hotels, textiles, cigarettes, wholesale operations, and of course, retailers. Companies where the product takes precedence (generally speaking) are the makers of food, drugs, apparel, cleaning agents, sweets, books, and movies.

There is little doubt that the average consumer is often unaware of the company making product. For skeptics, here is a simple test to show that such is the case. Indicate which of the following pairs of products are produced by the same parent company:

Pledge/Raid Insecticides	( )
Pepsodent/Rinso	( )
Salem/Winston	( )
Marlboro/Virginia Slims	( )
Mounds/Almond Joy	( )
Campbell Soup/Godiva Chocolatier	( )
Hanes Hosiery/L'eggs Products	( )
Coca-Cola/Minute Maid	( )
Benedictine D.O.M./B&B Liqueur	( )
Mountain Dew/Pepsi-Cola	( )
Smirnoff Vodka/Harvey's Bristol Cream	( )
Ballantine Beer/Narragansett Lager Beer	( )

If you guessed that in *every case* each two products belonged to the family of the same parent company, you were right.

There are those who argue that, with certain products, consumers couldn't care less about the manufacturer. This is a convincing argument, and one that is much substantiated by various studies (such as the test). It is doubtful if the average reader of a book is concerned about the publisher, a movie-goer about the film studio, and a whisky drinker about the distiller.

Usually, however, the name of the company plays more of a role in the general acceptance of a product — and most particularly, a service — than supposed. The influence may be a subtle one. Consumers do "believe" in many companies, particularly those that have been around for a while, have had successes in the past, have invested in advertising through the years, and have made civic contributions.

Just how much a company should advertise itself is usually a judgment call. Established identity has a great deal to do with the decision. It can be safely said, however, that many companies, especially in the low-ticket packaged goods field, stay needlessly in the background.

How to Advertise the Product and the Company at the Same Time

Advertising professionals often resist mentioning company names *and* the name of the product in the same ad. They insist such a double-identity signature serves only to confuse the audience, and often they are right. Studies show that complicated graphic devices can be a distraction and discourage readership.

There are ways to get around this identification problem, however. Here is a quick overview:

1. *Use the family name.* Levi Strauss calls its jeans Levi's Jeans. (Other products

are Levi's Sportswear, Levi's Youth-wear, Levi's Womenswear, Levi's Accessories, Levi's Activewear.) Pillsbury often puts its name in front of its individual brands, as do Gaines, Kellogg, General Foods.

2. *Look for continuity in packaging.* A red corner marks Nabisco's packages. Kellogg has its "K"; General Mills its "G"; Quaker Oats its good-natured Pilgrim. Workman publishing has made a name for itself putting out books strong on graphics; solid bold borders on the cover and pages inside the books have become the publisher's signature.

3. *"Own" a color scheme.* Yellow Pages features red and yellow. Coca-Cola specifies its own fire red combined with white; Pepsi-Cola added touches of blue to it; Seven-Up opts for green. And where would Howard Johnson be without its green and orange combination? The same colors consistently show up in literature, store interiors, trucks, letterheads, uniforms, paper plates, napkins.

4. *Develop a signature flexible enough to be used in a variety of ways.* The telephone companies' "walking fingers" appear in print, television, billboards. General Foods' red-white-blue emblem has a way of making quiet appearances next to brand logos in magazine and newspaper ads. So do Green Giant, Mr. Clean, Betty Crocker.

5. *Create a typeface. Vogue* has proprietary rights over a Bodoni-like typeface designed especially for the magazine. Guess jeans uses a hand written signature.

6. *Let it be known that the parent company stands behind all its brands.* P&G provides a toll-free number along with its name on the back of all its products —no matter what the brand— encouraging users to call one of its

150 service representatives covering everything from stain removal to working a microwave oven. Over a million buyers pick up the phone every year, asking for information four times as often as lodging a complaint.

7. *Coordinate advertising and corporate public relations.* Chrysler's Lee Iacocca has only reiterated in the company's car commercials what the press has been saying all along. Everyone knows what IBM stands for— as a company, and in its products.

8. *Sure, let brand managers run their own show—but look over their shoulders once in a while.* Procter & Gamble makes its policies clear up and down the line; its brand managers know just how far they can go without bumping up against the corporate stone wall. There are times when brand managers (or their corporate counterparts) could do with some gentle prodding, even a hand. Tact, of course, is essential here.

A distinctive symbol can identify a company quite effectively. Nabisco's red triangle has managed to work its way into public consciousness through years of constant use. It lends unity to all its public expressions, including advertising.

Obviously decentralization is a fine management technique but one that calls for discretion in advertising. It can give rise to many different advertising campaigns in different parts of the country, each created autonomously. Common themes may be lacking. This is why certain decisions on advertising, or policies regarding its use, best come from a single source, possibly corporate headquarters. It is to be hoped that there will be no scarcity of talent and good judgment at the top. One solution is to give advertising its due. Perhaps this is why so many successful corporations with consumer products have on their board at least one director with a strong background in advertising and marketing.

To Sum It Up

Good advertising not only sells the product but—directly or indirectly—reflects the philosophy of the company that makes it. Every corporation has its own "personality"—and the public tends to evaluate it in human terms. These percep-

tions play an important part in the success of the product.

Corporate attitudes in regard to advertising vary greatly. It is an important function in some. Others treat it more like a "necessary evil"—or not treat it at all. No one is personally more affected by the management's approach to advertising more than the corporate advertising manager. His standards are as often as not dictated by his environment: his relationship with other key figures in the corporation (in marketing, brand management, sales, promotion, public relations). The closer his involvement with top management, the higher the corporate awareness of advertising.

Functions of advertising managers vary from one corporation to another, depending on size, nature of the product, and company policy. Be that as it may, it behooves the corporation to invite the advertising manager's full participation in setting budgets, selecting agencies, and deciding on future sales strategies.

7

To Find the Problem Is to Find the Solution

Ask a company executive about the purpose of his company's advertising, and more likely than not, the answer will be that "the purpose of advertising is to sell." The motto (attributed to Al Hampel while he was creative head of Benton & Bowles) "It Is Not Creative Unless It Sells" has in fact become a favorite catchall maxim in advertising itself. Students in marketing classes are given that as the rationale for advertising; account executives use it in setting their art directors and copywriters straight; it is an oft-repeated statement at creative board meetings. Let it be said that the motto should find a permanent place on the walls in every advertising agency. Let it also be said, however, that it is also something of a truism. Of course advertising is supposed to sell, but that is like saying that the purpose of getting married is to procreate. Is that all there is to it?

Sell What?

It is absolutely essential that the advertiser have a *clear* idea *what* it is that is being sold. To say that advertising is to sell a product or a service would be a gross oversimplification of what is rarely that simple a problem. More important to the advertising professional are the specific attributes of the product that he is supposed to promote. The prime function of advertising is *not* to explain the product but to motivate a purchase. Facts are relayed to the consumer but only to create a *perception* about the product. In the final analysis, that and nothing else clinches the sale.

Your Product Is a State of Mind

An engineer or a scientist will define a product in terms of size, color, material, structure, motion. His description is apt to be strictly accurate, with no allowance for a subjective evaluation. But those in advertising take a different approach. If advertising presented only a precise definition of the product, then the best product on the market would invariably emerge as the winner. It doesn't work that way. The product that fails — and eight of ten new ones fail every two years — does so not because of lack of quality but because it leaves the consumer unconvinced that he or she needs it. In other words, the problem lies in the message as much as in the product itself.

Product attributes are *only* as good as consumers' perception of them. If the

147

consumer cannot convert claims into special *personal benefits,* then for all practical purposes, the fault probably lies in advertising. Such is not a matter of accuracy or completeness. No scholarly description will ever convince the consumer that the product excites his senses — tickles his palate, pleases his nostrils, or feasts his eye — unless he himself *feels* it.

The annals of advertising are replete with projects that never served the product well. Their failure to reach the consumer on a basic emotional level — viscerally, if you will — proved to be the problem, and that in face of well-laid-out marketing plans and products par excellence. The quick demise of Ford's Edsel was such a case. Quantitive research showed there was a niche for such a car. Little qualitative research was done, however, concerning the state of mind of prospects. While it is true that buyers began to look for a compact car at the time, Edsel failed in convincing the public that it was that. It tried to straddle two worlds simultaneously: The car was sold as *both* roomy and racy, low price and high price. The result was an automobile the average car buyer couldn't quite understand. Sybaritic drivers missed the heavy solidity of an oversized car; the sporty thought Edsel not racy enough both in looks and performance. The name *Edsel* did not help matters either; what did it mean? The car had no definite "personality" — the public was confused. In the end, the company was forced to pay for its failure in accurately assessing the mood of prospective buyers.

Coca-Cola conducted thorough taste tests before deciding to come up with a different kind of Coke after two decades. Considerable publicity and promotion touted the arrival of the new drink. There was retail excitement, plenty of shelf space waiting for the entry, publicity worth millions of dollars, but the company mistook its own extensive in-depth research. Sure, consumers liked the new flavor — but has the "old" Classic Coke become popular purely because of its

taste? Or has it long been an American tradition (and part of happy childhood memories) no longer possible to do away with?

Once Again, Left Brain vs. Right Brain

We made much of the two hemispheres of the brain in the opening chapter of this book: the fact that each performs a given set of functions; that it was helpful for the creator of advertising to be aware of the differences between the two sides of the brain — the logical and the imaginative. The same observations hold true with the consumer, too. He "thinks" and "feels" about the advertising in ways dictated by the duality of the brain.

Smart advertisers appreciate the fact that it is possible to reach an audience on either level, and that the choice rests with them. Obviously, some products more readily lend themselves to the rational approach, while others work the emotions. Generally, the less expensive the product, the less cognitive the purchase. For example, it is highly unlikely that the purchaser would deliberate at length about buying a

In the consumer's brain, messages shuttle back and forth between its two halves — consciously and unconsciously. Dominance of one side over the other largely determines product perceptions.

piece of candy (unless he happens to be on a strict diet). On the other hand, purchasing life insurance is largely a left-brain activity; the decision is reached by use of "logic."

That is why some ads contain a lot of information (even if this calls for long copy) while others prefer to use pictures to get the story across. A mouthwatering color photograph of a chocolate cake will probably sell itself; words may prove to be redundant. On the other hand, a prospect for a Mercedes-Benz ("Engineered Like No Other Car in the World") would be more willing to work his way through a lengthy description of the car and its recent performance.

The reason that direct mail advertisers thrive on seemingly tedious explanations of products is that in their case pictures in themselves rarely produce the hoped-for response. Readers want to learn about the product in detail before committing themselves to part with the money. They *need* the precision of the printed word, which leaves less to interpretation. To fur-

ther demonstrate what goes into purchasing products, consider the following:

LEFT-BRAIN DECISION	RIGHT-BRAIN DECISION
Financial	Fashion
Appliances	Cosmetics
Hardware	Flowers
Medical	Art
Tires	Accessories
Insurance	Travel
Fertilizers	Games, toys
Machinery	Music

It is important to remember that this list is not complete. Variations exists even within a product group. "Food," for example, may be bought both on an emotional, and intellectual level:

LEFT-BRAIN PURCHASES	RIGHT-BRAIN PURCHASES
Flour	Chocolate
Salt	Fish
Pet foods	Poultry
Milk	Salad dressing
Fresh potatoes	Fruits
Margarine	Bottled water

Both hemispheres may be put to work when purchasing coffee, sodas, canned foods, vegetables, bread, or cold cuts.

Sometimes it is more effective to do the unexpected and use an emotional appeal to sell a "rational" product. AT&T has done just that for years. While it stresses service and the technical superiority of its equipment, it never lets us forget that there is more to making a phone call than electronic impulses; it can also mean friendship and love.

Weyerhaueser's long-standing award-winning campaign offers another outstanding example of addressing both sides of the brain. The company is in the business of producing and processing timber, hardly an "emotional" product, yet this advertiser has had an extraordinary success in combining appeals. In a

149

series of full-color magazine ads showing the beauty of forests on the West Coast, as well as in its television commercials, Weyerhaueser has voiced its environmental concerns.

Product Attribute vs. Consumer Benefit

To further clarify the important differences between product attributes (inherent in the product) and consumer benefits (attributes as perceived by the consumer), the following is cited here for purposes of comparison.

These are product attributes:

Size	Elasticity	Vapor
Weight	Roughness	Fragrance
Texture	Brittleness	Tone quality
Shape	Pulpiness	Strength
Density	Moisture	Design
Rigidity	Dryness	Elegance
Pliancy	Color	Tactility

Now listen to verbatim reactions to products (as noted at various focus group interviews): "I like the way it looks . . .," "it saves me time . . .," "it'll fit into my shelf . . .," "it goes with my outfit . . .," "red is my favorite color . . .," "it won't tip over . . .," "the kids can't break it . . .," "it'll help me lose weight . . .," "I just love that smell . . .," "I can buy it on credit. . . ." These reactions are perceived as *consumer benefits*.

How to Tell the Difference

To find out about product attributes is a relatively simple matter; just ask your engineers or your people in R & D, and they will probably have the facts you're looking for. To find out the consumers' perceptions *about* the product, however, may involve a little more than that. Here, the answer calls for both instincts and solid consumer research. Most agencies can provide both. Reaction to the product and the advertising that goes with it all can be found out before the product is launched and the campaign is created. Here is how:

Pretesting Advertising Campaigns. This can be done at various stages of execution. A concept alone can be tested in its infancy, with or without the help of pictures and words. Some advertisers carry their campaigns into nearly complete form, so that the reader or viewer can see the ad exactly the way it would appear.

The three basic effects measured are *perception* (what does the advertisement mean to the respondent?), *comprehension* (do consumers understand the message?), and *reaction* (will the consumer react favorably to the brand advertised?).

Interviews can be conducted on location (shopping malls, street corners, home, supermarkets), or at some other convenient location, such as an office (focus groups, prerecruited consumer panels), or by telephone or mail.

Other forms of pretesting are *split testing* (the same ad placed in two different publications, reaching two different audiences), *on-air commercial tests* (actual commercials shown on home television sets), *trailer tests* (instead of showing the planned commercial in a theatrical setting, trailers are set up at shopping centers), *scanner tests* (number of sales are monitored with the aid of a coded card and scanner among those who have viewed the commercial recently), and *mechanical tests* (measuring respondents' involuntary physical responses to advertising exposure by means of psychogalvanometer, pupil dilation, or voice quality).

A relatively small sample often proves adequate for projection. Television commercials are normally pretested with audiences no larger than 130 to 150 people. The average focus group consists of 10 to 15 participants; in fact, more than that may create unnecessary confusion and can turn the session into a hard-to-follow open discussion. Street interviews of 300 to 500 produce a better than 90% statistical accuracy. Inquiry-based mailing tests of 2,000 to 3,000 usually suffice to project the future, provided the list accurately reflects the type of consumer using the product. The same holds true of coupon advertising.

Such research may require the help of an experienced professional, particularly for designing questionnaires and conducting long in-depth interviews. There is always the possibility of an overly subjective evaluation of the results on the part of a less experienced researcher. Interviewees are not always capable of verbalizing their emotions and they may wish to give the "proper" answers to please the interviewer or to demonstrate their sophistication. Moreover, they may also harbor built-in feelings against certain activities, not the least of which may be advertising itself.

Research shows that consumers react both to *what* the message tells them and *how* it is told to them. They relate to product features primarily in terms of personal benefits. Self-interest and subjectivity play a major role — more so than the learned reports that come from R & D.

"Before I'll ride with a drunk, I'll drive myself." —Stevie Wonder

Driving after drinking, or riding with a driver who's been drinking, is a big mistake. Anyone can see that.

This public service poster appeals to reason — but more than that, it reaches people on the deepest of emotional levels. Taking the wheel in an inebriated state has more to do with feelings than "logic"; love for fellow beings, fear of killing others or oneself, ostracism by one's peers.

THE PRIVILEGED CLIENT'S MORTGAGE.

THE BOSTON COMPANY HAS A SIMPLE APPROACH TO PERSONAL INVESTMENT BANKING:

SERVE EVERY CLIENT AS IF THAT CLIENT WERE OUR *ONLY* CLIENT.

TO THAT END, THROUGH OUR SUBSIDIARY BOSTON SAFE DEPOSIT AND TRUST COMPANY, WE OFFER THE BOSTON COMPANY RESIDENTIAL MORTGAGE.*

OUR ONE-YEAR ADJUSTABLE RATE RESIDENTIAL MORTGAGES ARE DISTINGUISHED BY EXCEPTIONALLY ATTRACTIVE, COMPETITIVE RATES. YOU'LL LIKELY FIND OUR JUMBO MORTGAGES OF OVER $500,000 HAVE THE MOST FAVORABLE TERMS AVAILABLE ANYWHERE.

FOR A COMPLETE DESCRIPTION, CONTACT US AT 1-800-CALL BOS (1-800-225-5267, EXT. 200).

AND ENJOY THE ADVANTAGES OF BEING A PRIVILEGED CLIENT.

*Certain products may not be available in all states.

A subsidiary of Shearson Lehman Brothers Inc. An American Express company

THE BOSTON COMPANY
Boston Safe Deposit and Trust Company
Member FDIC. An Equal Housing Lender.

Most investment decisions are processed through the left side of the brain. In this ad, the prestigious Boston Company chooses to refer to its "favorable terms," "jumbo mortgages of over $500,000," "attractive, competitive rates," and other factual information to set itself apart from competition in the mind of its sophisticated audience.

153

Friendship

as little as **10¢**

She's your best friend. And you haven't spoken to her in, well, hours. So give her a call now. For as little as 10¢, you can call anywhere within any of these regions: New York City, East Suffolk, West Suffolk, Nassau, Rockland, Upper Westchester & Putnam, or Lower Westchester. It's even less after 9 p.m. and on weekends. Flat-rate customers pay 2¢ for each minute past the first. Go ahead. Pick up the phone. You've got a lot to catch up on since this morning.

A call can make a difference.

New York Telephone
A **NYNEX** Company

This ad reaches *both* sides of the brain.

154

Positioning: Don't Leave Home Without It

Much has been written about positioning under various names (*major selling point, competitive edge, brand personality*) for years. Rosser Reeves, the moving force behind Ted Bates in the fifties and sixties, called it *Unique selling proposition* or USP. Here is the way he defines it in his classic treatise *Reality in Advertising:*

1. Each advertisement must make a proposition to the consumer. Not just words, not just product puffery, not just show window advertising. Each advertisement must say this to each reader: "Buy this product and you will get this specific benefit . . ."
2. The proposition must be one that the competition either cannot or does not offer. It must be unique either in the brand or in the claim . . . .
3. The proposition must be strong enough to move the mass millions, i.e. pull over new customers to your brand . . . .

David Ogilvy takes the idea one step further in his book *Confessions of an Advertising Man.* Less predisposed to Rosser Reeves's "hard-sell" approach, he prefers a softer, more long-range method of selling.

Advertisers who fail to develop *and* claim a product difference may find their voices lost on the consumer. Product differences must be hammered in, not once but over and over again. Consumers rarely discover the distinction on their own.

Where to Put the Emphasis

Funny things can happen on the way to the market. The product difference you or your R & D put on top of the list may slide down a notch or two in your search for a meaningful product benefit. Attributes that seemed minor at first may move into the forefront at second thought.

It takes a finely honed advertising mind to discover deeply buried consumer benefits of the product. In the beginning, Pampers had set out to design a diaper easy to fasten on the baby; it emphasized "convenience" in all its advertising. But sales rose as the company switched its advertising strategy to "keeping babies dry." Obviously, this was more important to the mothers of America. For years, Dannon lived under the impression that it was taste that separated it from its competitors, until management and the agency discovered that nutrition played an even more important part in its success. Today, Dannon is looked upon as "health food."

When Less Is More

It is probably more effective to promote one major benefit than to try selling two, and two get through better than three. Giving five or six benefits equal emphasis can so diffuse attention as to be counterproductive. There is an understandable temptation to tell all. "But look at all the advantages our product has over competition," one company executive told his advertising agency, which was arguing for simplicity. "Why not list them all and satisfy not one but a variety of needs?" This argument carries conviction yet rarely proves true on the open marketplace. An ad is not a confession booth. In fact, ads are often skimmed over. Twenty percent readership of half of copy would be considered exceptional according to studies made by Starch Advertisement Readership Service. Thirty percent recall of a television commercial a day after appearance is better than par. The truth is that the average consumer is not holding his breath waiting for the advertiser's next announcement. He is too busy doing other things.

Your Advertising Style

Technique of advertising—words and pictures—may tell as much about your product and your company as the substance of the message. Brash advertising bespeaks a brash company. A low-key voice suggests the presence of a thoughtful, avuncular management. Trendy commercials imply that the company is as "cool" as most of its customers probably expect it to be. Grand, spirit-stirring claims bring big-league companies to mind, while frequent allusions to competition point to the presence of an underdog. Some advertisers turn masculine in their brand advertising campaigns, others talk woman to woman. And finally, there are companies with a sense of humor. To illustrate:

Brash advertising / brash company: Crazy Eddie, Midas Muffler, and local car dealerships. *Low-key advertising/thoughtful company:* Johnson & Johnson, McGraw-Hill, and Gallo Wines. *Trendy advertising / "with-it" company:* California Wine Cooler, Pepsi-Cola, and Calvin Klein. *Grandiose advertising / important company:* IBM, Shearson-Lehman, GTE. *Comparison advertising / underdog:* Sprint, Southern Bell Telephone, US West. *Masculine advertising / masculine company:* Marlboro, Chrysler, Anheuser-Busch. *Feminine advertising / feminine company:* Chesebrough-Ponds, Revlon, Beatrice Foods, Scott Paper. *Emotional advertising / company with feelings:* Hallmark Cards, McDonald's, Eastman Kodak. *Light-hearted advertising / company with a sense of humor:* Federal Express, Wendy's International, Dunkin' Donuts.

Few companies are as skilled in positioning their products as is Philip Morris. Marlboro has changed its image from "feminine" to "masculine" through advertising, establishing its identity as a "macho smoke." Virginia Slims carved a respectable niche for itself, too, concentrating on women celebrating their status of economic independence and the self-confidence that it brings.

All communication in advertising follows the "PPP Route" — beginning with the Product sold to People through means of building a clear-cut Perception (an advertising task). Of the three "P's", the center one is most amenable to change. Success stories abound where thorough change in the *image* of the product, *not the product itself,* has created a whole new market. (Marlboro is an example.) Defining the identity of the product should be the first step in launching an advertising campaign.

This announcement of a concert was prepared by Scali McCabe Sloves — with the sponsor wisely given a low profile. The perception created here reflects the civic-mindedness of a major corporation. Goal-oriented Apple Computer television spots (Chiat/Day) play up the same theme over and over — the user-friendliest computer money can buy. The advertiser knows not only where it is coming from but where it wants to go.

157

Maybe It's Time To Sell Your Rolex.

swatch® ✚
Holding steady at $35.

In this newspaper ad, Swatch boldly confronts its competition. Our perception is of Swatch as a confident, enterprising company, as well as a fine watch.

MICHELIN. BECAUSE SO MUCH IS RIDING ON YOUR TIRES.

Nancy Stahl is a graphic designer, which the logo effectively suggests without spelling it out.

WIFE: Honey?

HUSBAND: Hmmm.

WI FE: You have Michelin tires in your car, don't you?

HUSBAND: Yeah.

WIFE: How come?

HUSBAND: I don't know. They're terrific tires. Why?

WIFE: How come I don't have Michelins in my car?

HUSBAND: Oh sweetheart, they cost more. I drive to work, I go out of town a lot. All you use your car for is shopping, driving Amy around . . . I'll get you a set tomorrow.

WIFE: You sure you want to spend the extra money on us?

HUSBAND: Come on.

ANNCR VO: Michelin. Because so much is riding on your tires.

Michelin emphasizes its concern for safety by letting its tires speak for themselves. A favorable impression of the company has a ripple effect.

SHE'S VERY CHARLIE.

Charlie
REVLON

Nike loves athletes, athletes love Nike. Glorifying its users, Nike has developed an image all its own: the footwear that knows the needs of its wearer. Revlon has taken an equally successful route, if with a difference. Charlie personifies the fragrance she sells — she is the quintessential woman of today, fun-loving, feminine, but in control. There are many would-be Charlies in this world — why not begin with the perfume?

In a disposable world, is there a place for a vase designed to last centuries?

Some Waterford patterns available
today were designed over 200 years ago.
To many, this ability to transcend
time may seem remarkable.
To us, it's simply the criterion that
determines whether or not a design
is worthy of the designation "Waterford."

Waterford
Steadfast in a world of wavering standards

The quiet elegance in this ad is part of the message. The Waterford tagline, "Steadfast in a world of wavering standards," sums up the company's philosophy.

Art and copy set the tone in this newspaper advertising campaign by Odd Couple Advertising. Going to a pub is fun — and so should be looking at and reading ads that so represent the institution.

Our lightweight Summer suits
ideal for travel or business

The Summer suit, a concept we introduced
in the 1930's is favored for its light weight
and crisp looks. And we feel our selection
is the largest, and of the highest quality, in
America today. Each is tailored for us on
our exclusive models. Coat and trousers.

New cotton-polyester tan poplin suit, $210
Blue-and-white cotton seersucker suit, $215

Use your Brooks Brothers card, American Express,
Diners Club, MasterCard or Visa

346 MADISON AVENUE • LIBERTY PLAZA • MANHASSET
PARAMUS • SCARSDALE • SHORT HILLS • STAMFORD

**Brooks Brothers has used the same for-
mat in its advertising for many years,
creating an image neither of tomorrow
nor yesterday. The technique suggests
stability—a company whose fashions
wear well and long.**

Close Your Eyes—What Do You See?

A good way to test the impact of your
advertising is to lean back and close your
eyes. Now, think of the name of your own
company. What comes to your mind first?
Look for one or two adjectives, a simple
definition. Congratulations! You have just
read your customer's mind.

Keep Asking Yourself: What Is It That My Advertising Is Trying to Accomplish?

As we said at the beginning of this chapter, the word *sell* is too general a word to
describe the function of advertising. A
more exacting definition is needed. This
definition should be developed and refined as soon as possible. Research,
media, copy, art will all come to naught if
not following a consistent strategy. Hoping that everything will fall into place later
is a sign of an incurable optimist, not a
good manager.

Keep asking yourself these questions as
you are mulling over strategy:

1. *What is it that this advertising campaign is supposed to accomplish?* Is the
   goal short or long range?

161

2. *If it's short-range results you want, so be it.* Move the product off the shelf quickly? Consumer and trade promotions may just be your answer. If it's the image of a company you want to build up, so be it. Most advertising is designed for the long pull. Rarely is an ad a one-night stand.

3. *Is the company's advertising consistent with its philosophy?* Even quick, put-out-the-fire promotional campaigns can—and should—reflect your corporate image. As we said earlier, advertising and promotion are separate disciplines, but they can have similar goals.

4. *Is advertising designed to confront specific claims made by the competition?* If so, it must be specific.

5. *Is the product new, on its way to being established, or well established?* Each situation calls for a different approach.

To Sum It Up

To say that the function of advertising is to sell the product is somewhat of a truism. Sell, yes. But sell *what?*

The "what" is for the advertiser and his advertising experts to decide. Obviously, every product has several attributes, some more meaningful *to the customer* than others. The problem must always be clearly defined before the solution is sought. The key is to set priorities as to the selling features. Decisions should not be subjective, close as some product attributes may be to the advertiser's heart. The consumer must be able to convert product attribute into a clearly defined benefit to himself or herself.

It is the perception of the product that counts, even more than factual information. Perception can be built up by advertising: the positioning of the product on the marketplace. Everything must work in tandem toward creating a simple, easy-to-remember image of the product: the theme, use of media, execution.

Sophisticated research techniques are available today to gauge audience reaction to products both before and after the advertising campaign. These can be either quantitative (sales volume, results of test marketing, coupon returns, etc.) or qualitative (focus group interviews, in-depth psychological studies, reactions to commercials, etc.). Modern technology makes it easier to relate today's advertising to tomorrow's sales, an important step toward measuring advertising effectiveness.

8

Consumer, Who Are You?

Among the profound changes in advertising in recent years the concept of segmentation stands out—the use of the rifle instead of the shotgun approach to reaching the ultimate customer. No product represents everything to all people. While there are commodities that everyone uses (toothpaste, soap, salt, toilet paper), not everyone uses the same *brand*—a vital distinction to the advertiser interested in selling his brand, not the entire category. No marketer, unless he is an incurable optimist or the greatest spendthrift who ever lived, would try selling the same item to over 240 million people—and especially not in a culture as diverse as ours.

There are three key elements in segmentation approaches, Geographic, demographic, and psychographic.

The three often overlap but for the sake of clarity, we will discuss each separately.

Geographic Segmentation

In this type of segmentation, the customers' whereabouts are used as a prime factor in pinpointing their demographic and psychographic characteristics. Obviously, people living in certain areas share common interests. But it is only recently that marketers are beginning to pay serious attention to this phenomenon—and with telling results.

One of the most conspicuous examples of cultural bonding shows up in the difference between the urban and rural population. Each of these groups has its own distinctive needs, life-styles, attitudes, and product preferences.

Generally speaking (and in trying to classify people, allowances must be made for stereotyping), the typical urbanite is more willing to experiment with new products, more upwardly mobile, and more skeptical of advertising claims. He is less likely to have a large family, or stay married to the same partner for life. With more discretionary income than his country cousin, he carries, on the average, three credit cards in his pocket. Per household, he owns fewer cars.

A separate *geodemographic* (the word connotes common demographic characteristics in a geographic area) group living within the confines of the city but with its own characteristics is the so-called "inner-city" population. Feeling less secure about the future, these urban dwellers are more likely to make impulse purchases (when they feel "the money is there"), and pay in cash. Their brand loyalty runs high, as does their commitment to "their" store. As a whole, they are more susceptible to product claims and have a singular preference for television over other advertising media. Radio and posters come in as distant seconds, newspapers third.

Suburbanites are basically urbanites, but with a difference. The new breed of suburbanites is not nearly as dependent as the generation before them on nearby metropolises for jobs (more and more are being offered close by), entertainment (movies and various entertainment centers have moved to the suburbs), and shopping (shopping malls are growing faster than downtown retail districts). This is the market for family-oriented products and home and driving amenities. As their city neighbors, they also listen to advertising none too attentively, but because of a slower pace of life, they at least stop and think about the claims when they hear them.

The rural population is a less important market in terms of purchasing power: The average income is lower and buying habits are more difficult (and therefore, more expensive) to change. Traditional values still reign supreme among the countrybred. Popular media are television and radio, perhaps because of their easy access, with home-delivered newspapers in close pursuit. Marketers who concentrate on selling to this group usually do so with rural-specific products: i.e. farm supplies, tools, magazines, food and household staples.

Regional Approach

Different parts of the country tend to develop their own buying patterns. Modern computer technology is now providing entirely new insights into the many subtle and not-so-subtle differences that exist between various areas. Here's a quick look at the United States — from the point of an advertiser:

All things considered, the two most culturally watchful regions in the country are its two "coasts" — or more specifically, New York City and the two largest cities in California, Los Angeles and San Francisco. Those living on either side insist, of course, that theirs is the last word in new trends. Both have a case. According to *Sunset*, a West Coast magazine with an understandable bias, all that is worthwhile in a civilized world began in the Golden State, including indoor-outdoor architecture, body building, year-round suntan, the push-up bra, jeans, the air hostess, the dry martini, Mickey Mouse, self-service supermarkets, the no-fault divorce law, and the topless bathing suit. New Yorkers are quick to respond with an equally long list of their own, similar in nature.

All three cities are a launching pad for over a 1,000 new products every year. Their population are not only willing but eager to experiment. They can be reached easily through local media. Californians are consummate radio listeners while New York City has three major newspapers and nearly three dozen minor ones — no small achievement in a country of few two-newspaper towns. Retail stores abound and keep specializing to a finer and finer degree to satisfy specific — and increasingly exotic — tastes. Ideas introduced here flitter as quickly from one city to another as do electric sparks between poles. A trend in New York may show up in Los Angeles and San Francisco in a matter of a few weeks or even days and vice versa. Chicago, Dallas, Houston, Washington, Boston, Atlanta, Philadelphia, Denver, and Seattle follow suit — in that order. New ideas, new attitudes, and new buying habits then hopscotch from here to there, as they become an integrated part of grass roots America. The process of an idea to be accepted nationwide may take several months or as much as a year. And curiously enough, by the time the innovation has sunk into public consciousness throughout the nation, it has often become a memory among those who started it in the first place.

Disco offers an example of just such a crazy-quilt pattern. The Latino population of New York initially developed both the music and the dance, which spread from there throughout the nation. Today, the big city is beginning to show signs of wearying of its own progeny; ballroom dancing is now trying to make a comeback. Yet discotheques are still the in-thing in many smaller communities and new clubs are still opening up.

Americans are far from being a homogeneous lot. Different places, different folks. The West Coast prefers yellow; Texans, red; Michiganites, green; Vermonters, blue. (Typically, New Yorkers have no favorite color.) Southeasterners go to church on Sundays and constitute the largest market for ladies' full slips;

A great many products and services have had their beginnings at either coast of the United States, notably Los Angeles, San Francisco, and New York City. New ideas often leap right across the land in a few days, with regions in the rest of the country absorbing them at their own accustomed pace. It may take an innovation several years before gaining nationwide acceptance.

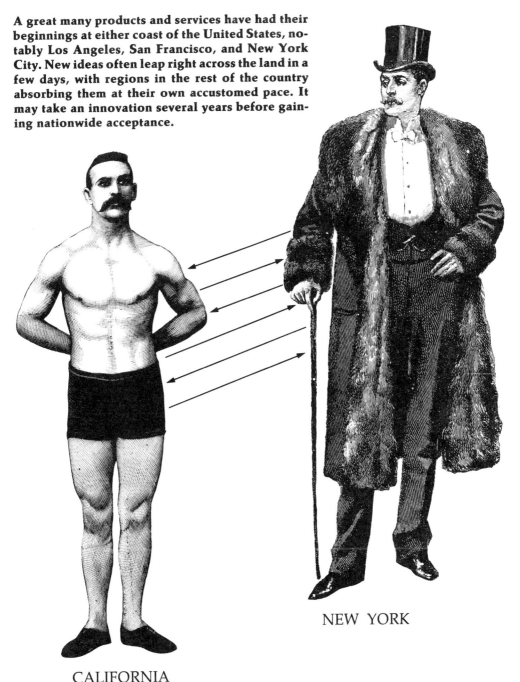

CALIFORNIA

NEW YORK

165

Southwesterners buy pickup trucks but Northeasterners ask for vans. Texans drive big cars, unlike New Yorkers forever in search of a place to park. Insecticides sell best in New York and Houston, the two roach capitals of the nation, while fleasprays go over big in Birmingham and Tampa. Raid has carved out a new marketshare in 16 or 18 regions by paying attention to just such local peculiarities; overall it has increased its insecticide marketshare by over 5% in little over a year.

Joel Garreau, an editor at the *Washington Post*, argues that it is possible to divide North America into nine "nations" as defined by a population that shares the same distinct values, attitudes, and styles. His definitive book on the subject, *The Nine Nations of America* (Houghton Mifflin), is in fact mandated reading among executives of a number of large consumer product companies. His "nations" are:

The Foundry: industrial Great Lakes Region

Dixie: what used to be the Confederate States of America; sometimes also referred to as the Bible Belt

The Islands: Southern Florida and the Caribbean

MexAmerica: Mexico

Southwest: including somewhat cavalierly southern California

Ecotopia: the temperate region between the Pacific Coast and coastal mountain ranges

Quebec: the French-speaking population in Canada

The Breadbasket: the huge wheatgrowing areas in the Midwest

The Empty Quarter: New England

To complete his list we feel compelled to add two more of our own:

Texas: a region with its own one-of-a-kind attitudes

New York City: a nation within a nation and then some

This commercial for Anheuser-Busch Bud Light warms the heart of grassroots America. Two farmers watch an athlete carry the Olympic torch across the land. Feelings of pride and patriotism run high. Mid-America talking to mid-America, this ad was created by Needham Harper's Chicago office.

"Local" advertising is often best left to the locals. This commercial by Loeffler Marley Mountjoy for South Carolina Federal was created for native consumption — a smiling banker is still considered a friend there. A jaded New York creative would be less prone to explore the same idea in this day and age.

ANNCR: *Pronto Ristorante's Chef Tomaso.*

TOMASO: *After exposing Minnesotans to many new Italian words through my big new menu, I would like to take a little time to recognize all of the people who have been helping me with my Minnesotan. Bill and Shelly of Minnetonka — thank you for telling me about dust bunnies — I look forward to seeing them the next time I am at the zoo. Paul of Blaine contributed Uff-da, Ish and Mopar, very nice words. A special thanks to my friends at the Shriners for all those Sven and Ole jokes — Italians think the Irish are funny, too. I'm sorry if I left anybody out. If you have a Minnesota Phrase, please write it down and bring it to Pronto the next time you have dinner. If I am out, just leave it with the hostess. She is, as you say, my main man.*

ANNCR: *Pronto Ristorante, an Italian-Italian restaurant. For reservations, call 333-4414.*

TOMASO: *"Let's have lunch" — that's good-bye, yes?*

This Minnesota radio "talk", aired for a Minnesota client (Pronto Ristorante), was written and produced by Minnesotan Jarl Olsen toiling away at an agency in — where else? — Minneapolis, Minnesota (Fallon McElligott Rice).

VOTE FOR A TURKEY.
YES ON ZOO BONDS.

Bumper stickers produced for the Woodland Park Zoo in Seattle were created by an agency located there. Livingston & Company. A touch of local chauvinism perhaps — and why not?

A Case History: Campbell's Soup

Campbell's established 22 geographically defined regions with an eye on regional differences in less than a year after management had decided to "go local." Having wide decision-making powers, regional managers instituted their own promotions. Examples of such programs include a car giveaway in Pittsburgh tied to a local TV station, billboards atop a ski lift in upstate New York, film spots for Campbell's dip soups and brand name mushrooms in two moviehouses in Sacramento, and a Spanish-speaking radio and giveaway campaign for V-8 Juice in northern California. Says Jon Ready, a regional sales manager of the company: "We work, live and breathe Cleveland-Pittsburgh. Nobody from Camden makes the final decision for us; we are allowed to do what makes sense for this area. With all our brands together, we have a better collective power base with them and better ad support. We've been able to turn marketing programs around in a few weeks, which is something you can't do with a national program."

The company has created several products to satisfy staunch regional tastes. When a local competitor cut into Campbell's pork and beans with his Mexican-style pinto beans in the Southwest area, management swiftly eliminated the pork in favor of more chili pepper and ranchero beans. Sales of pinto beans shot up from virtually nothing to 75,000 cases. Following the same logic, subsidiary Vlasic bought out Zesty Pickles mostly for Northwesterners, who for reasons known only to themselves like their pickles more sour than do most Americans.

Demographic Segmentation

Even simpler than using geographic segmentation to predict buying preferences is the use of demographic information as a base. According to the American Association of Advertising Agencies, this way of dividing the population into manageable units is based on such categories as:

Age	Income
Sex	Number of children
Education	Ages of children
Marital status	Household size
Occupation	Household income
Race	Geographic

These categories would provide for a minimal breakdown, just slightly more inclusive than that of the U.S. Census Bureau, hampered by laws on privacy. Most advertisers demand more detailed data to draw up their consumers' profile. A more comprehensive list of categories is provided by various research firms. For example, one of the largest, Simmons Market Research Bureau, Inc., examines no less than 27 different demographic categories to measure media audiences. Paying close attention to the consumption patterns and purchasing habits of almost 20,000 households in the United States, the company is able to cover some 800 product categories and 3,900 brands cross-tabulated by demographics and media and many other data bases.

Finely honed information such as this is particularly valuable for clients of determinate demographic targets; i.e. movies, insurance, investments, retail stores, fashion, cosmetics, publications. Using just such data, *U.S. News & World Report* celebrated its media reach by laying claim to these 100 demographic categories in a full-page ad in the *New York Times*.

1. Total Adults
2. Total Males
3. Professional/Managerial
4. Managerial/Administrative
5. Top Management
6. College Educated
7. College Graduate
8. Household Income $25,000+
9. Household Income $35,000+

10. Household Income $50,000+
11. Individual Earned Income $25,000+
12. Individual Earned Income $35,000+
13. Individual Earned Income $50,000+
14. Adults Employed in Company Size 1–99 Employees
15. Adults Employed in Company Size 100–999 Employees
16. A&B County Adults
17. C&D County Adults
18. Household Heads
19. Parents
20. Employed Full Time
21. Married Adults
22. Own a Home Worth $100,000+
23. Age 25–34, HHI $25,000+
24. Age 25–34, HHI $30,000+
25. Age 25–34, HHI $35,000+
26. Age 25–34, HHI $50,000+
27. P/M, IEI $30,000+
28. P/M, IEI $35,000+
29. P/M, in Manufacturing
30. P/M, in Other Industrial
31. P/M, in Business Services
32. P/M, in Public Administration
33. Professionals
34. P/M, Company Size 100–999 Employees
35. P/M, Company Size 1000+ Employees
36. P/M, HHI $50,000+
37. Metro/Suburban Adults
38. Adults in Households of 3–4 Adults
39. Adults in Single Family Dwellings
40. P/M, Male
41. P/M, Attended College
42. P/M, Graduated College
43. Top Management, Age 25–64
44. Age 25–49, HHI $25,000+
45. Age 25–49, HHI $25,000+, Att/Grad College
46. Age 25–54, HHI $25,000+, Att/Grad College
47. Age 25–34, HHI $25,000+, Att/Grad College
48. Age 25–34, HHI $50,000+, Att/Grad College
49. Age 25–49, HHI $35,000+, Att/Grad College
50. Involved in Purchase Decision of Telecommunications Eq. & Srv.
51. Involved in Purchase Decision of Word Processors
52. Involved in Purchase Decision of Office Copiers
53. Involved in Purchase Decision of Office Equip/Furn.
54. Involved in Purchase Decision of Corp. Investments/Fin. Serv.
55. Involved in Purchase Decision of Property/Group Insurance
56. Household Income $30,000+
57. Men, 25–49, IEI $25,000+
58. Men, 25–49, IEI $35,000+
59. Men, 25–34, HHI $25,000+, Att/Grad College
60. Individual Earned Income $75,000+
61. Individual Earned Income $100,000+
62. Age 25+, HHI $40,000+, Graduated College.
63. Own a Vacation or Weekend Home
64. Age 25–54, IEI $50,000+, Att/Grad College
65. Age 25–49, IEI $35,000+, Att/Grad College
66. Age 25–49, HHI $25,000+, Att/Grad College
67. Age 25–49, HHI $35,000+, Att/Grad College
68. Age 25–49, HHI $50,000+, Att/Grad College
69. Age 25–54, IEI $35,000+
70. Men, Age 25–34
71. Men, Age 25–49
72. Men, Age 25–54
73. Men, Att/Grad College
74. Men, Top Management
75. Men, 25–34, HHI $25,000+
76. Men, 25–34, HHI $30,000+
77. Men, 25–34, HHI $35,000+
78. Men, 25–34, HHI $50,000+
79. Men, 25–49, HHI $25,000+
80. Men, 25–49, HHI $30,000+
81. Men, 25–49, HHI $35,000+
82. Men, 25–49, HHI $50,000+
83. Men, 25–54, HHI $25,000+
84. Men, 25–54, HHI $30,000+
85. Men, 25–54, HHI $35,000+
86. Men, 25–54, HHI $50,000+
87. Men, IEI $25,000+
88. Men, IEI $35,000+

89. Men, IEI $50,000+
90. Men, 25–54, IEI $25,000+
91. P/M, IEI $25,000+
92. P/M, IEI $75,000+
93. P/M, IEI $100,000+
94. P/M, Age 30+
95. P/M, IEI $45,000+
96. P/M, Graduated College, Age 25–44
97. P/M, Att/Grad College, Age 25–44
98. P/M Involved in Purch. Dec. of Personal Computers for Bus.
99. P/M Involved in Purch. Dec. of Other Computer/EDP Equip.
100. P/M Involved in Purch. Dec. of Software for Bus.

American Marketing Association (New York)
Crain Communications (Chicago)
McGraw-Hill Book Company (New York)
John Wiley & Sons (New York)
Prentice-Hall (New York)
Fairchild Publications (New York)
Rand McNally & Company (Chicago)
Dow Jones Books (New York)
Random House (New York)
Harcourt Brace Jovanovich (New York)
Harvard University Press
Reuben H. Donnelley Corporation
F. W. Dodge Company
Sales Management Inc.
Industrial Marketing Inc.
Government Printing Office (Washington)
Postal service

The most popular trade and professional publications containing demographic information are:

Advertising Age
AdWeek
American Demographics
The Gallagher Report
Journal of Retailing
Journal of Marketing Research
Market Digest
Consumer Reports
Consumer Bulletins
Chain Store Age
Marketing News
Marketing Communications
Advertising & Sales Promotion
Sales Management
Industrial Marketing
Direct Marketing
Management Review
Public Relations Quarterly
Broadcasting
Media Decisions
Medical Marketing & Media
Variety
Television/Radio Age
Media/Scope
Client/Media News
Journal of Advertising Research

Demographics: Where to Find It

There are numerous sources for demographic information, such as research firms, information-based direct marketing services, government agencies, computerized data bases (over 1,000 of them), business newspapers and magazines, directories, and advertising agencies. Books like *Where to Find Business Information*, John Wiley & Sons, New York; *Names & Numbers*, John Wiley & Sons, New York; *Information U.S.A.*, The Viking Press, New York; *National Directory of Addresses and Telephone Numbers*, Bantam Books, New York; and, of course, the *World Almanac* in its various editions provide additional information.

Publishers most likely to have books on demographics are:

Media: The Best Source of Information Yet

Few organizations know more about their consumers than media; their livelihood depends on their fresh insights. Both publications and broadcast stations are continually compiling updated demographic and psychographic information, so they can spot an up-and-coming trend — or perhaps start one of their own. This information is readily available; ask sales representatives to send or bring you their "media kit." These kits contain reams of data, material that will be useful in the quest for just the "right" audience.

Psychographic Segmentation

The psychological makeup of today's consumer can be just as important as — and often more so than — the demographic profile. Demographic data help to define status but fall short on explaining buying motivations. Take income, for example. A garbage collector in New York City earns the same salary as a college professor, but they spend it in two entirely different fashions. They would not necessarily be interested in the same product or, for that matter, listen to the same advertising message.

WHO IS MINDING THE TV SET?

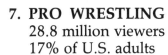

1. **PRO FOOTBALL**
   63.2 million viewers
   37% of U.S. adults
2. **BASEBALL**
   62.7 million viewers
   37% of U.S. adults
3. **COLLEGE FOOTBALL**
   48.9 million viewers
   29% of U.S. adults
4. **BOXING**
   37.2 million viewers
   22% of U.S. adults
5. **COLLEGE BASKETBAL**
   36.2 million viewers
   21% of U.S. adults
6. **PRO BASKETBALL**
   34.7 million viewers
   21% of U.S. adults

7. **PRO WRESTLING**
   28.8 million viewers
   17% of U.S. adults
8. **BOWLING**
   28.6 million viewers
   17% of U.S. adults
9. **TENNIS**
   26.3 million viewers
   16% of U.S. adults
10. **AUTO RACING**
    25.8 million viewers
    15% of U.S. adults
11. **GOLF**
    25.8 million viewers
    15% of U.S. adults
12. **DRAG RACING**
    18.4 million viewers
    11% of U.S. adults

Looking for his target audience, the advertiser often looks to information gathered by media or syndicated research employed by media. Simmons Market Research Bureau prepared this index.

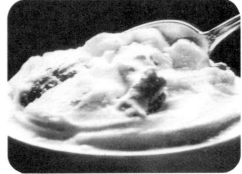

(MUSIC: UP)

(SFX: DOOR OPENS)

ANNCR VO: If you don't feel guilty, it wasn't that good

MAN VO: Hi, Honey.

WOMAN: I ate all the Frusen Gladje.

MAN VO: You ate all the what?

WOMAN: I ate all the Frusen Gladje.

ANNCR VO: Frusen Gladje, the ice cream under the dome. So creamy; so delicious; so rewarding.

WOMAN: And I'd do it again.

ANNCR VO: Enjoy the guilt.
Frusen Gladje.

Lear's has swiftly carved out a place for itself: the sophisticated forty-plus woman who knows life still holds a few surprises for her. Früsen Gladje heralds still another new psychographic arrival to the scene: the health-conscious, self-indulgent, baby-boom generation.

This magazine ad for DeBeers mirrors a subtle but basic fundamental change in women's attitudes. Diamonds have always been considered the gift of gifts, but it was usually the "girl's best friend," not the man's. Roles are reversed in this ad: the woman is the giver. An interesting sideline that shows how exacting research pays off is the tagline; "the gift of success" was changed when the agency, Ayer's, found out that women, too, perceive diamonds as a gift of love, more so than a symbolic celebration of "getting ahead."

An unusual ad for bridal gowns but one that touches the heart of today's newly wed. Prepared by *Bride* magazine's in-house agency for The Diamond Collection.

For people who like to smoke...

BENSON & HEDGES
because quality matters.

Few cigarette campaigns have aroused as much controversy as the one prepared by Wells Rich Greene for Benson & Hedges, a Philip Morris brand. The agency decided to forgo the visual clichés so prevalent in much of tobacco advertising. The campaign proved to be a resounding success. Pictures accurately reflect the attitudes and lifestyles of the audience the advertiser is trying to reach.

ONE OF THE PLAIN JANES WHO
READS McCALL'S.

McCall's
MORE THAN THE EXPECTED.

ONE OF THE OLD-FASHIONED GIRLS
WHO READS McCALL'S.

McCall's
MORE THAN THE EXPECTED.

McCalls has changed its image by hand-picking lively, known celebrities to represent its typical — and changed — reader.

All you have to be is you.

All you have to be is you.

All you have to be is you.

Campaign for Liz Claiborne created by Altschiller Reitzfield Advertising firmly establishes a contemporary image. It shows each women as a distinctive individual. Each has a mind of her own, especially when it comes to choosing her favorite fragrance.

175

Life-Style Dimensions, Activities, Interests, Opinions

Today's marketer can no longer base his decisions on demographic information alone. He must learn what the customer *thinks,* how he *feels,* and what he *does,* regardless of his background. Almost literally, he must get inside the head of his customer — much like a psychologist.

The Leo Burnett Advertising Agency uses these criteria to find out about the consumer's lifestyle dimensions:

ACTIVITIES	INTERESTS	OPINIONS
Work	Family	Themselves
Hobbies	Home	Social Issues
Social Events	Job	Politics
Vacations	Recreation	Business
Entertainment	Fashion	Economics
Shopping	Food	Products
Sports	Media	Culture

Research companies go even further in their analysis at the behest of their advertising clients. Using values and a life-style method of interrogation, it is now possible to measure (and cross-index) such esoterics as the respondants' *self-concept* (affectionate, broad-minded, creative, efficient, funny, kind, reserved, sociable), *buying habits* (ad believer, brand loyal, conforming, frugal, adventurous, style conscious), and both his *pleasure and work-related activities.*

The Psychology of a Pill-Taker

Pill-takers offer an excellent example of attitude segmentation — with demographics at best only tailgating the psychographic profile. In this case, we are talking about the most common — and perhaps the most effective — headache medicine of all: plain aspirin tablets. Demographically, users cut accross the board; psychographically, they fall into several distinct categories.

Severe Sufferers. This group takes medication to alleviate recurrent pain, usually on a doctor's advice. Opting for prescriptions, they do not like to take generic drugs and are unlikely prospects for such an "ordinary" drug as aspirin. Of the four groups listed here, Severe Sufferers take the largest number of dosages. Yet advertising may fall on a deaf ear here; they "know" their medication and a commercial or two is not about to win them over. Approximately one-fifth of them have two or more medical checkups a year.

Active medicators listen to advertising claims and are willing to experiment with variations of the same basic drug, aspirin. They will look for a brand they perceive as best for their specific problem: Bayer, Bufferin, Tylenol, Excedrin, Anacin, Advil, Nuprin, or other painkilling drugs. Less educated, they make less income, and are second in the number of dosages per month. They are more likely to switch brands than the Severe Sufferers.

Hypochondriacs are by far the largest and most important market for analgesics. Most television commercials — if not all — are targeted at this psychographic cluster. Figures vary, but some medical authorities estimate that over half of all headaches are of psychosomatic origin. This does not mean that the pain is absent; muscles, nerves, blood circulation all actively respond to the mind, causing physiological changes in the body. The fact remains, however, that people vary greatly in their tolerance; those unfortunate enough to have a low pain threshold usually look for validation of their suffering, a sympathetic ear. That is why commercials showing anatomical drawings are so effective — they "scientifically prove" what takes place inside one's body, not only the Hypochondriac's but any "normal" person's.

Practicalists are the most apt to purchase generic drugs, including aspirin. Subtle product differences claimed by makers of various headache remedies leave them relatively unimpressed. They are the least likely to develop side effects, including allergies, constipation, and muscle cramps. Of the four groups, they are most apt to purchase pills on the basis of price, and will shop around for bargains. They take the lowest number of dosages per month, and make the fewest visits to the doctor, about one-fourth that of the Hypochondriacs.

Another Psychographic Study: "Please Release Me, Let Me Go"

Chapel Hill, a small family-owned funeral home in New York City, was struggling to find "clients" for its prearranged funerals. Competition in this field is keen. Since larger homes offer a wider range of funeral services, including cremation, Chapel Hill designed its own simple but dignified cremation service. At first, its advertising stressed low price—ads appeared in publications such as the *New York Daily News, El Diario,* black-oriented *Amsterdam News, Daily Challenge,* and *Black American.* The copy explained that it was altogether proper to wish to economize; the Lord has always received the poor and the rich without distinction.

The campaign ran for over a year but failed to increase business. The few who responded would resist cremation and could not be persuaded to arrange for a prepaid funeral. Even though most represented lower-income families, their objections to the concept of cremation were more psychological than economical. Many claimed that incineration of the human body went against their religious beliefs; the flames would consume not

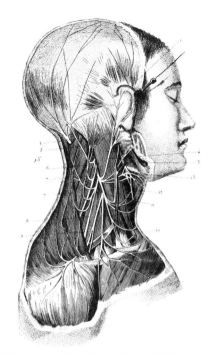

This meticulously rendered illustration (by medical illustrators of the last century) may impress a scientifically-minded audience, but less so the average user of pain-killers. It fails to convey the *sensation* of pain—the very way the sufferer feels.

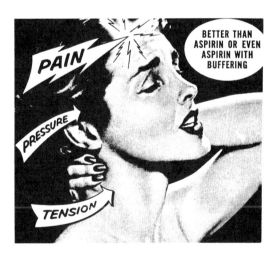

This illustration dramatizes pain; the advertiser sympathizes with its audience. Validation is important to the headache-prone who may feel that his or her complaints are dismissed as psychological in origin, and thus trivial in nature.

'Yes' answers could be a sign of a medical problem.

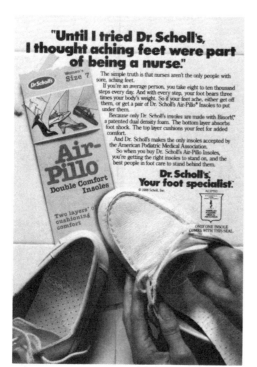

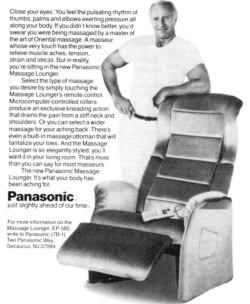

All of the advertisements on this page effectively play up the feel-good effect of their product more than the product itself. Readers who *feel* the pain, respond. Glaxo sends the sufferer symptom hunting, encouraging him to listen to the "message from your body." Thorlo stresses "pain-free walking." Dr. Scholl's Air-Pillo uses a nurse's experience to lend its message believability. Panasonic waxes positively poetic about getting a massage.

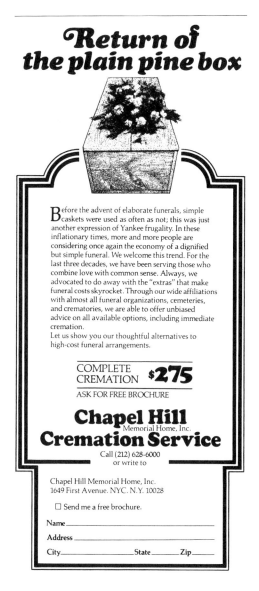
Public opinions shift — even about long-cherished funeral rites. More and more people accept cremation as they become better-educated, more accepting of death, and — last but not least — more sophisticated about the industry's worshiplike ways. Response to this ad was the largest of any ever run by the funeral home — and, interestingly enough, laywers, doctors and business executives clamored the loudest for a simple ceremony — the very same group that could most afford elaborate funerals.

only the body but the soul itself. Perhaps unconciously, they imagined that burning would cause them or their beloved terrible pain. They also thought that absence of a long and involved memorial service clearly would indicate lack of love and respect for the deceased. The majority of respondents came from large Italian and Spanish families.

A decision was then made to change the thrust of the message. The *New York Times* and *Our Town* were chosen as the prime vehicles to reach a different mind set. The headline "The Return of the Plain Pine Box" and the illustration of a wooden casket that accompanied it reintroduced the venerated concept of a simple, unpretentious funeral.

Response increased more than fiftyfold in the week following the first insertion. Callers admitted that they had long been looking for a simple funeral and they "liked the idea." A vigorous man in his seventies joked that, considering his checkered life-style, a pine box would be all he deserved anyway. Surprisingly enough, the majority of respondents could have well afforded a more elaborate funeral. Three out of four were successful professionals; almost one out of four was a doctor, two out of ten were lawyers. Most opted for cremation on the basis "of principle." More able to confront their mortality than those in lower income brackets, they were psychologically better prepared to make arrangements for their own funerals far in advance.

To Fit the Product to the Person? Or the Person to the Product?

Obviously, information about the consumer enables the manufacturer to seek out his customers with a minimum of waste. This also works the other way around. Information about consumers' needs and wants inspires new inventions, new commercially viable enterprises.

Many new products are born just that way — and often at the prodding of advertising agencies with their finger on the pulse. "If enough people want it," an executive at P & G said, "we'll invent it."

Hitting the Bull's Eye — Demographics or Psychographics?

For the most part, demographics holds out greater dangers for risky generalizations. Psychographics — from an advertising point of view at least — makes for more accurate targeting. Evidently, if people think or feel alike, they will react in a like manner to the same selling message.

Computers Make It Possible

It is not only the vast reservoir of information about the customer that has profoundly changed marketing techniques, but the fact that advanced technology allows the user to store and apply the data to his best advantage many different ways. It is entirely up to the manufacturer how much information he wants to have on file — or more accurately, in the memory banks of his computers. Some manufacturers — cereal makers, for example — may be satisfied with only two or three bits of information, such as age, size of family, and location of their customers. But the vast majority of marketers — automobile manufacturers and renters, hotels, schools, financial institutions, travel agents, and so on — want to know a great deal more. An airline, for example, may be looking for seven or eight bits of information about its "frequent flyer": location, age, income, profession, position in his company, number of overseas offices, favorite meals, ideas about service. Companies like these develop an almost one-to-one relationship with their customers — a love affair that can last a lifetime.

Sophisticated data bases now make it possible for the marketer to focus in on the "heavy user," keep in occasional touch with the "light user," and — most important — pass by the "nonuser." Never has the 20 – 80 rule (20% of customers are responsible for 80% of the purchases made) been put to use more effectively. Direct mail advertisers — a highly result-oriented bunch — have long since discovered the importance of sizing up the customer before making their move. Direct mail readily lends itself to preselection. Those who respond to a mailing are deemed to be "users"; their names would be included on the "active list." Those who do not are relegated into the nonuser category — the marketing equivalent of a deadbeat, undeserving of attention, too costly to pursue. All information is cross-indexed to arrive at the most effective mailing list possible. For example, an outboard manufacturer can specify a list of (1) boat owners (2) living with their families (3) in Connecticut (4) near the shoreline (5) in a home worth at least $200,000.

Retailers too have long been aware of the importance of establishing contact with their customers. They know that his or her long-term loyalty is like having money in the bank. Satisfied customers return to buy not only the same product, but new ones as well. They are more apt to respond to special promotions and appreciate extra services.

Thus, selling has come full cycle. The old small-town corner store, where everyone knew everyone else by name, is still with us, if not in fact, then in spirit. The modern version comprises hundreds — sometimes millions — of names, neatly tucked away in RAMS and ROMS. The archetypical shopkeeper, peering over his half-glasses from behind the counter, has moved to sit in front of the electronic machine. That he knows so many of his customers so intimately and can call them in at the touch of his fingers makes him the most effective marketer the world has ever known.

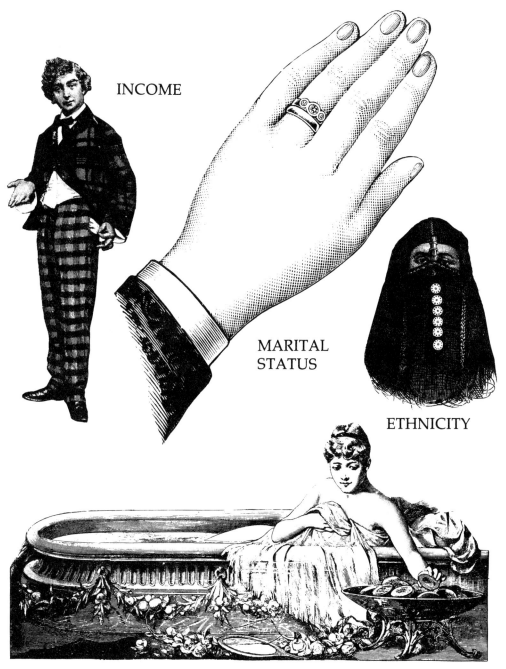

INCOME

MARITAL
STATUS

ETHNICITY

LIFESTYLE—ATTITUDES—PERSONAL PREFERENCES

At the time of this writing, information on up to 85 million households may be collected by computer-driven databases. Electronic cross-indexing enables the advertiser to get to know his customer's buying habits, demographic profile, lifestyle, product preferences, and aspirations. Never before has there been so much in-depth information accumulated so fast about so many.

To Sum It Up

State-of-the-art information gathering makes it possible to define markets accurately — to shoot at a target.

The United States may be one nation, but a homogeneous marketplace it is not. Its population is among the most diverse in the world. It can be broken down into hundreds of smaller and (from the advertiser's point of view) more manageable groups, depending on geographic location and demographic and psychographic predilections.

Buying habits in different parts of the country gave new meaning to regional advertising. "National" advertisers often turn "local" for that reason — and with excellent results.

Thanks to computers and cross-indexing, it is possible today to reach various demographic and psychographic groups at a cost lower than ever. And so, the segmentation is no longer a mere sociological exercise. It has become one of the advertiser's most effective money-saving marketing tools.

9

So Swings the Pendulum

These are not the times for a marketer to take a nap; the marketplace is astir. Always there have been changes, but never as many—and in such rapid succession—as in recent years.

The reasons are multifarious and subtle, frequently overlapping one another. Here is a quick overview of cause and effect, the parts of the sum.

Technological Advances. In almost every human endeavor the rate of progress has accelerated: medicine, science, entertainment, communications, marketing. Advertising is simply keeping up with the pace.

Better-Informed Population. By nature, each generation is a little smarter than the one preceding it (though some skeptics will take issue with this). Civilization feeds upon itself; it always has. More educated consumers make more sophisticated—and pickier—buyers.

Profound Changes in Demographics. Incomes, schooling, changes in emphasis from manufacturing to servicing, and population shifts make the difference. The babyboom generation is entering middle age.

Improved Economy. Fluctuations in economy bring about new demands. The United States is wealthier than ever before.

Keener Competition. Business is feeling the pressure, not only from within the country but from foreign manufacturers as well.

Quicker Reaction. It takes less time to develop a new product or service and put it on the market. The result is that today it is just as easy to be left behind as to get ahead of everyone else.

How Long, Oh, How Long?

A good marketer is part observer, part soothsayer. He has the genius to judge the mood of the public as it is and as it is about to turn. Predicting the future has never been easy, but planning without predicting can play havoc with the future of an organization. Large and successful corporations have disappeared because of their managements' inability to predict the life cycle of their products and react swiftly to market changes. By one estimate, in the year 2000 four-fifths of today's manufacturers will have faced "technological discontinuities," i.e. the need to let their primary product line go because of competition and new buying habits.

The reason for the product's exit from the marketplace may be purely technological. This was the case, for example with National Cash Register when the invention of electronic registers turned the company's mainstay product into a relic of the past in less than five years. Scientific obsolescence, however, is rarely the root of the problem. As often as not, it is management's unawareness of — and sometimes, indifference to — the ever-changing moods of the buying public that brings a product line to an end.

Like animals or plants, each product has its own life expectancy. The product may live for decades (as has Coca-Cola), or a few years (as did Wham-O's hula hoops), or sometimes only a few months (as do hit records). It should be noted here for the benefit of get-rich-quick dreamers that short-lived products can bring financial rewards, also, as the success of Pet Rock, Wacky Wallwalkers, est seminars, CBs (over a million sold), and countless toys and boardgames so eloquently testify. Be that as it may, an educated guess about life of the product almost always saves post mortem grief.

An advertising agency too had better make a fair prediction as to the rise and fall of the product. A campaign based on what turns out to be a fleeting fad can play havoc with the best laid of marketing plans. An example is Coca-Cola's tie-in campaign with Max Headroom (the electronic hero) which came to an untimely end when the show built around him abruptly collapsed.

Who Calls the Shots?

Is the public responsible for the birth of a trend? Or does a trend come about independently and then find a large enough following to make an impact? The answer is that trend making can work in either direction.

The most lasting of trends are those that are legitimized by institutional recognition, usually expressing broad public support. The physical fitness craze is more than a public fancy; it was refined, and eventually sanctioned, by the medical profession to help prevent health prob-

lems. Once the feminist movement received legislative and judicial approval, it became a part of our social matrix. Similarly, the "born-again" fundamentalist view gained in momentum when embraced by the Moral Majority and then by the political establishment.

Keep an eye on the mood swings of the following:

Church — the slowest to approve of change

Law — also slow — deliberation and precedent-setting are built into the system

Government — responsive to public opinion

Science — sets the pace but insists on empirical data

Press — powerful but unpredictable, and most likely to misinterpret trends

Education — willing to try anything once

Arts — artists, writers, entertainers are an adventurous lot. Many trends make their beginnings here.

Business — Always looking for new profit centers, it often initiates a trend or a fad. Many companies plough a large part (up to 50% at times) of their earnings back into Research & Development.

A Fad Is Not a Trend; a Trend Is Not a Fad

The difference between a "fad" and a "trend" is more than just a matter of semantics. A fad can look forward to a relatively short life, bursting on the scene amid considerable press coverage and disappearing just as quickly. Trends, on the other hand, tend to stay around for a while — sometimes for generations. Almost always they tap into a need, real or imagined.

The difference between "fad" and "trend" becomes clearer in hindsight. How do you rate as a crystal-gazer? Have your predictions come true? Here is a quick rundown of some of the fad and trend movements of the not-so-distant past, in addition to the ones already mentioned:

FADS	TRENDS
Nehru jackets	Overseas vacations
Hot pants	Home offices
Jazzed-up jeans	Casual fashions
Granny glasses	Shopping at home
Zen Buddhism	Ethnic food
Smile buttons	Compact cars
Transcendental	Moral majority
meditation	Morning soda
Pac Man	breaks

Sometimes one trend gives being to another, and then another—all from the same mother of invention. For example, here are but a few of the trends that the health industry started, and all in a relatively short time:

Health clubs	Jogging
Low-calorie food	Sports medicine
Foods low in	HMOs
sodium	Herbal teas
Foods low in	Breastfeeding
sugar	Sneakers
"Natural" foods	Diet support
Exercise videos	groups
Books on exercise	Home diagnostic
Health food	tests
sections in	Diet sodas
supermarkets	Decaffeinated
Moderation in	coffee
smoking	Bottled water
Vitamin dosages	"Health" pet
Health food	foods
stores	Wine coolers
Home gyms	(Low in alcohol)

Quite a few crazes disappear for seemingly no reason at all—except for the fact that they lose their novelty status—at least for the moment. Young people's fascination with dinosaurs is an example of just such an on-again, off-again phenomenon. At the time of this writing, these prehistoric monsters have again entered the scene. One company has sired no less than 14 versions of this giant but cuddly creature in plastic, rubber, vinyl inflatable, and of course, an easy-to-assemble version—for do-it-yourself enthusiasts. Response to their simple one-page mailing piece has ran into many thousands.

For the most part, the American public responds quickly to new ideas; especially if they are "fun." But it also tires of them sooner than most other populations. Pace of life, extensive media hype, and an economy that allows a relatively indulgent life-style are responsible for our short attention span. The rapidity with which our interests, tastes, and values change has been a constant source of amazement to visitors coming from all corners of the world—among them such men of learning as Alexis de Tocqueville, Charles Dickens, Oscar Wilde, and Sigmund Freud.

How to Spot a Trend—or Latch onto a Fad

Marketers are often able to spot trends in the making and their instincts can prove to be immensely profitable. Palmer House and Towers Hotel, a Chicago landmark for the last five decades, for example, has set aside 150 rooms—an entire floor—as a preserve for its nonsmoking guests. Bloomingdale's in New York has put in its own "Lick Your Chops" boutique to vend veggie acorns; liver, beef, and ham cookies; and vitamin nuggets to its canine customers, or to be exact, owners of canines. Coca-Cola has distributed 5 million copies of Nancy M. Lee's *Tele-Photo Phone Book*—a simple picture book that teaches the ever-growing population of latchkey children how to dial important numbers, including those in case of emergency. People's Resources, a New York dating service, uses private video viewing booths to help its clients "meet" one another through state-of-the-art communication; the audio-videotape on the television is accompanied by a printed version of the "applicant's" personal and professional résumé for further study. And when Morris, the cat, announced his candidacy for the presidency, thousands of people joined the fun and sent their "yes" votes to Nine Lives Cat Food; for quite a while, the feline presidential hopeful had better name recognition than any of the Democratic Party candidates.

Trend spotting is an acquired art. As in bird-watching, identification gets easier with practice. Here are some of the prime sources from which ideas flow:

Entertainment. Watch the current movies, theatre, and television. Today's public appears to respond to visual experience more than any other kind — a product of our talk-to-the-eye technology. A single visual message can change lifelong habits. When Clark Gable undressed in front of Claudette Colbert in the movie *It Happened One Night* and was seen not to be wearing an undershirt, the T-shirt industry suffered a severe setback; it took World War II to put the industry together again. John F. Kennedy's uncovered head — at his Inauguration ceremonies and after — upset not only the experts on good manners but also the owners of haberdasheries throughout the country.

But one does not have to reach that far back to find examples of quick fashion changes brought about by a single event, a single personality. MTV — watched mostly by the young and the restless — does in days what it used to take couturiers months to establish. Popular serials like "Dynasty" and "Miami Vice" and game shows like "Wheel of Fortune" have spawned fashion trends (or fads) of their own. When Jane Fonda displayed her anatomy in a bathing suit in the movie *On Golden Pond*, it didn't take the women in

the audience past their 40th birthday to get the message, and a multimillion-dollar fitness industry was born.

It is not only fashion that responds to star performers. Singer Madonna has given the bustline a new boost — a trend that had already began. Out goes the Twiggy/Annie Hall look, in comes the full figure again — heralding the greatest boom in breast augmentation in the history of plastic surgery. (The operation has become the second most popular in the United States, with only lipectomy beating it out by a slight margin.)

By the same token, Arnold Schwarzenegger and Sylvester Stallone brought back biceps, Oliver North the crew haircut, Michael Fox and Billy Joel the sex appeal of average height, Catherine Deneuve glamour over forty, Lauren Hutton the space between front teeth and the beauty of a less-than-perfect face, Don Johnson the carefully dishevelled look, Willard Scott and Don Rickles the balding pate.

CURRENTS

Swiss company finds time to branch out with introduction of wooden watch

First the rock watch; now the wood watch.

Following the success of another Swiss

company selling watches with a movement installed in a hunk of rock cut from a Swiss Alp, Piquerez-Bourquard, a watchmaker in Bassecourt, Switzerland, has announced plans to market a wood watch; the movement resides within a piece of wood carved from an Alpine tree. Not just any trees will do, however: Those destined to become timepieces are chosen for their lack of flammability and resistance to aging.

Production of some 50,000 watches a year has begun; the marketing effort first will be tested in Western Europe, with the possibility of moving to the U.S. and Canada later this year.

First stone, then wood. From what will the next Swiss timepiece be made? There's always chocolate . . . .

John Parry

'Tortillagrams' a palatable way to reach illegal aliens

With only one month left in its amnesty program, the Immigration & Naturalization Service is taking every avenue to get information about immigration reform to the public.

Some of those avenues are slightly off the beaten track.

Hispanic radio stations in border states are broadcasting programs from INS offices. An "amnesty fair" was held recently at a Fort Worth, Texas, community center offering attendees cotton candy and free fingerprinting.

But the most imaginative promotion is the one that Texans have dubbed "tortillagrams." Five regional bakeries are distributing fliers explaining the amnesty program inside their tortilla packages.

A total of 580,000 stuffers will be passed out in this manner, according to Jane Friday, public information officer for the Dallas INS office. She says the idea originated in a "brainstorming" session in which "we were just talking about anything and everything.

No Pierda Tiempo!
Aprovéche Del Programa De Legalización Antesde la Fecha Límite El 4 de Mayo, 1988

Si usted ha vivido en los Estados Unidos ilegalmente antes de Enero 1, 1982 quizá usted será elegible

Estar Legal Es Vivir Tranquilo!

Fliers detailing INS' amnesty program prove to be an unusual stuffing for tortillas distributed in Texas.

"We're calling this our local, grass-roots campaign," she says.

Joe Trujillo, owner of La Poblanita Tortillas in Lovington, N.M., says he agreed to participate in the promotion as a public service to his customers. His company has received quite a bit of publicity as a result.

Both Friday and Trujillo say they've gotten positive feedback from leaders in the Hispanic community. The tortilla-eaters themselves, however, have yet to be heard from.

Louis Weisberg

Right answers cure players' problems in 'Therapy' game

Some pastimes are obviously therapeutic: Swimming clears the mind, singing lifts the spirits, square dancing rejuve-

nates the soul.

But playing board games?

Therapeutic indeed, if you're playing "Therapy: The Game" (Pressman Toys, $19.95).

Moving plastic couches around the board, players pick cards from piles representing all stages of psychological development, including infancy, adolescence and adulthood.

Players also land in one another's "therapy offices" where they pick cards with questions like: "So tell me, [name], which player do you think would be most likely to have a dream about a large snake?"

Patient and therapist each scrawl their answers on a "prescription pad" and when they agree, the player leaves therapy.

Yes, that seems a little too easy (and cheap). But all games are simplified versions of real life, says one of the game's inventors, Canadian psychiatrist Edward Brown.

"We test reality by games. Who knows how many tycoons began with Monopoly?" he says.

Who knows how many of us need Therapy?

Lenore Skenazy

Plastic couches, cards with psychology questions and prescription pads are integral components to "Therapy: The Game."

Top Oscar categories too close to call— but we do anyway

You can skip the Kentucky Derby this year; the Preakness and the Belmont, too. If you want to see a real horse race, just tune into the 60th annual Academy Awards on ABC-TV April 11.

Look for photo finishes in most major categories:

Best Picture and Best Director. We all know the nifty "Broadcast News" is in trouble because its director, James L. Brooks, failed to get a nomination; the last movie to win Best Picture without its director being nominated was "Grand Hotel" in 1932. But "News' " main competition, Bernardo Bertolucci's shallow epic, "The Last Emperor," is also vulnerable. Only one movie (1958's "Gigi") has won Best Picture and Director without having been nominated in at least one of the four acting categories.

So which will it be? Norman Jewison's enchanting "Moonstruck"? John Boorman's gooey "Hope and Glory"? Adrian Lyne's sleazy "Fatal Attraction"? A "News"/Bertolucci split? Take your pick. My guess is "Moonstruck"—everybody loves it, and Jewison's been around forever. Fifth director: Lasse Hallstrom ("My Life as a Dog").

Best Actor. Michael Douglas ("Wall Street") looks strongest, buoyed by his equally gritty performance in "Fatal Attraction." But it's hard to work up enthusiasm for an actor who didn't show anybody he could act until last year. My own favorite is William Hurt for his lightly comic turn in "Broadcast News." He'll have a helluva time whipping Douglas' double whammy. Other nominees: Marcello Mastroianni ("Dark Eyes"), Jack Nicholson ("Ironweed") and Robin Williams ("Good Morning, Vietnam"). Why Williams, but not Steve Martin ("Roxanne")? Could it be that Williams shows the sweat in his work and Martin doesn't?

Or could it

be . . . Satan?

Best Actress. My fantasy is a tie between offscreen pals Cher ("Moonstruck") and Meryl Streep ("Ironweed"), because if you put them together you have the perfect actress: pure intuition meets pure technique. But I think the real race is between Glenn Close ("Fatal Attraction") and Holly Hunter ("Broadcast News"), who are so neck-and-neck they might leave an

The way the nominations fell, 'Broadcast News' may be in trouble; so keep your eyes on 'Moonstruck' to capture the big one.

®MGM Pictures   ®20th Century Fox   ®20th Century Fox/Kerry Hayes

Nicholas Cage and Cher in "Moonstruck" in Norman Jewison's delightful comedy. Michael Douglas takes young Charlie Sheen under his wing on a swing through the canyons of "Wall Street," directed and co-written by Oliver Stone. Cher's parents, also are in the running for Oscars.

It's tough being a power broker. Michael Douglas takes young Charlie Sheen under his wing on a swing through the canyons of "Wall Street," directed and co-written by Oliver Stone.

William Hurt (seated), Holly Hunter and Albert Brooks gather in a newsroom scene from "Broadcast News." As the woman in the middle in this romantic comedy, Hunter was cheered for her "lovable" role.

opening for Cher. On Close's side, three prior nominations; on Hunter's, a sizable, "lovable" role. Is it too close to be Close? Probably.

Fifth nominee: Sally Kirkland ("Anna"), who has waged the most shameless self-promoting campaign since Chill Wills was up for "The Alamo."

Best Supporting Actor. Last year in this category, Michael Caine finally took home the gold for "Hannah and her Sisters."

This year, Sean Connery is favored to do so for his splendid work in "The Untouchables." Will this category become a Hall of Fame for neglected icons? It has done worse. Remember, this is Connery's first nomination. Other nominees: Albert Brooks ("Broadcast News"), Morgan Freeman ("Street Smart"), Vincent Gardenia ("Moonstruck") and Denzel Washington ("Cry Freedom"), whose near-starring performance poses the only threat to 007's mission.

Best Supporting Actress. If Connery has cause to complain about past slights, Ann Sothern ("The Whales of August") has reason to sue: This is her first nomination after 60 years in films. Unfortunately, she wasn't as well served by her script and director. The prize should fall to Olympia Dukakis ("Moonstruck"), who not only lead tip-top writing and directing to back her up but also a lifetime on the New York stage. She's the only sure thing of the evening. Other nominees: Norma Aleandro ("Gaby—A True Story"), Anne Archer ("Fatal Attraction") and Anne Ramsey ("Throw Momma from the Train").

Michael McWilliams

Helping readers to keep up with, and stay ahead of, trends is *Advertising Age*. It regularly publishes a page or more on new products and services, current events, movies, top videos, TV shows, records, and best-sellers. Other worthy features include calendar of events, global gallery, MediaWorks, Public Relations Beat, Slices, The Next Trends, and Special Reports on various aspects of the industry.

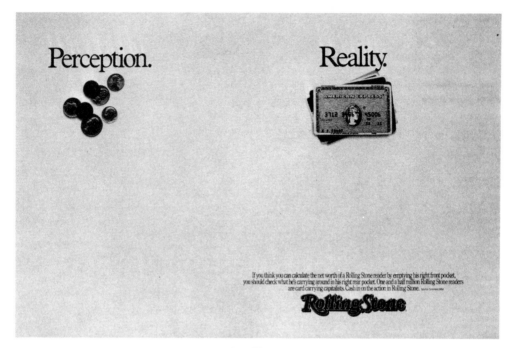

Sensitive to the needs of its readers is *Rolling Stone*. Aimed at the babyboom generation, its editorial approach has kept in tune with a maturing audience. Today, the
magazine devotes more space to discussing social, political, and economic issues.

As astute observer of its readers is *Cosmopolitan*. Its "Cosmo Girl" — symbolic of its
reader — has gone through an interesting metamorphosis in recent years. She is still
as attractive as ever, but more professional and sophisticated — as the objects behind
her back so eloquently allude to. Copy tells of the person she has become: "A girl
who drinks success as easily as she drinks imported water."

Just a reminder that the most impressive thing about Chivas Regal is what's *in* the bottle, not what's on it.

What are you saving the Chivas for?

BEFORE	AFTER

For over a quarter of a century, Chivas has advertised its snob appeal. Times have changed. As Edgar Bronfman, Jr., president of The House of Seagram puts it: "We want people to drink and serve Chivas to make everyday events more rewarding, too."

Always a marketer, Campbell's is as aware of America's preoccupation with health as anyone. The company even tried slimming down its "Campbell Kids", but nostalgia won out. The Campbell kids today are once again their old-fashioned chubby selves.

This Week	Nonfiction	Last Week
1	**LOVE, MEDICINE & MIRACLES,** by Bernie S. Siegel. (Harper & Row, $17.95.) A surgeon stresses the importance of the patient's mind and emotions in treating serious illness.	1
2	**MOONWALK,** by Michael Jackson. (Doubleday, $15.95.) The autobiography of the celebrated performer.	
3	**A BRIEF HISTORY OF TIME,** by Stephen W. Hawking. (Bantam, $18.95.) A British scientist's review of efforts to create a unified theory of the universe.	2
4★	**WASHINGTON GOES TO WAR,** by David Brinkley. (Knopf, $18.95.) A social and political portrait of the nation's capital during World War II.	4
5	**TRUMP,** by Donald J. Trump with Tony Schwartz. (Random House, $19.95.) The career and business style of the New York entrepreneur.	3
6	**THE RISE AND FALL OF THE GREAT POWERS,** by Paul Kennedy. (Random House, $24.95.) How economic and military forces affected the fortunes of great nations in the past 500 years.	6
7	**CITIZEN COHN,** by Nicholas von Hoffman. (Doubleday, $19.95.) The life and times of the New York lawyer and political figure Roy M. Cohn.	5
8	**WINFIELD,** by Dave Winfield with Tom Parker. (Norton, $16.95.) The autobiography of the New York Yankee outfielder.	9
9	**THRIVING ON CHAOS,** by Tom Peters. (Knopf, $19.95.) The author discusses ways for companies to survive in today's and tomorrow's turbulent world.	7
10	**THE POWER GAME,** by Hedrick Smith. (Random House, $22.50.) How the Federal Government has evolved over the past 15 years.	12
11	**BATTLE CRY OF FREEDOM,** by James M. McPherson. (Oxford University, $30.) A history of the American Civil War era.	8
12	**1999,** by Richard Nixon. (Simon & Schuster, $19.95.) The former President outlines a program to assure the survival of the United States.	16
13	**SPEAKING OUT,** by Larry Speakes with Robert Pack. (Scribners, $19.95.) The experiences of President Reagan's former spokesman.	15
14	**CHAOS,** by James Gleick. (Viking, $19.95.) An account of a fast-developing new science that involves disorder, arrhythmia and the bizarre and the random in nature.	10
15	**THE TRIAL OF SOCRATES,** by I. F. Stone. (Little, Brown, $18.95.) The Greek philosopher's life and death, with an unfavorable assessment of his ideas.	11

Advice, How-to and Miscellaneous

1	**THE 8-WEEK CHOLESTEROL CURE,** by Robert E. Kowalski. (Harper & Row, $17.95.) How to lower your blood cholesterol level without drugs.	1
2	**SWIM WITH THE SHARKS WITHOUT BEING EATEN ALIVE,** by Harvey Mackay. (Morrow, $15.95.) Strategies for succeeding in business.	2
3	**CONTROLLING CHOLESTEROL,** by Kenneth H. Cooper. (Bantam, $17.95.) A physician's program to prevent heart disease through exercise and diet.	4
4	**WHAT'S NEXT?** by Paul Erdman. (Doubleday, $14.95.) An economist's prescription for preparing yourself for "the crash of '89" and profiting	

The **New York Times Book Review's** *Best Sellers list* often proves to be an accurate guide as to what is in favor at the moment, particularly in its Nonfiction and Advice, How-To, and Miscellaneous sections. For the most part, book publishers are much aware of current likes and dislikes; they have to be. Sometimes they deal with an already existing trend and on occasion they are actually instrumental in creating a new one. Today the hot subject is biography, tomorrow it may be business and industry, cooking, nutrition, inspirational books, or what have you. Typically, 8 of the top 12 hardcover best-sellers between 1985 and 1986 in the How-To category had to do with dieting and exercise.

This author had a revealing (and amusing, depending on your point of view) experience in launching a series of profit-making books on account of a trend. Cat titles were beginning to appear on the best-sellers list with increased regularity —thanks largely to the genius of Jim Davis and his fat, wisecracking feline called (though not necessarily responding to) Garfield. It was then that this author borrowed a cat from his neighbor and forthwith put together a book on the subject entitled *Names for Cats* (McGraw-Hill), following this up with *How to Live with a Neurotic Cat* (Warner) and *My Cat: The First Twenty Years* (Geis), the latter based on the established format of human baby books. He is now seriously considering getting a cat.

Magazines are usually on the cutting edge. For example, here are some of the subjects that appeared in a single issue of *Cosmopolitan:* twelve sexual types of husbands; update on hypnosis; quickspeak —the art of opening a conversation; footloose and freelancing; dental update; glamorous eyebrows; best jeans for the silhouette; October horoscope; and cosmetic surgery.

About the same time, *Modern Maturity,* a magazine that caters to the 50-plus crowd, took it upon itself to instruct and entertain its readers with features on

Medicare, home care of elderly parents, travel fever, pot making as a hobby, tourism in China, mushroom watching, recipes for low-cholesterol fish dishes, car buying caveats, spas, staying well, and building dinghies as a pastime.

Obviously these magazines either echo or accurately foretell the mood of certain segments of the U.S. population. The ability of a publication to speak its readers' language usually pays off in increased circulation.

Here are some of the other magazines consummate trend watchers may find it worth their time to follow:

American Health	*Mademoiselle*
Changing Times	*Business Week*
Connoisseur	*Esquire*
Money	*Playboy*
Psychology Today	*Time*
Town & Country	*New York*
Travel & Leisure	*Magazine*
House & Garden	*Advertising*
Metropolitan Home	*Age*
American	*AdWeek*
Demographics	*Savvy*
Penthouse	*Seventeen*
Omni	*Working*
Ebony	*Woman*
Glamour	*Fortune*
New Woman	*Inc.*
Self	*GQ*
Vogue	*Advertising*
	Research

Advertising executives do well subscribing to anywhere from a half dozen to a dozen such magazines. Time may keep them from reading each of the publications from cover to cover but even one or two articles an issue worth reading pay for the cost of subscription.

Sources for information, too, are **newsletters.** Some are no more than a platform for the opinions of a single individual—an expert in the field. Others represent a collection of vast amounts of timely information culled from a wide array of sources.

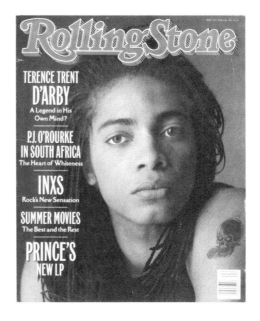

Alert, trend-watching advertisers include dozens of publications in their daily reading fare. The subjects may or may not bear direct relation to the field. Some of the best and most original ideas come from magazines that deal with changing lifestyles.

1. A.C. Nielsen Co.
2. IMS International
3. SAMI/Burke
4. Arbitron Ratings Co.
5. Information Resources
6. MRB Group
7. M/A/R/C
8. Market Facts
9. NFO Research
10. NPD Group
11. Westat
12. Maritz Marketing Research
13. Elrick and Lavidge
14. YSW/Clancy Shulman
15. Walker Research
16. Chilton Research
17. ASI Market Research
18. Decisions Center
19. Louis Harris and Associates
20. Opinion Research Corp.
21. Ehrhart-Babic Group
22. National Analysts
23. Harte-Hanks Marketing Services Group
24. Mediamark Research
25. Data Development Corp.
26. Custom Research
27. Decision/Making/ Information
28. Decision Research Corp.
29. Gallup Organization
30. Market Opinion Research
31. Admar Research
32. Starch INRA Hooper
33. National Research Group
34. McCollum/Spielman Research
35. Guideline Research

A look at statistics that shape your finances

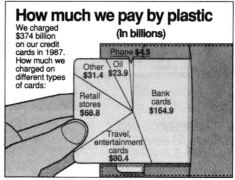

How much we pay by plastic

We charged $374 billion on our credit cards in 1987. How much we charged on different types of cards:

(In billions)

Phone $4.5
Oil $23.9
Other $31.4
Retail stores $68.8
Bank cards $164.9
Travel, entertainment cards $80.4

Copyright 1988, USA TODAY. Reprinted with permission.

A look at statistics that shape the nation

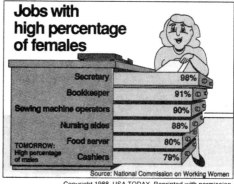

Jobs with high percentage of females

Secretary	98%
Bookkeeper	91%
Sewing machine operators	90%
Nursing aides	88%
Food server	80%
Cashiers	79%

TOMORROW: High percentage of males

Source: National Commission on Working Women

Copyright 1988, USA TODAY. Reprinted with permission.

A look at statistics that shape our lives

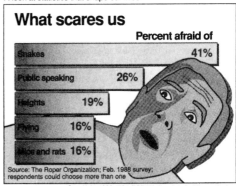

What scares us

Percent afraid of

Snakes	41%
Public speaking	26%
Heights	19%
Flying	16%
Mice and rats	16%

Source: The Roper Organization; Feb. 1988 survey; respondents could choose more than one

Copyright 1988, USA TODAY. Reprinted with permission.

Top research companies constantly scan the market to spot trends. They provide both syndicated and customized information. Listed here, in order by size, are the 35 leading organizations in the U.S. at the present time.

Polls reflect the latest sentiments. Several major newspapers publish them on a regular basis, often initiating them themselves. *USA Today* **is such a publication; its U.S.A. Snapshots provide a quick visual glimpse at statistics that shape the lives of Americans day after day.**

Not all **newspapers** can afford the luxury of you-heard-it-here-first-folks articles; those with lesser circulation must rely on information passed down to them by wire services, syndicated sources, or other newspapers. All of them, however, augur the arrival of new developments, shifts in the wind.

The vast resources of the *New York Times* allow this publication to cover the news in detail, but also in its analysis. Close second is *U.S.A. Today.* Its polls make interesting reading, its graphics (much of it computer generated) exciting to behold. The two newspapers just mentioned lead in number of by-lined articles — always a sign of originality. *Washington Post, San Francisco Chronicle, Boston Globe, Philadelphia Inquirer, Denver Post, Los Angeles Times, Sacramento Bee,* and *Dallas News* follow. All have an excellent "Living Section" — an important source of information to those eager to keep up with changes in consumer psychology.

Television provides an important window to the world. Viewing TV — particularly its documentaries and commentaries — can be one of the best sources of information to the advertiser.

Schools, particularly adult education, provide another glimpse at the current scene. These institutions cater to a wide range of interests, only some of which are academic, and their courses are designed to answer existing needs. The New School, long a leader in feeding information to the after-office-hours crowd, offers an agenda of over 2,000 courses ranging from *Herb and Spices Workshop* to *T'ai Chi Ch'uan: General Principles of Body Movement.*

Another institution, Learning Annex, conducts 2- to 4-hour-long classes in cities throughout the nation that hold up a mirror to society. The Annex's vending-machine-distributed catalogue reaches an audience of far over a million, and its list of courses offer a wealth of advertising, marketing, and new product ideas to business people with fertile and flexible minds. A few examples:

How to Survive on $50,000 to $150,000 a Year — An opportunity to compile a valuable mailing list of affluent buyers . . . A travel club or dating service exclusively for the $50,000 plus crowd . . . Special piggy banks designed for the poor rich.

How to Make Money Even when the Market Goes Down — Computer software based on the same idea . . . Stuffed toy bear as a gift to winning "bear huggers" . . . Grin-and-bear-it newsletter during down-market periods.

Co-ops and Condominiums — Completely furnished ready-to-occupy apartments available for sale for corporate executives new in town . . . An across-the-board landlord-association-sponsored advertising campaign promoting the advantages of condominium over co-op ownership, or vice versa.

Massage for Couples — A television campaign featuring a young couple massaging one another while conversationally extolling the virtues of the sponsor's product — i.e. underwear, hosiery, mattress . . . "The Massage is the Message" love-posters for live-in couples . . . Special oil sold to massagers — bottled in the stylized shape of a male or female torso.

White Collar Boxing — Franchise operations to provide training facilities to white collar boxers, possibly as part of a health club already in operation . . . White boxing gloves to match the "white collar" . . . Amateur three-bout White Gloves contest among Wall Streeters.

The World At Large. Fads and trends are burgeoning everywhere you look — if you only look long and hard enough. Let your imagination go free.

Supermarkets? Watch for the new shopping habits that are making news as of late. More men than ever are in the aisles, with shopping habits nothing like women shoppers' — they want to get on with it, balk at studying each and every label, buy more in less time. (Why not design labels and instructions more appealing to the male shopper? What about

("masculine" color schemes? An advertising campaign for food directed at the male shopper?)

Gone are the "good old days" when one shoe fits all.

The Chop-Chop Theory

More-varied tastes—and larger pocketbooks—demand more of different kinds of products. The average supermarket today carries 11,000 different kinds of items, more than ever in its 76-year history. New products arrive at an ever growing rate (there has been a 234% increase since 1980), a fact that makes retailers more selective, and more wary, than ever before. In fact, the bewildering array of new products is one of the reasons why deal-hungry retailers are gaining the upper hand in deciding what goes on the shelf—and what does not.

Today's automobile buyers are offered over 800 different makes of cars for their consideration. They are given choices of payment schedules, options, warranties, services, and discounts. No doubt about it: The days of the Model T Ford ("Give 'em any color . . .") are gone for better or worse. No fewer than 300 colors today are there for the picking—and with the increase of color-conscious female visitors in showrooms, this could be only the beginning.

Mustard used to be mustard in the good old days (ten years ago). But no more. Like ice cream, mustard today comes in a multitude of types: peanut, creole, black olive, anchovy, Russian style, hickory-smoke, green peppercorn, garlic, honey combined, Dijon, white wine, salt free, and, of course, "all natural."

White bread, the staple of households for over a half century, is losing its all-purpose status in the bakery department by about 5% a year. About half of consumers insist on such staff-of-life anomalies as whole wheat, rye, pumpernickel, unleavened, sourdough, French, corn, or the Mexican version of bread, tortilla. Are bakeries in supermarkets far behind?

Nearly 300 brands of cigarettes line the shelves. A store in Manhattan sells over 2,500 different light bulbs (with disarming modesty it admits that this is the "only" merchandise it sells). Not even the most natural food of all, milk, can afford to ignore the proliferate-or-perish theory any longer. More than a dozen varieties tempt the consumer's palate. Some of today's supermarkets even offer milk with fizz and flavor, so as to take your mind off your favorite soda. Even coloring has been added. Who says milk has to be white? Elsie the cow?

Now Hush Puppies come in just as many styles and sizes.

In 1958, Hush Puppies introduced a comfortable basic suede shoe. It was a big hit. In fact, so big that thirty years later a lot of people still think of that shoe when they think of Hush Puppies. In reality, there are over 130 other Hush Puppies styles. Some just as traditional as the original, others more contemporary. There are stylish heels and classic business pumps for women. Dressy loafers and power wing tips for men. Even a full line of children's shoes. Look for us at the National Shoe Fair and FFANY. See what good breeding has done for the Hush Puppies line. Men's Line: Booth 2818, Jacob Javits Center. Women's Line: Hush Puppies Showroom, 717 5th Ave. at 56th Street.

Corporate Hush Puppies.

Sophisticated Hush Puppies.

Hush Puppies typifies the proliferation of products, each satisfying a perceived and real need. The company produces over 130 different styles of footwear, not to mention a wide range of sizes and colors. The campaign, prepared by Fallon McElligott, stresses variety. Corporate Hush Puppies "will make someone at the office drool." Sophisticated Hush Puppies are for "those with a nose for finer things." And so it goes.

To Sum It Up

The marketplace is in perpetual motion. The population is in flux, political and economic winds blow; developments bring new challenges, new products arrive on the scene. There is no sign of the pace abating.

Attention spans can have short lives, especially in the United States, the land of opportunity. It is important that the marketer be able to predict the impact of shifts in taste. Some represent nothing more than a fleeting fad. Others signal trends. Still others herald the arrival of a new era.

Few products, however, live in perpetuity. Even if they are here to stay—automobiles, for example—they must usually be modified within their lifetimes to accommodate new life-style and to stand up against ever-alert competition. The lives of many brilliant products end prematurely because of the inability of managers to heed the warning signals.

New ideas come from everywhere. It is for the advertiser to look for them. Listen to suggestions made by arbiters of public taste: media and other means of mass communication, fashion, entertainment, education, retail, and entrepreneurs.

Advanced technology, popular demand, and modern research techniques make it possible for advertisers to introduce new products faster than ever in marketing history. More than 1,000 new products and services enter the fray every month in this country alone; not all survive. Those based on a real (or even imagined) need flourish; those that do not, flounder.

10

Around the World in 30 Minutes

Advertising is going international to a greater extent than ever before. In the past practically all advertising originated in this country; over 90% of the agencies were located here. "Overseas advertising" was looked upon as an offshoot of the main business reaching the United States. If agencies maintained foreign offices, they were for special clients with global needs, not primarily to add to the agencies' coffers. Until recently, nondomestic ad spending growth has lagged behind domestic.

Not so today. It is estimated that in the not so distant future advertising growth outside the United States will outstrip domestic. In fact, even today most "domestic" growth comes not from serving domestic clients but businesses abroad. Increasingly, clients demand international sophistication from their U.S.-based agencies. The need for this kind of servicing has taken on a new sense of urgency.

"Global" vs. "National" Advertising

Much has been said and written about these two approaches to international advertising. One tries to accommodate local tastes and attitudes, the other delivers the same message to all nationalities more or less the same way. The subject is controversial; almost anyone involved in international marketing and advertising has an opinion as to which of the two is more efficient. Roger Matthews, a director at Collett, Dickenson, Pearce & Partners in London says, "One single strategy, brand name, and advertising through the world is but absurd nonsense. National differences are too great for even a single European message, much less a global one." Peter Scott, CEO of Britain's WCRS Group is even more emphatic: "Business, but not advertising or creative solutions, is becoming global." On the other hand, Keith Reinhard, chairman of Needham Worldwide, Inc. says, "People are more alike than different, so creating one ad that has universal appeal is much more efficient."

The debate will probably go on as long as there is advertising on a global scale, simply because both sides have a case. The danger, in fact, may be in subscribing totally to one point of view or the other.

As the World Turns

The *global* approach usually works when our cultural heritage—the "American

Way"—is an integral part of the product's sales appeal. An example would be Coca-Cola. A completely different campaign for every one of the 134 countries where this beverage is sold would prove to be not only exorbitant in cost but probably also a waste of creative effort. The same theme works everywhere modified only slightly for better comprehension. With 60% of its business overseas, the hourglass-shaped bottle is as familiar a sight the world over as the Star Spangled Banner. A sip of the ice-cold drink turns the drinker into a Yank, at least for that instant; he or she has just tasted America.

Marlboro—the best-selling cigarette worldwide—is another case in point. Its cowboy heroes have long since become part of the American lore; they have galloped into global consciousness through the years by way of Hollywood shoot-'em-ups, Louis L'Amour's widely translated Old West stories, and John Wayne's drawl in translation on television screens.

On the other hand, some companies are less fortunate for having chosen the "one voice, one message" route. Avis's classic "We're Number Two" campaign confused the Japanese, who equate underdog status with inferiority. IBM's highly successful Chaplin campaign (in this country) failed to sell computers to the Chinese; humor and high technology do not mix in that part of the world. When IBM replaced its little tramp with venerable Lau Pan, the patron god of Chinese craftsmen and toolmakers, and Zong Shi, a Taoist sage, sales took a turn for the better.

Cars Spoken Here

Automobile manufacturers too have given up using the "global approach" in their international advertising when they found out the hard way that drivers are different the world over.

Dramatizing the suspension system of cars worked in Brazil, the land of bumpy roads, but not in France, which has one of the most advanced highway systems in the world. Celebrity endorsements worked best with the Japanese, who relate to their cars in human terms—*shitashimi yasui*, literally "feeling close." Germans looked for technological superiority in their own Mercedes-Benz and BMW tradition. The Chinese were primarily interested in the price of the car and delivery time. In Scandinavian countries, emphasis was put on the car's long life; in Italy, on design; and in southern Asia, on utility. In fact, it appears that different cultures call for altogether different car names. Ford's lineup in Taiwan includes a van named "Load More" in translation, a truck called "Good Helper," and the Ford Granada, imported from Europe, is identified as the "Thousand Mile Horse." Because of such diversity the two largest automakers of the world, Ford and General Motors, opposed unifying their message throughout the world. Ford uses 24 agencies—with J. Walter Thompson dominating the scene—and GM has McCann-Erickson handle its assignments in 37 countries.

USA, I Love You, I Love You Not . . .

Understanding what others think of us is the first step toward understanding what advertising works overseas. In nearly all countries in the world, Americans are viewed with mixed feelings. Survey after survey shows that over two-thirds of the world's population would choose the United States as their second home, but that doesn't keep the same aspirants from questioning our ways, envying our success, and loudly opposing much of what we do.

Admire, They Do

Here is what most of the world likes about the United States:

The popularity of the United States varies among the countries. Great Britain consistently tops the list.

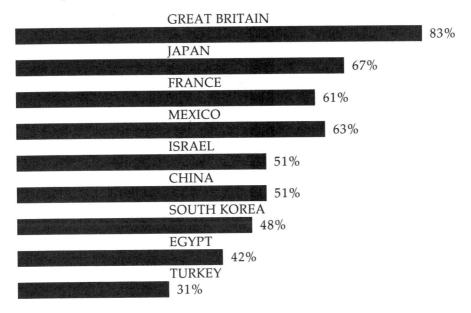

GREAT BRITAIN — 83%
JAPAN — 67%
FRANCE — 61%
MEXICO — 63%
ISRAEL — 51%
CHINA — 51%
SOUTH KOREA — 48%
EGYPT — 42%
TURKEY — 31%

Prosperity. We are the largest importers of goods in the world; the only country that buys more than it sells — about twice as much at the time of this writing. Curiously enough, not all countries feel that our wealth is the result of hard work and free enterprise. There is a widespread belief (taught in most foreign schools) that our natural resources are responsible for the good life we enjoy — that, and the fact that we have never had to fight off a foreign invader.

Advanced Technology. Though we have lost leadership in some areas, we are still high on the list as far as the rest of the world is concerned.

Power. Our political and economic strength, real or perceived, is much respected abroad. This is especially true in countries outside Europe — in Asia or Africa, for example, where power is often equated with military might.

Entrepreneurship. More new companies go in — and out — of business in the United States per year than in all other developed countries combined. New ideas are encouraged; venture capital (an almost unknown concept elsewhere) is available. Our domestic consumption in itself is large and rich enough for a new company to turn a profit in a relatively short time.

Innovation. Our artistic leadership is held in high regard the world over, perhaps even more so than by some of our homegrown critics. We still tend to underestimate our cultural heritage.

Classless Society. Other nations may give lip service to the idea but, for the most part, are less successful in implementing it. We had the advantage of starting fresh some 200 years ago, wiser for the mistakes of the imperious regimes we left behind. No other country offers the opportunity for upward mobility that we do.

High Living Standards. The United States no longer leads the world in per capita income (Japan does), but it is second only to Switzerland in income adjusted to purchasing power.

An outstanding example of the power of a single but telling global advertising message is provided by Marlboro. No need to change the basic theme here — the image of a cowboy has long been a symbol of much that we stand for: rugged individualism, spirit of adventure, and freedom of choice. A taste of Marlboro is a taste of America. This ad appeared in *Jeune Afrique* magazine, covering French-speaking Africa. (Reprinted by permission of Philip Morris, Inc.)

Subtle distinctions in lifestyles and sensibilities show up in advertising, too. This scene shows an indigenous French-style apartment, a man practicing martial arts (unusual in France), and a woman commenting in typical Parisian *dégagé* that he looked "cuter" to her while swimming (a popular pasttime in France).

Admire, They Do Not

Materialism. Money is obviously an important commodity in the United States, even though in itself it produces nothing. Accumulating it is a favorite pastime; we speak and write about it openly and use it as a yardstick of success. That wealth ipso facto builds character and bestows wisdom seems like a strange notion to the rest of the world.

Pace of Life. Too hectic and outward oriented for most outside our borders.

Individualism. Ours is an open society; people are allowed—and even encouraged—to pursue their own lifestyles. Many foreigners think we are much too easygoing in this respect and point to the rise of the "Me Generation" as the inevitable by-product of self-indulgence.

Less Emphasis on Social Graces. Our culture encourages direct communication with others, getting to the point fast, using the vernacular freely. Most other cultures savor the subtleties in human relations, looking to establish long-term human relationships lasting perhaps for generations. Our blunt approach is often misinterpreted both in our one-on-one business dealings overseas and in the advertising we create.

And This the World Doesn't Know What to Make of

The People Speak. It is difficult for foreigners—especially those in seats of power—to appreciate the emphasis we place on public opinion. More decisions are made by fewer people in other countries, and more expeditiously.

Tolerance of Extreme Poverty. That the hungry and homeless would still exist in a rich country such as ours perplexes those living under more socialistic forms of government.

Freedom of Speech. Our tendency to air grievances by way of public debates confuses those living in a closed society. Our slow, convoluted ways to reach agreement suggests a flawed system in countries more accustomed to taking orders.

"Lack of Patriotism." Criticism—and even public ridicule—of political figures is often interpreted as a sign of a nation divided, a population on verge of a rebellion.

Power of the Press. The propensity of our press to print whatever comes to its collective mind befuddles those who read and see only government-approved news.

What You Know vs. Whom You Know. In cultures where influence and power routinely passes from one generation to the next and where personal contacts are a mainstay in success, our tendency to accept people on the basis of their ability is viewed with skepticism.

Unbridled Idealism. The combination of solid pragmatism and blue-sky idealism that exists in our culture strikes foreigners as a paradox.

A Look at Overseas Markets: A Quick Overview

With all due deference to the many exceptions, here is a glance at the world at large from the point of view of an advertiser:

Less-Sophisticated Marketing Techniques. Advertising campaigns built for targeted audiences are not the norm in countries other than the United States Marketing research as we know it is just beginning to take hold. That includes direct mail.

More Limited Selection of Media. Matching media to specific audiences is no easy task in foreign countries. Size of readership does not justify special-interest magazines. Television stations are fewer, and in many countries are subsi-

201

dized by the government, which views broadcast primarily as its main conduit to the public. Commercial television wholly supported by advertising (as all network and most local and cable stations are here) is a concept still grappled with. Over two-thirds of companies use newspaper as their major or near-major advertising medium. Only about one-third buy television time. Direct mail is beginning to come into its own, but with less sophistication than in the United States.

Segmentation Less Applicable. Homogeneous populations, lack of demographic and psychographic data, and less developed marketing techniques make targeting a more difficult task, and in some cases, hardly the worth the effort.

Negotiated Media Costs. Rate cards do exist but few take them seriously. Nor is audience data on media as accurate (and well regulated) as it is in this country.

Soft-Sell vs. Hard-Sell. As said earlier, our no-nonsense approach in advertising does not go over well in most countries. Both the buying public and the government are philosophically against it.

Comparison Advertising Frowned Upon. With few exceptions, this kind of open, no-holds-barred comparison is discouraged. Some nations prohibit it altogether; others permit it but only in a limited way.

Government Ownership. Many public utilities, transportation, health services, media, and other institutions and companies are wholly or partially under government ownership. Nearly all airlines in the world are "official." This means more bureaucracy, more subsidy, and less vigorous competition on the open marketplace.

More Onerous Regulations. Advertising is still suspect by many a government that feels any kind of mass persuasion should come only from those in authority.

The laws are specific and change slowly; their complexity often confuses advertisers in the United States where industry prefers self-regulation to governmental interference. In some countries there is an absolute ban on commercial sponsorship.

Dependence on World Trade. Trade balance is reported regularly in foreign newspapers; it is an important part of the day-to-day economy. Our import/export imbalance astonishes foreign observers.

Jingoism Runs High. While cooperation between nations is improving (a United Europe is in the making), centuries-old traditions are hard to do away with. What would history be without its heroes? The nation's past plays an important part in its self-image.

"Made in the U.S.A." Has Lost Some of Its Luster. In the last decade or so, the products of other nations — particularly those from Japan, West Germany, France, Taiwan, and more recently, South Korea — have become truly competitive with ours.

Advertising Is Still Viewed More as an Art Form than a Science. There is less insistence on accountability and profit and a tendency to measure advertising effectiveness on the basis of dramatic impact alone ("If it's unexpected, it must be good"). It is generally held that creativity is an inherently subjective process, an art form like a painting or a stage play. Some people have it, some people do not. Sales projections are rarely included in creative presentation.

The Differences That Make a Difference

For a marketer to "conquer" a new territory, he must become thoroughly familiar with all aspects of the lay of the land: its geography, history, demographics, legal restrictions, costs, ways of doing business, and distribution patterns. Local advertising agencies and media can be very helpful in pointing the way, as can various authorities, including the government itself.

As in this country, it is psychographics that must top the advertiser's learning agenda; i.e. native attitudes, customs, lifestyle, values, buying habits, perceptions of beauty and fashion, and sense of humor. Overlooking any of these expressions of everyday life can lead to advertising that looks and sounds out of place.

What follows is a quick analysis of major foreign marketplaces from an advertiser's point of view.

United Kingdom

Ad spending: $8 billion (domestic)

Number of ad agencies: 1,200

Major marketers: Procter & Gamble, Mars, Kellogg

Major industries: steel, metals, banking, insurance, chemicals, distilling

Population: 57 million

Newspapers: 407 per 1,000 population

Television sets: 90 million

Passenger cars: 17 million

Life-Style. Class consciousness still lingers on, albeit less openly. Titles are still important, as is standing on ceremony. Most members of top management come from the aristocratic breed; few make it from the bottom of the ladder. The result is lackluster working habits. Those from the upper class insist on following their own well-entrenched, leisurely pace; those below them tend to resent it.

Traditional values often collide with the spirit of an unusually rebellious, restless youth. It was the British teenyboppers who took to the "total look" first in the heyday of the babyboom generation: high boots, white stockings, straight hair, Liverpool cap, and micromini skirt. Likewise, some of the most spectacular rock music came from here.

This is the land of gardeners; flowers bloom everywhere, even in thickly populated areas. London boasts more greenery per square acre than any other metropolis in the world. Homes are homey and comfortable but slow in adopting modern technology. Frequent travelers, avid readers, patrons of the arts and theatre, the British have developed a distinct lifestyle of their own.

Attitudes About the U.S. Perhaps Agatha Christie put the British opinion best: "An American is a sort of queer Englishman." Both nations have parliamentary democracy, yet our politics boggle the British mind. They admire our economic success but consider our way of doing business too fast, too blunt.

Fashion Sense. Not much among the older generation. Innovative among the young, both male and female.

Favorite Sports, Pastimes. Soccer, cricket, rugby, golf, hunting, sailing, fishing, horse racing, tennis, pub life, vacationing in the country, shopping.

Humor. Dry, understated, uninhibited, inconsistent.

Advertising Approach. Very traditional, or very creative. Irreverence toward authority spills over into client/agency relationships; the British creatives guard their turf with passion. Clients tend to let the agency have the last word on copy and art — which could be one of the reasons why so much of British advertising is so imaginative. Many creative "breakthroughs" got their start here; among them the fast-cut technique of MTV, use of pop music, self-mocking advertising, uninhibited authority bashing, and superior graphic techniques first introduced into publishing and animated movies. Proximity to Europe lends worldly sophistication to the British; that and a free-wheeling spirit helped their upstart entrepreneurs to buy and merge with larger and older U.S. advertising firms. Only 40% of the top 20 agencies are in the hands of U.S. managers, less than half as many as there were only ten years ago — an unusual development in the European advertising community so dependent on signals from this side of the Atlantic Ocean. The sun has yet to set on the empire.

Legal Quirks. Among its prohibited product categories are fortune tellers and hypnotists, private detectives, contraceptives, pregnancy tests, matrimonial agencies, undertakers, and the Bible. Which shows that propriety still lives in England. Television censorship, headed by the Independent Broadcasting Authority, is sensitive to public opinion. As in the United States, a half dozen complaints or so are enough for the commercial watched by millions to be yanked off the airways.

HUNCHBACK: Oh why was I born so ugly?
(SFX: RING RING.)
HUNCHBACK: The bells!?
VO: It's for you-ooo!
HUNCHBACK: For me??
CROWD: It's for you-ooo!
HUNCHBACK: Hello. It's Esmeralda!
(TO GARGOYLE) She loves me! Smack!
VO: The phone.
   It's for you to make someone feel wanted.

British sense of humor — a curious mix of under and overstatement — is a part of the advertising language there. This commercial for British Telecom is typical. The same instinct for satire shows up in U.S. advertising, too — a legacy passed down from our British ancestry.

Having gone through major social upheavals in the last few decades, British society shows signs of fundamental changes. Conservatism lives side by side with a rebellious, energetic, and talented youth thumbing its nose at long-cherished conventions. This advertisement for Raleigh bicycles features a properly dressed young lady with flowers in the front basket of her two-wheeler. In the ad for Easy, a clothing manufacturer, the photograph of a racially mixed couple suggests the freedom of personal choice, a breaking away from the dictates of society.

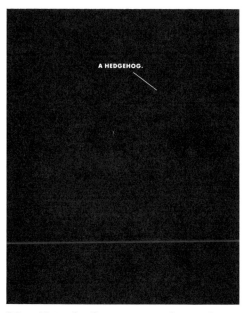

Most British advertisers prefer to play it safe and take the creative middle road — but by no means all of them. The same restlessness that has so changed fashion, music, and theatre also shows up in advertising. When that happens, it usually does so loud and clear. In this two-page magazine ad for Audi, the background is solid black. The word on the left hand page is A HEDGEHOG. Lines at the bottom on the opposite page explain: FOR THOSE OF YOU WITHOUT AUDI'S WIDEBEAM ASSYMETRIC HEADLAMPS, THIS IS WHAT A HEDGEHOG LOOKS LIKE AT MIDNIGHT.

For hand-delivery service in:
Atlanta · Houston · San Francisco · Boston · Los Angeles · Seattle · Chicago · Miami · Stamford · Cleveland · Minneapolis · Washington · Dallas · New York · Montreal · Denver · Philadelphia · Ottawa · Detroit · Pittsburgh · Toronto · Greenwich · St. Louis · Vancouver
Call toll-free 1-800-344-1144
(In Canada 416-283-2777)

FINANCIAL TIMES

LONDON – NEW YORK – FRANKFURT

No. 30,552 · Wednesday June 1 1988 · USA $1.00 Canada C$1.00 Bermuda $1.50

Unofficial solutions to a Chinese job puzzle, Page 6

World News

Armenians maintain protests in Yerevan

Thousands of people have been demonstrating daily in Yerevan, capital of Soviet Armenia, in a new upsurge of protests over the disputed enclave of Azerbaijani. **Page 4**

Punjab bombing

At least 21 people were killed and eight seriously injured in an explosion in Amritsar, northern Punjab state. Reports differed on the cause of the explosion.

Schlüter called

Denmark's acting Prime Minister Poul Schlüter was asked by Queen Margrethe to form a new government three weeks after an inconclusive election. **Page 4**

Gas explosion in China

Forty-nine people were killed in a gas explosion at a coal mine in China's northern Shanxi province, Xinhua news agency reported.

Yugoslav demands

Yugoslavia's trade union leader demanded an inquiry into allegations of corruption against Communist Party officials. **Page 3**

Gulf mine blast

A small fishing boat hit a mine in the Gulf of Oman and exploded, killing one fisherman and injuring two others. The incident occurred 32km south of the Strait of Hormuz.

Lebanon kidnap

A Norwegian relief group threatened to suspend activities in Lebanon if missing Belgian physician Dr Jan Cools, who disappeared on May 21, did not turn up.

Clergy campaign

Anti-apartheid clergymen in South Africa ended an unprecedented emergency conference with a church service at which they called for intensified non-violent resistance.

S Korean unrest

South Korea's labour unrest escalated when a striking union member attempted suicide by slashing his stomach in a dispute over wages. The Cabinet warned that violations would be dealt with strictly. **Page 5**

Strike in Beirut

A strike paralysed Christian east Beirut as 20 people killed in a car bombing were buried. Police said 78 people were wounded when a car packed with TNT exploded on a crowded street.

Algerian-Albanian ties

Algeria and Albania have signed a series of agreements on agricultural, economic, scientific and technical co-operation following the first session of the Albanian-Algerian Economic Co-operation Commission. Algeria is the only country with which Albania has set up such a commission.

Maghreb 'summit'

The leaders of the five North African Arab nations, the Maghreb, are planning to meet in Algiers next week on the sidelines of an Arab summit on the Palestinian crisis. The meeting would be the first since Algeria, Morocco, Tunisia, Mauritania and Libya became independent.

Rockets on Kabul

Anti-communist guerrillas this week lobbed more rockets into the Afghan capital of Kabul than any other week this year. Diplomatic sources also reported that the Soviets had begun supplying the Afghan army with more sophisticated equipment.

Lufthansa walkout

More than 1,800 Lufthansa ground staff staged token strikes at major West German airports to press their contract demands, causing cancellations and delays.

Business Summary

Wall Street soars above 2,000 as dollar firms

WALL STREET: The Dow Jones industrial average soared 74.68 points to close at 2031.12. Declining inflation worries, strength in the dollar, and hopes of no further interest rate rises in the immediate future helped the market to its largest one-day gain since January 4. Volume leapt to 250m shares, the second highest this year. **Page 42**

CHINA'S leading provincial telecommunications authority is to buy 10m shares in Hong Kong Telecommunications, a Cable and Wireless subsidiary. **Page 20**

MACMILLAN, US book publisher, unveiled a recapitalisation plan worth more than $1.66bn which it hopes will fend off a hostile takeover offer. **Page 21**

ALUMINIUM prices rose to record levels on the London Metal Exchange yesterday. The cash price of high-grade material

Aluminium
3 month price (US$)
2600 · 2500 · 2300 · 2100 · 1900 · 1700
Jan · 1988 · May

moved up by $340, to a peak of $3,535 a tonne. High-grade aluminium for delivery in three months rose by $160, to $2,655 a tonne, also a record. **Page 32**

TOKYO: Demand for stocks with specific incentives helped drive share prices sharply higher again, with volume reaching its second heaviest so far this year. The Nikkei average ended 193.6 higher at 27,416.7. **Page 42**

DOLLAR closed in New York at DM1.7325, Y125.2, FFr5.8295, and at SFr1.446. In London it closed at DM1.7290 (DM1.7180), Y125.10 (Y125.00), SFr1.4435 (SFr1.4360), FFr5.8200 (FFr5.7800). **Page 33**

STERLING closed in New York at $1.8352. In London it closed at $1.8385 ($1.856), DM3.1775 (DM3.1875), Y230.0 (Y232.0), SFr2.6550 (SFr2.6650), and FFr10.7000 (FFr10.7275). **Page 33**

US FARM prices rose 3.1 per cent in May after recording no change in April, and were 4.7 per cent above prices a year ago, the US Agriculture Department said.

SAUDI ARABIA'S oil industry contributed only 30 per cent of gross national product in 1987, compared with 55 per cent 10 years previously. **Page 5**

TELEFONICA, Spain's national telecommunications company, is poised to embark on two new ventures in the Soviet Union. **Page 6**

ALCATEL CIT, main French subsidiary of CGE-controlled Alcatel NV telecommunications group, increased parent company net profits from FFr198m to FFr265m (£45.8m) in 1987. **Page 22**

JAPAN'S eight biggest pharmaceutical groups reported increased sales and profits in spite of government-imposed cuts on drug prices. **Page 23**

STEEL consumption in Japan rose in 1987 by 8 per cent, the largest increase among the main industrial nations. **Page 3**

JAPAN AIR LINES, privatised national airline, reported a nine-fold rise in annual pre-tax profits to Y32.4bn ($259.2m). **Page 23**

AUSTRIAN AIRLINES' 24.2 per cent flotation has been substantially oversubscribed, said Oesterreichische Laenderbank, lead manager for the sale. **Page 24**

INTERNATIONAL BUSINESS Machines is this week expected to announce additions to its Personal System/2 personal computers range and to cut the prices of some existing models. **Page 21**

Leaders signal hope of strategic arms deal by year end

BY ROBERT MAUTHNER, QUENTIN PEEL AND STEWART FLEMING IN MOSCOW

A FULL progress report on the latest state of the US-Soviet discussions on strategic arms cuts will be published today in Moscow as the series of summit meetings between President Ronald Reagan and Mr Mikhail Gorbachev, the Soviet leader, draw towards a close.

The aim will be to boost superpower negotiations in Geneva, leading, it is hoped, to the conclusion of a strategic arms reduction treaty by the end of the year.

Neither side has made a firm forecast, although President Reagan and Mr Gorbachev yesterday reiterated their desire to sign the treaty by the time President Reagan leaves office in January 1989.

In the meantime, the two leaders have registered their first concrete result since the five-day summit began on Sunday, with the signing of two relatively minor arms control agreements and seven other bilateral accords.

The agreements concern the advanced notification of test launches of intercontinental ballistic missiles and submarine-launched ballistic missiles to avoid accidental conflict, and a joint verification scheme permitting ratification of two longstanding nuclear test explosions limitation treaties.

A further gloss to the proceedings will be given today when President Reagan and Mr Gorbachev exchange the instruments of ratification of the Intermediate Nuclear Forces Treaty, banning all land-based medium range nuclear missiles, which they

Continued on Page 20
Further summit news, Pages 2 and 3

President Ronald Reagan (centre) and Soviet leader Mikhail Gorbachev (right) watch US Secretary of State George Shultz (seated left) and Soviet Foreign Minister Eduard Shevardnadze signing accords on nuclear and missile test controls in the Kremlin yesterday

Scandinavian banks plan to form new finance group

BY SARA WEBB IN STOCKHOLM AND OLLI VIRTANEN IN HELSINKI

TWO of the biggest banks in Scandinavia, Kansallis-Osake-Pankki (KOP) of Finland and the Gota Group of Sweden, yesterday announced plans for the creation of a major new Nordic banking and financial services group.

In view of the increasing internationalisation of the financial services industry, the two banks have agreed to a measure of cross-ownership through a holding company and have agreed to co-operate in retail, corporate and investment banking and in data processing.

Both partners hinted that a more solid partnership could result once Swedish legislation permits foreigners to own direct stakes in Swedish banks, a recommendation expected to be made by the country's credit market committee shortly.

"After 1992, there will be much more competition so we need to be large – we aim to build a substantial Nordic group", said Mr Gabriel Urwitz, managing director of Proventus, the investment group which has a 44 per cent stake in the Gota Group.

The deal, in which Norwegian and Danish banking partners might also eventually participate, reflects growing concern in Swedish financial circles that the spate of acquisitions and mergers among Spanish, West German, Dutch and Belgian institutions could leave Sweden at a serious disadvantage in the European financial services market.

The prospect of European market integration in 1992 has already provoked talk of closer collaboration between banks within the EC. However, the Nordic deal indicates the extent to which banks in third countries expect to be affected by the move towards a unified market, and the steps they feel compelled to take to protect themselves.

Proventus is transferring a 38 per cent stake in Gota Group to a new holding company called Proventus Nordic, in which KOP has agreed to buy a 40 per cent holding for SKr896m ($150m). Proventus will take the remaining 60 per cent of Proventus Nordic and will also buy a 2 per cent shareholding in KOP for SKr300m, making it one of the larger shareholders in the Finnish bank.

Mr Urwitz said the agreement would lead to close co-operation in Sweden and Finland between KOP, Finland's leading bank, and the banking and financial operations of the Gota Group, which is Sweden's fourth largest banking and financial group with majority stakes in Wermlandsbanken, Skaraborgsbanken and 100 per cent of Gotabanken.

KOP had total assets of FM117bn (SKr172bn) while the Gota Group and Skaraborgsbanken had assets of SKr95bn at the end of 1987.

The two banks have a complementary international network which should open up wider possibilities for trade financing abroad. KOP has offices in New York, Moscow, Tokyo and Singapore, whereas Gota is represented in Peking, Shanghai and Bangkok. The banks will probably merge their operations in Hong Kong and Luxembourg, while leaving their London operations separate.

Merger talks pave way for Beazer control of Koppers

BY JAMES BUCHAN IN NEW YORK

BEAZER, the ambitious UK housebuilding and construction group, is poised to gain control of Koppers the US chemicals and aggregates group, following an announcement yesterday that the two companies were holding talks on a merger.

Koppers, which for three months has campaigned through courts in Pittsburgh and California and enlisted local officials and Congressmen in its defence against Beazer's $1.7bn bid, said executives of the two companies held "serious negotiations towards a merger" over the long Memorial Day weekend.

Koppers' decision to start talking with Beazer follows a string of reverses, which culminated in a small but potentially dangerous setback in a California court on Friday.

Koppers' stock rose sharply in heavy trading yesterday morning amid rising confidence on Wall Street that the management of the Pittsburgh-based group had been forced to drop its bitter hostility to a Beazer takeover.

Stockbrokers' analysts believe Beazer, which has grown more than 10-fold through acquisitions engineered by Mr Brian Beazer, its chairman, can now capture Koppers, whose sales total $1.52bn a year, if it makes a small increase in its offer of $60 a share.

"This thing is winding down at last," said Mr Robert Kanters, an analyst at the Pittsburgh offices of Legg Mason Walker. "But we may see a point or two above $60 so that management can feel it has extracted a bit more."

As of May 29, about 80 per cent of Koppers' stock was owned or had been tendered to BNS, the consortium of Beazer, Shearson Lehman Hutton and NatWest Investment Bank through which the bid has been mounted. Beazer's offer expires at midnight tonight New York time, but is expected to be extended once more.

On Friday, a federal appeals court judge in San Francisco in effect removed anti-trust objections to the takeover by ruling that he would lift a lower court injunction if a trustee were appointed for some Koppers quarries in southern California. A second injunction, imposed by a federal judge in Pittsburgh, remains in force but Wall Street believes that Beazer can satisfy the court's objections which concern financing.

The point at issue in the Pittsburgh court is some $540m of preferred stock which may be sold by BNS to finance the bid. The court is trying to decide if these are debt securities, in violation of takeover borrowing rules. But Beazer has called a meeting of its shareholders for June 13 to ask them to guarantee a $540m bridging loan, which would get round the injunction.

Campbell Soup buys UK frozen food group for $202m

By Christopher Parkes in London

CAMPBELL SOUP of the US yesterday took over the British frozen foods group Freshbake Foods in an agreed cash bid valuing the target at about £109m ($202m).

The link between of one of the world's biggest food processors and the number three in the UK frozen sector would give both an opportunity to expand and compete in the pan-European market place, the companies said in a statement.

It follows warnings from many quarters that British food companies – as shown in the battle for control of Rowntree – were likely to become targets for predators seeking market opportunities in the run-up to the completion of the European Community's internal market in 1992.

However, Mr Mike Manley, chief executive of Freshbake, welcomed yesterday's deal and the "splendid" price. "It puts us under the umbrella of one of the world's biggest food groups," he said.

Mr Manley is to be chairman of a new company, Campbell Foods UK, which will incorporate Freshbake, all Campbell's existing UK businesses and the Groko frozen foods business in the Netherlands.

With acceptances from Freshbake directors and their families for the 162p-a-share offer, plus a 2p second interim dividend in lieu of a final payment for the year ended April 2, Campbell was assured of a 31.12 per cent holding.

Purchases of further shares at 164p in the Stock Exchange yesterday morning gave Campbell a controlling interest of 50.7 per cent. Freshbake's shares were quoted at 124p at the close last Friday.

Freshbake makes a wide range of frozen foods including uncooked savoury pastry products, dough, desserts, confectionery and vegetables and also has interests in chilled foods and food process engineering.

Its assets include 11 factories accumulated mainly in the past five years during a series of 14 acquisitions of mainly small and loss-making companies.

Pre-tax profits this year are expected to be around £6.4m compared with £5.09m last year. Sales in 1987 were £147m.

Campbell Soup ranks with Heinz, General Foods, Nestlé and Unilever among the world's top food makers. Even so, its European interests have been relatively slow to develop since it first set up in the UK in 1933.

Details, Page 26

OECD says $ should not fall further

BY ANTHONY HARRIS IN WASHINGTON

THERE IS no case, in the near term, for any further depreciation in the dollar exchange rate, according to the Organisation for Economic Co-operation and Development. If downward pressures appear in the market it should be resisted, the OECD urges in a report on the US economy published today.

The OECD forecast suggests that US export growth will be near the limit of manufacturing capacity, although domestic demand is relatively subdued, so that import volume growth this year is put at only a quarter the rate of export growth. The report comments bluntly: "The stock market crisis seems to have helped the US economy to move towards better balance."

In these circumstances, the report argues, a further devaluation would not improve the trade balance at all unless it was backed by a strong monetary squeeze. This would risk inflation in the US and recession in other countries, and would be dangerous, given the present fragility of the financial markets.

The deficit should be tackled through higher domestic saving, by way of budget cuts and reduced consumer borrowing, the report argues. It suggests specifically that the US should act to stop the use of second mortgage borrowing to finance consumer spending.

The report, based on a study presented to the OECD's Economic Development and Review Committee on February 22, projects a 15¾ per cent volume increase in exports this year, which would add three per cent to manufacturing output, in addition to the increase required to meet home demand.

Real GDP growth is forecast to slow gently to 2¾ per cent in the current year and 2½ per cent in 1989, and at these growth rates little pressure on costs and prices is foreseen. In the event, export and output growth in the first quarter of 1988 has been well above the OECD projections, and the Federal Reserve has tightened monetary policy.

The report repeats the trade balance projections published at the time of the Interim Committee meeting in March, showing the trade balance narrowing by about $20bn in each of the next two years, and only slowly thereafter. This is in line with IMF forecasts, but the OECD report also sketches more favourable scenarios.

On more optimistic assumptions about US private sector saving, cost competitiveness, and about growth outside the US, progress would be sustained after 1989. Under the most favourable assumptions projected, the external deficit would largely disappear by 1993.

This "best case" assumes that the Gramm-Rudman budget targets are met, that long-term price elasticities for imports and exports are larger than short-term, and that the US gains another 10 per cent in competitiveness between 1990 and 1993, through wage restraint, productivity and possibly some rise in the real exchange rate of the Asian middle-income countries.

The report says that the disappointing progress of the US trade account in 1987 is entirely explained by the abnormally weak response of import prices to the dollar devaluation. If the forecasters had made the right assumptions about import prices, the OECD model would have produced an accurate projection.

Manufactured imports are now expected to go on growing at about 6 per cent a year in volume terms, with manufactured exports rising four times as fast in 1988 and three times as fast next year.

Our foreign staff adds: The dollar was supported yesterday by speculation about higher interest rates. It strengthened further in Europe and consolidated the gains later in New York.

In London the dollar closed at DM1.7290 compared with DM1.7180 on Friday, and finished in New York at DM1.7325. It was largely unchanged against the yen, closing just above Y125.

Earlier the Bundesbank, the West German central bank, had intervened when the dollar was fixed against the D-Mark and sold a small amount of dollars.

The Budnesbank's intervention, although minor, was the first time since January 13 that the bank had been detected in Frankfurt currency markets. At that time it had bought dollars to support the US currency.

Over the weekend, Mr David Mulford, a senior US Treasury official, said that currency markets should be aware that the major industrialised countries would co-operate closely to preserve exchange rate stability. Separately, the French and West German finance ministers also endorsed the necessity for stabilising the dollar

Background, Page 6; Currencies, markets, Section II

CUTTING A DASH TO PARIS: FROM THE HEART OF LONDON.

London City Airport provides the base for an exclusive partnership. Brymon Airways, an experienced operator of short take-off and landing De Havilland Dash 7 aircraft and Air France, offering the efficiency and convenience of Terminal 2 at Charles De Gaulle Airport where there's the shortest distance between aircraft and exit of any major international airport.
The service is called Cityclass and we're now operating a new improved schedule to Paris.
Cityclass completes the picture for Air France, as we're now the only airline to operate out of all four London airports. Four different ways to cut a dash to Paris.

AIR FRANCE

CITYCLASS DEPARTURE TIMES

London City Airport – Paris		Paris – London City Airport	
0700	Mon-Fri	0800	Mon-Sat
0900	Mon-Sat	1000	Mon-Fri
1100	Mon-Fri	1200	Mon-Fri
1300	Mon-Fri	1400	Mon-Fri
1500	Mon-Fri	1600	Mon-Fri
1700	Mon-Fri	1800	Mon-Fri
1900	Mon-Fri	2000	Mon-Fri
1540	Sun	1500	Sun
1900	Sun	1820	Sun

Summer schedule

For direct flights from London City Airport to Charles de Gaulle Terminal 2, call Air France on 01-499 9511, or Brymon Airways on Linkline (0345) 717383.

CONTENTS

GRECO-TURKISH RELATIONS: RECONCILING THE MIRROR IMAGES

Greek Prime Minister Andreas Papandreou who meets his Turkish counterpart later this month, Page 18

The appearance of publications in England reflects a culture searching for identity. The front page of the *Financial Times* — an important daily in England — is laid out in the same traditional way, much like it has been for years. At the other end of the spectrum are the newspapers that use sensationalism for mass appeal — an approach that did not go unnoticed by certain publishers in this country.

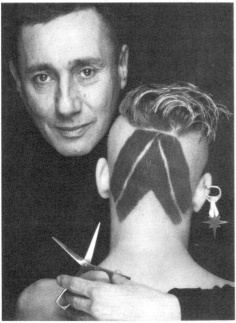

There is nothing "traditional" in these promotional ads for Stella Premium Lager Beer. Shown here is a shoe designer who used the logo — red inverted chevron — to embellish the heels of her hand-made "Stellatoes." In the other ad, a well-known coiffeur transforms the back of his pupil's head into a living Stella logo.

France

Ad spending: $8 million

Number of ad agencies: 2,600

Major marketers: IBM, Renault, Carrefour

Major industries: steel, chemicals, autos, textiles, wine, perfume, aircraft, ships

Population: 55 million

Newspapers: 237 per 1,000 population

Television sets: 19 million

Passenger cars: 21 million

Life-Style. Sense of history gives the French unshakable national pride (the word *chauvinism* was born here), but that is not to say that the French welcome authority. The average citizen is both critical and cynical about its leaders, and is not afraid to vent his or her opinions. Heady exchanges about politics are as routine at French bistros as they are about last night's baseball game at a bar in the United States. Spirit of individualism is firmly ingrained in the French psyche. *"Chacun a son gout"* goes the proverb; each to his own taste. Typically, the nation's reaction to the influx of English words (at least 2,000 in general use) is none too friendly, even though they have contributed at least 40% of their own to our dictionary.

The French forever keep searching for just the right balance between business and pleasure, with the latter getting more attention. A two to three-hour rest period after the midday meal is the norm and shops close during lunch hours. Low productivity has become somewhat of a national embarrassment to the French government, but not its people.

Attitude About the U.S. Quietly aloof. In true Tocqueville tradition ("No stigma attaches to the love of money in America . . ."), the French disapprove our preoccupation with accumulating material wealth. The consensus is that the United States is a nation still in its adolescence; a case of youth wasted on the young.

As in many countries, however, the new generation is more accepting of our ways. Parisian preppies, or the BCBGs (*"bon chic, bon genre"*) as they are called, consider anything from the United States to be *branché*, or "plugged in." Brunch, bagels, power lunches, chocolate chip cookies, tight jeans, Harvard MBA degrees, disco, tacos, and California wines are rapidly winning new converts.

Fashion Sense. French couturiers have long been the leaders of fashion and are still making important contributions. What you wear is almost as important to the French as what you do not.

Favorite Sports, Pastimes. Soccer, bicycling, car racing, mountain climbing, skiing, horse racing, nightlife, erotica, vacationing at the seashore, haute cuisine, and cuisine bourgeoise.

Humor. Open, relaxed, cheerful. French humorists are national heroes as are athletes in this country. Words like *satire, lampoon, burlesque, parody, caricature,* and *comedy* are all a legacy of the Gallic language.

Advertising Approach. French agencies call the shots, even more so than in the United Kingdom. If a client objects to an idea, the agency feels duty bound to set him straight. The result is advertising at its best or most bizarre. Convinced that the prime—if not only—purpose of advertising is to entertain, the French will not stand for a "dull," simplistic message; i.e. one that focuses on the attributes of the product. French creative Jacques Seguale sums up this attitude: "The act of buying one brand over another is an act of love, like marriage." Sex is considered a prime mover of goods. Its use in French advertising would raise the eyebrows of most U.S. television censors.

Legal Quirks. The logic of regulations leaves U.S. ad executives at a complete loss. Tourism outside the country cannot be touted—it would encourage French vacationers to spend their francs outside the borders. Supermarket advertising is discouraged for fear that it may drive the smaller, family-owned stores out of business. Children can be used only in ads that sell children's products, and even then the young performer cannot make the pitch. Auto spots are not allowed to entice drivers with the potential speed of the car. Not too surprisingly, few restrictions apply to nudity. In a recent election, the socialist party featured naked men and women in its campaign.

HYACINTHE RIGUAD: LOUIS XIV. THE LOUVRE, PARIS

French aesthetics—in music, art, theatre, literature—have dominated the European scene for many a century. Creativity is highly regarded, a gift from God bestowed only on a selected few—which explains the power French agencies have over their clients, when it comes to creative.

THE LOUVRE

Wine, women and song have long been part of the French psyche. Success in business is not equated with success in life. This attitude shows up in French art, as in the posters by Toulouse-Lautrec. Illustration (originally in blue) is from an ad for Tampona, a tampon product. The model's pose is chic, provocative, and very French. Copy explains matter-of-factly that she is wearing Tampona "à la bande bleue".

Il a fallu 20 ans de recherches pour que l'homme soit bien cou ché, il n'a pas fallu longtemps pour que tout le monde le sache.

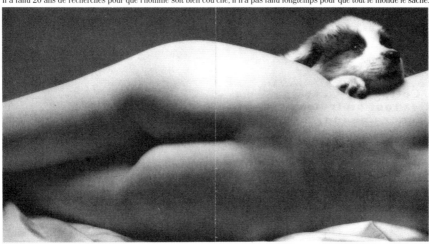

Few nations have developed as relaxed an attitude about matters sexual as the French. Bodies *tout ensemble* frequently appear in advertising, not only to titillate but to be touted for their beauty. This ad for Firelli beds shows a woman in repose, while the headline tells of research done for the product.

209

West Germany

Ad spending: $6 billion

Number of ad agencies: 330

Major marketers: Volkswagen, Procter & Gamble, Henkel

Major industries: steel, ships, autos, machinery, coal, cement, chemicals

Population: 61 million

Newspapers: 141 per 1,000 population

Television sets: 22 million

Passenger cars: 25 million

Life-Style. Germans are justifiably proud of their cultural past. The belief that a nation should be governed by strong leaders is firmly entrenched in the national character; human "weakness" (physical and emotional) may be considered a serious character flaw. Work ethic is strong, as is respect for education, technological excellence, scientific discipline. Living standards are high in Germany; few emigrate to the United States today.

Germany is not as mobile a population as ours. Bonding and "belonging" are an important part of the fabric of life; clubs and associations thrive in Germany. Even older people have not lost their zest for having a good time in the intimate company of one's family and friends. "Gemütlich" is a German word without English equivalent. It connotes easygoing friendliness, perhaps helped along by a few *Biere, Rindfleisch, und Lieder.*

Attitude About the U.S. A high percentage of Germans speak English—fluently. Germans are genuinely fond of Americans, though they tend to explain our postwar generosity in their own terms; i.e. that our approach remains the most realistic way to keep history from repeating itself. Still, Germany feels close to the United States—an attitude based partially on the fact that German immigrants have always played an important role in

U.S. history. Today, Americanisms are as accepted here as the ubiquitous presence of U.S. soldiers. A few random examples of our cultural influence: *die Jeans, die Boots, das Teeshirt,* and *der Stereo.*

Fashion Sense. Utilitarian approach to fashion inhibits originality among the older set. But the coming generation assiduously tries to emulate U.S. fashion styles, with an eye on the provocative.

Favorite Sports, Pastimes. Soccer, hiking, bicycling, track, tennis, nightlife, music.

Humor. Difficult to appreciate by our standards. It leans toward the grotesque, as witnessed in the works of such artists as Albrecht Dürer, Pieter Brueghel, George Grosz, and many German contemporary filmmakers. Impatience with human frailty discourages friendly, easygoing bantering between people.

Advertising Approach. As methodical as the German mind. Creativity is stifled, graphics is inbred. Realism in illustration dominates, less so in photography. Fine artists are still thinking grandiosely—a legacy of a glorious past. Germany has produced some of the greatest artists, writers, architects, musicians in the world. Today much of artistic inspiration comes from this side of the Atlantic, especially in advertising.

Legal Quirks. The German Advertising Federation (ZAW) publishes entire books on regulations. Advertising may not inspire fear, promote superstition and discrimination. Showing athletes drinking alcoholic beverages is prohibited. Conspicuously absent from German advertising are children. Product claims must be scrupulously documented. A European joke has it this way: "In Germany everything is forbidden that is not permitted (vs. "In France, everything is permitted even if it's forbidden; in Russia, everything is forbidden, even if it's permitted").

Perhaps because of its past, Germany has had little chance to develop a sunny, optimistic outlook on life, say, the way the French, Italians and Americans have. Weltschmerz pervades German art and literature, and even its music. The works of Albrecht Dürer (top left), Pieter Brueghel, and even satirist George Grosz, could hardly be considered cheery. German advertising is as serious-minded as those who create it.

Partially as a reaction to the excesses of the Baroque style, Germany developed its own stark, simple, "logical" Bauhaus style. The approach shows up in much of today's art, as seen here in a poster for an experimental film series and an advertisement for a school.

Italy

Ad spending: $3 billion

Number of ad agencies: 155

Major marketers: Fiat, Alfa Romeo, Parmalat

Major industries: steel, machinery, autos, textiles, shoes, machine tools, chemicals

Population: 57 million

Newspapers: 124 per 1,000 population

Television sets: 14 million

Passenger cars: 21 million

Social Mores. National pride is not as fierce as in some of the other countries in Europe but there is a strong identification with anything "Italian" nonetheless. A pragmatic approach to politics and life in general, prevails. Shortcuts are for the wise. Historically, Italy has switched alliances during wars more often than any other nation; that tendency prompted Klemens von Metternich to call this nation "only a geographic expression." Life is to be lived, not to be pondered. Work, too, is to be enjoyed, and not to be taken in prohibitively large doses. Shops are closed between 1:00 p.m. and 4:00 p.m. and then again at 7:00 p.m., but typically, bars stay open into small hours of the morning. One should make an effort only if absolutely necessary. *"Chi non fa, non falla"*: "The man who does nothing makes no mistakes."

Family units are strong, with the lady of the house quietly (or not so quietly) running the family. Men act macho, but deep down are an easy mark for the carinas of the land.

Attitude About the U.S. Italians look up to Americans. They are well aware of the contributions their fellow countrymen made on this continent (including discovering it), and can rattle off the names of famous American-Italians at the drop of

un cappello. A seafaring nation, they think little of hopping across the ocean to visit a relative or friend. Our ways find ready embrace with the young and the young in heart. A high percentage of the population speaks English, and as in France, our words easily slip into "Italian." A few borrowings: *il supermarket, il marketing, il drink, la TV, lo slip, il popcorn.*

Fashion Sense. Some of the best fashion designers live in Italy; almost half of the nation's export is fashion-related, with Milan as the center of activity. Bold designs, bright colors dominate the scene. The younger the wearer, the better she looks in her Italian-made garb; as in the United States, designers' attention flags when faced with wearers past their 40th birthday. Biannual fashion shows generate as much excitement in Milan as the Super Bowl does in this country.

Favorite Sports, Pastimes. Soccer, bicycling, skiing, sailing, fencing, horseback riding, hiking, auto racing, sipping wine and eating alfresco, and watching the opposite sex pass by on the streets.

Humor. Irrepressible, gleeful, carefree. Much is based on everyday occurrences, human foibles, the absurdity of life. Italians are consummate teasers of one another. Never have they lost the ability to laugh at just about everything, including — God bless them! — themselves.

Advertising. As spirited and light-hearted as the Italians' disposition. Strong on design and illustration, less strong with the still camera. As in France, illustrators are put on the pedestal here. Within their province fall both the layout and finished art, as often as not. Art directors are frequently fine artists at heart. The nation's rich artistic heritage plays an important role; for centuries, Italy has produced some of the greatest painters and sculptors, singers, and entertainers. The word *conversazione* (slowly becoming part of the English language from necessity) means "a meeting for conversation, especially about art." Agencies feel their major contribution to advertising lies in their creativity. Sure sense of taste shows up everywhere: fashion, furniture, architecture, fine art, jewelry, the streamlined breed of the Italian greyhound — and, of course, advertising. An Italian-made ad can be recognized on sight; it is always well designed; the difference between a magazine ad and a poster may be virtually imperceptible.

Legal Quirks. One of the few countries in the world that tolerates comparative advertising. However, "deceptive" advertising is against the law; claims must be provable. Only authenticated testimonials are allowed. Ads banned in Italy include a Johnnie Walker ad that suggested an executive relaxing with a bottle in his office, and a ritual talisman that guarantees "the attainment of all your dreams." The former was considered to encourage imbibing, the latter blatant exploitation of superstition. Cigarette advertising on television is banned. The fine is nearly $50,000.

This full-color magazine ad for Alfa Romeo embodies much of the Italian spirit. The photographer has changed the landscape to create the mood he wanted; the colors are predominantly blues and pinks. Clouds cover much of the sky as if put there by expert ceiling painter Michelangelo himself. The car — a machine designed as carefully as a piece of sculpture, fits right in for a *compozione perfetto.* Psychologically, too, this picture meets with the approval of the typical Italian driver whose foot drops heavily on the pedal at the sight of long stretches of unobstructed road.

Design is important to the Italian artist — which is why poster-style graphics dominate advertising. He tends to think in terms of the total page.

(MUSIC)
(OPEN ON MAN SITTING IN DOORWAY)

ANNCR: (VO) The Italians know that the classics are made

to enrich one's life every day. That's why they enjoy Bolla.
(MAN CHECKS POCKET WATCH)

(MAN PEERS LONGINGLY DOWN DESERTED STREET)

The Bolla Family has been making
(CUT TO BOLLA)

classic premium wines for over a century.
(MAN POURS GLASS)

Maybe that's why the most popular premium wine from Italy is Bolla.

Just one of the classics
(CUT TO BEAUTIFUL YOUNG LADY NOW COMING DOWN STREET)

that can enrich your life...
(MAN LOOKS UP TO SEE HER)

every day.
(CUT TO CLOSE UP OF WOMAN AS SHE PASSES BY HIM)

(CUT TO MAN AS HE TOASTS HER)

Bolla. The Italian Classic.

You don't have to be Italian to understand an Italian. This commercial was created by Ammirati & Puris — an American agency employed by the Brown-Forman Beverage company. An elderly man sips his glass of Bolla as he notices a comely young lady pass by. He looks up and, with a knowing smile as Italian as the wine he is savoring, he toasts her.

Japan

Ad spending: $11.5 billion (?)

Number of ad agencies: 2,900

Major marketers: Kao, Toyota Motor, Matsushita

Major industries: electrical and electronic equipment, autos, machinery, chemicals

Population: 121 million

Newspapers: 125 per 1,000 population

Television sets: 30 million (three times as many radios)

Passenger cars: 25 million

Social Mores. The Japanese too have a strong national identity, a sense of the past almost 2,000 thousand years old. Historically, the country has always encouraged isolation and has viewed "foreign influence" with suspicion. Legacy of a rigidly structured feudal system has left its mark on society even under present democratic rule. The Japanese cling to the concept that directions and final instructions best flow from the top down. At the same time, corporations invite workers' free and easy participation; there are no "supervisors" in Japan, only "managers." Dismissals from one's job are rare, except for outright violations; demotions, lack of promotion, or just plain losing face are the conventional forms of penalty for shoddy performance.

Much has been written about the "Japanese way" of doing business; we have little to add. Suffice it to say that their cultural traditions are very different from ours, sometimes to the bewilderment of both parties. Theirs is the belief that any human activity, thought, or aspiration is but an expression of one's higher inner self; nature leaves nothing to chance. Everyone is part of a whole, the Japanese society. Education determines one's lot in life; competition to get into the best of schools (and thus, into the largest of companies after graduation) is keen enough to induce some of the failing students to put an end to their lives. Average school attendance is 12 years, higher than ours. There is better than 99% literacy in Japan. Office politics in the sense that it is practiced in the United States would be considered disruptive. One must try to "fit in."

Managers are elected on the basis of their ability to gain consensus among employees, more than their professional skills. Decision making is a communal affair; "decisiveness" in an executive, a highly desirable trait in this country, may prove to be counterproductive in a Japanese working environment. Outright rejection of an idea is a traumatic experience with many Japanese; polite ambiguity is a learned response that will keep the respondent from making a commitment. Our insistence in "getting to the point" grates on the Japanese; they call this deplorable habit of ours *rikutsupi*—"too logical."

Work ethic runs high, second only to Korea's and Taiwan's. One's professional associations and position in the company define his worth; titles are featured prominently on name cards and often mentioned before the bearer's name when introduced socially. Women have long been accepted in the work force but it is still rare to find a female executive in high position; American corporations with a female executive representing them at important summit meetings may run up against subtle resistance.

It is difficult to explain in simple terms the success of the Japanese in the international marketplace; the reasons are many. Hard work is one, of course. Others are loyalty to the company, ambition to advance in the organization (or perhaps fear of humiliation that goes with being left behind), team spirit, mind-over-matter philosophy, attention to (and even a fascination with) minute detail, and the ability and willingness to think long range.

216

Attitude About the U.S. The Japanese are still not sure what to make of a conqueror turning benefactor after a bitterly fought war; nothing like it had ever happened in their experience. Our ways are emulated everywhere, perhaps with more intensity than in any other part of the world. Magazines, cigarettes, restaurants blazon Anglo Saxon; cosmetics and plastic surgery strive to attain the "American look" (including unslanted eyes) that brings a woman's face closer to the current Japanese ideal: *tamago kato no kao* — "an egg with eyes." About 10% of ads use a U.S. celebrity. Translations of U.S. books are popular, particularly nonfiction. The Japanese hold a record of words adopted from English — almost 10,000 of them — even though the two languages have no common roots. A few examples: *ado* ("ad"), *rajio* ("radio"), *teipw rekoda* ("tape recorder") and *komu* ("computer"). There is a realistic chance that Japan will soon be our closest economic ally, superseding even our geographically nearest but economically less vigorous no-tariff neighbor up north, Canada.

Fashion Sense. Japanese designers are becoming an important force in women's attire. Much of the fashion is designed for export — aimed particularly at their largest and richest customer, the United States.

Favorite Sports, Pastimes. Dancing and jogging among the young; gymnastics, martial arts, sumo wrestling, swimming, golf, skiing.

Humor. Difficult for us to understand — broad, pejorative, and relying on coxcomb sight gags. Our ability to mix tears with smiles yet eludes Japanese scenarists.

Advertising Approach. The Japanese have yet to develop their own distinctive style of advertising; many ideas come from the United States. Illustrators are strong on symbolism, no doubt inspired by the stylized approach to fine art of past masters. (Even Japanese letters have their own history — they are based on the Chinese *kanji,* a series of pictorial symbols.) Color reigns; the brighter, the better. Almost all Japanese newspapers are printed in color, as is print advertising. Their feel for the abstract shows up in photography, too, which is one of the reasons why Japanese photographers handle still life and fashion photography so well. In cinematic picture taking, Japanese craftsmen are among the best in the world. If the U.S. moviegoer, watching a Japanese film, finds it too slow paced or short of narrative force, that is only because his view of life is more hurried, less contemplative. Pacing and narrative force are less important in a 30-second spot, and here the Japanese are at their best. Commercials made there are consistent award winners at international festivals.

Always willing to learn, the Japanese have mastered our marketing techniques better than have others in the world. While segmentation is not overly important on the domestic front (over 99% of the population is ethnically Japanese and over 90% belongs to the "middle class" — very rich and very poor are few), the Japanese apply their marketing with consummate skill on world markets. Credit should go to the Japanese business community for being among the first to admit that "global advertising" often stands in the way of reaching local markets effectively. Even though Japanese advertising agencies abound (among them is one of the largest in the world, Dentsu), they have a record of appointing U.S. agencies to prepare advertising for the U.S. marketplace.

Legal Quirks. Hard sell is discouraged in Japan, as is even the slightest hint of comparison advertising. The rules are lax, however, and surprisingly permissive for a nation with a history of absolute rulers. Showing a topless female body is all right as long as "good taste" prevails. There are no laws designed to make sure that spokespersons actually use the product. Firmly ingrained honesty keeps a lid on grossly exaggerated claims.

EARLY 18TH CENTURY WOODCUT

Traditional Japanese design has a distinctive character. Symbolism is a large part of the visual vernacular. Their lettering is in itself representational. Skillful use of the modern version of the *Ryumin* typography is used in the advertising poster above.

Japanese humor often befuddles the Western mind. It gravitates toward overstatement, even the grotesque. In an advertising campaign for *Prevent* sweetener (note the English name) short stories tell about the lives of people portrayed in each ad. Shown here is a man who claims he is the son of Marilyn Monroe and Marlon Brando, and so he doesn't have to worry much about calories.

The giant monster Godzilla is a Japanese invention. Brave warriors usually bring him down. Messages are rarely subtle in Japanese movies.

Designs by Issey Miyake/photos by Irving Peng

There Is More to Translating Advertising Copy than a Literal Translation of the Words

Said Frank Perdue with a straight face, down under in South America: "It takes a sexually excited man to make a chick affectionate." It was his writers who translated the slogan "It takes a tough man to make a tender chicken" literally. The translator, who learned her Spanish in school, forgot about slang and local use of the language.

It is important that native speakers do the translations. Only they have complete command of the vernacular — the lingua franca advertisers speak. Budweiser became the "queen of beers" in Spanish, while another brewery was caught by surprise when told its slogan read "the beer that would make you more drunk" in Spanish. Still another beer — this one of the light kind — boasted: "Filling. Less delicious."

If no expert is available in the agency, it should turn to an outside professional. Translation services usually have an ample supply of native speakers on staff, or they know how to find one fast. What's more, they have the typewriters, word processors, and other typesetting facilities to put the words on paper the way native readers are used to seeing them. The American Translators Association can tell you where to find such services.

Another thing: Nearly all translation from English to another language results in a text longer than the original version. That's because our language is by far the richest in vocabulary — over a million words by the latest count. Other languages have fewer words and so they need more of them to get from one end of the sentence to the other. German, the second-richest language in the world — has only half as many. French — *langue du pays,* a favorite with the literati — has

Japanese fashion designers are gaining international repute for their use of bright colors and artistic abandon.

even fewer. Be prepared to make a few adjustments in your print layout to accommodate foreign translation of the text.

To Sum It Up

Income derived from overseas is becoming increasingly important to U.S. corporations; the days of corporate isolationism are fairly over. Almost all large companies do business overseas and the trend will continue.

Advertising, too, has gone international. An increased number of U.S. agencies have overseas affiliation. The wish to have worldwide presence is probably one of the most important reasons for agencies' growing propensity to merge; clients demand representation outside the country and this yet may be the simplest answer to the problem.

Thus, it is becoming increasingly important for agencies to develop "global consciousness." At times this grates on U.S. sensibilities, since our tradition favors self-sufficiency. But circumstances have changed. Competition today comes from all corners of the world.

It is important to know what works overseas—and why. Mistakes can be costly. Cultures differ greatly from one country to another. Opinions and sentiments about the United States affect sales, too. While global advertising—one voice throughout the world—works effectively in some instances, as often as not cultural and language differences block effective communications. Most companies find that localized advertising is more effective. Major differences exist in life-styles, values, manners, and the character of people. Generally speaking, other nations tend to put events into a larger historical perspective. They are less responsive to "hard sell" and more apt to appreciate art in execution. Governments have mixed feelings about commercial influence, and local regulations often reflect this attitude. Compared to the United States, advertising is still a relatively new industry.

11

Making Sense out of Media

Pick the wrong media and, no matter how good the creative execution, the ad will not live up to its potential. Poorly conceived media plans are usually the costliest mistakes in all of advertising; about 70% of budgets are allocated to buying space and time. And so, while media buying may not have the drama and excitement of giving birth to an ad, it yet deserves a great deal of attention.

Most advertisers delegate media buying to outside professionals because it is an activity that calls for a full commitment. Prices fluctuate wildly with changes in supply and demand, new programs and stations come to the fore, audience tastes change—the amount of data can be overwhelming. Computers can help in sorting it out but at times even they are overwhelmed. It takes a professional to sort it all out.

This does not mean, of course, that the advertiser—be that an individual or an organization—has no choice but to stay completely on the sidelines. He can—and many times, he should—get involved, if not day to day then at least at judicious intervals. As a generalist, he always should be qualified to ask the right questions. The answers may surprise him.

Media Buying Is Done Scientifically, But It Is Not a Science

Numbers can tell you the amount of people reached, the frequency with which they are reached, speed of audience accumulation, coverage, cost efficiencies, and so on. They can also be helpful in converting geographic, demographic, and at times, psychographic clusters into meaningful statistics, making it possible to compare, cross index, plot, locate customers, analyze and rank relative market potentials, and suggest integrated solutions. But numbers are seductive for their authority; it is all too tempting to take the computer screen at face value and leave out judgment and common sense.

In arriving at your media decision, always consider these two questions no matter what the numbers say:

1. Who and where are the prospects I'm trying to reach? (You should already know that at this point.)

2. Does the medium of choice best reach them?

Segmentation—Help or Hindrance?

In today's many-faceted society, media buying has become a true art form. While quantitative audience data still play a vital role, it is *qualitative* data that lead to intelligent choices.

The 80%/20% rule (80% of purchases are made by 20% of the people) should not be a prime consideration when buying media. Ideally, the target should be 100%. Why pay for the delivery of 10 million people when only 20% of them are interested in purchasing the product? The goal is to reach 10 million people, the majority of whom are prospects.

Take a VCR as the product to be marketed. Audience characteristics are fairly easy to define. The prospects have (a) a home, (b) at least one (but preferably two) television sets, (c) enough money to afford to buy the equipment, and—it is to be hoped—(e) interest in watching tape-recorded material on the TV screen. This is a mixed bag of requirements, but you should be able to choose media that will reach this person.

Here are the questions you must ask of your media *and* of your market experts—simultaneously (each will be able to give you only a partial answer):

Geography. Is your distribution "in place"—is it *where* the product can reach your customers? If no stores for it are nearby, how far would your prospects have to travel to find the product? Can they be reached through direct mail? How keen is the competition in the area?

Demography. What is the median income of the audience reached by the media of choice? Dominant age? (Older people, while having more discretionary income, are less apt to install a VCR.) Occupation? (Students may not be able to afford to buy the equipment.) Size of family? (The larger the family, the more likely that a purchase will be made.) Number of TV sets per household? (The more sets, the better.) Education? (A well-educated audience is more likely to make a purchase. With higher education goes higher income.)

Psychography. How strong an inclination is there to buy the equipment? Buying space in a magazine catering to buyers of antiques, for example, could be a less than prudent investment (antique collectors show less interest in having a VCR in their homes). In a medical journal, the ad may look out of place unless the message aims at the needs of doctors (i.e. to record medical programs for later viewing). Even a magazine reaching video professionals could prove to be an unwise purchase— VCR ownership among its readers may have peaked, or your particular type of VCR may not appeal to their sophisticated and expensive taste.

Of the three measurements, the easiest to get an accurate reading on is the geographic coverage of the media. Demographics also lends itself to statistical scrutiny, and so it is second on the list. The most resistant to quantitative interpretation is psychographic data. That is where insight into human nature and common sense play the most important role.

How the Chop-Chop Theory Works in Media

All media today are targeted toward a niche in the marketplace—even television networks through their choice of programming and timing. Segment-minded advertisers insist upon media taking this tack. Ten years ago, there were about 350 notable consumer magazines published, including some that sold themselves to advertisers on the basis of their mass circulation and little else. With television in nearly all homes, magazines must now look for a niche in the marketplace, just as any other product would have to; as a result, the number of consumer magazines has almost doubled.

Publications moving into smaller voids in the marketplace generally do better. In pursuit of geographic segmentation, 220 regional and city magazines have been started in recent years, according to the City & Regional Magazine Association. The computer industry alone has spawned over 300 new publications during the same period, some that received financial support from makers of computers. Real estate, another business that has enjoyed a boom for some time, has given birth to over 30 new titles in the last three years, each that appeals to readers of various incomes and personal tastes (one that speaks to Japanese real estate investors only), while expectant mothers and mothers of small infants now have a choice of 15 titles.

Typically, a vendor store in New York (on the concourse level in the Pan Am Building) sells no less than 2,500 different magazines. Among them are *Bird Talk, Hot Water Living, Biblical Archeology Review.*

Television audiences, too, are getting increasingly choosy in their program selections. With nearly 3,000 cable systems reaching over half of television households, it is possible today to reach the "right" people with just the "right" program, be that for sport fans, armchair travelers, tickertape watchers, home exercisers, 24-hour weather buffs, or medical practitioners.

If You Know Your Product, You Know Your Media

Media representatives will not only compare their wares with those in the same media *category* (*Woman's Day* vs. *Family Circle*), but in true American entrepreneurial spirit will take on anybody in the house. A vendor of television will tout the *reach* of the medium, a vendor of radio will stress *frequency*, a vendor of magazines will concentrate on *selectivity*, and

so on. Such comparisons, while informative, rarely provide sufficient insights for the preparation of a sound media plan. The advantages and disadvantages of every media category are contingent on the specific marketing goals of the advertiser. No single "advantage" is so overwhelming that, ipso facto, it makes a particular media category superior to all others. Television may reach more people (for a price) but are they true prospects?

Here is how to make comparisons between one media category and another — this combined with good judgment and common sense:

Cost per Thousand (CPM). This figure reflects the cost of reaching 1,000 individuals (or homes, or any other units of measurement) through the medium of choice. The measurement is purely quantitative, however, and tells little about the composition of the audience.

Selectivity. This reflects the medium's ability to reach the advertiser's target audience. Usually (though not always), the larger the audience, the less discriminating the medium.

Coverage. Quantitative measurement of people (or homes, or whatever) the medium is targeted to cover. The goal may be defined in geographic (i.e. "trading area"), demographic, or psychographic terms, or more commonly, combinations of the three.

Speed of Audience Accumulation. Some media are "faster" than others in reaching their audience. A weekly publication is faster than a monthly, a daily newspaper is faster than a billboard posted for 30 days. Frequency of impressions within a given time period determines audience accumulation.

Geographic Flexibility. This is important for advertisers wishing to match media coverage with product distribution patterns, branch office locations, sales territories. Most national magazines offer "regional" editions in narrowing down geographic coverage.

Timing Flexibility. Ability to move in and out of media quickly may be important to an advertiser, especially in retail. "Lead time" (period between receiving and showing an ad) is the briefest among newspapers, the longest among the monthly magazines.

Comparing Media Efficiency: The Quick Way

The chart shown below will enable you to make a quick comparison between one media category and another. It is based on *average* use of each; if used for different purposes in a specific way, the results may be entirely different.

For example, "outdoor" would rate poorly in audience selectivity since normally it is not possible for this medium to define its audience demographically. Thousands of cars may pass a highway poster. But advertise on top of the mountain at a ski resort—as Campbell Soup did—and the situation changes. It is possible to define skiers by age (15 to 45), education (higher), income (higher), lifestyle (sport and outdoor oriented), and attitude (more adventurous than average). They were the people this advertiser was trying to reach.

Television, too, rates low on audience specifics, but astute buying can partially overcome this weakness of the medium. Selection of programs is one way to attract the "right" demographic and psychographic audience. In a single year, Coca-Cola has bought commercial time on no less than a dozen popular programs, each aimed at a specific segment of viewers. Aetna Life and Casualty sponsored a 30-second commercial in support of S.A.D.D. (Students Against Driving Drunk) addressed to families during four games of the World Series reaching about 18 million parents and 17 million teenagers. Merrill Lynch and Cadillac have both been major sponsors of televised golf tournaments watched by an affluent audience.

On the other end of the spectrum of selectivity are magazines, but even in this group, definitions blur at times. *Prevention* magazine is read by both the old and the young; the target is more psychographic than demographic. The "average" reader of the *Wall Street Journal* is the executive in the $50,000 plus bracket, but more than half of the readership is made up of the upwardly mobile still standing at the first rung of the corporate ladder.

More About Media Categories: Creative Opportunities

Each media category offers a different challenge to the creative. No one knows

	TV[a]	Radio[b]	Magazine[c]	Newspaper[d]	Outdoor[e]	Direct Mail
CPM	Average	Low	Average	High	Low	High
Target-hitting ability	Fair	Good	Excellent	Fair	Poor	Excellent
Coverage	90%	60%	75%	85%	95%	95%
Speed of audience accumulation	Excellent	Good	Poor	Excellent	Fair	Excellent
Geographic flexibility	Excellent	Excellent	Fair	Excellent	Excellent	Excellent

[a]30-second, [b]60-second, [c]Full page in four-color, [d]1,000 lines, [e]24 sheets

this better than the writers and artists whose job it is to make the message fit the media. A true love/hate relationship exists between those who create the ads and those who publish them.

The medium that is most popular with both art directors and copywriters is television. When it comes to other types of media, the two professions go their separate ways. Art directors prefer posters, magazines (four-color), newspapers, direct mail, and radio—in that order. The larger the ad, the better. Copywriters, on the other hand, list radio as their second favorite, with newspapers, magazines, direct mail, and posters following after. Any writer worth his word processor puts high value on words, and radio allows them to deal with words in their purest form.

But it is television that, for the most part, creatives will vote for the major media advertising that promises maximum exposure—and wins awards. (Even judges are influenced by degree of exposure.) Art directors and copywriters who create storyboards for network commercials are the heroes in an agency; they have recognition and the salaries to match. The fact that television may not be the most cost-effective medium for the client may not always be the prime concern of those concentrating on exposing their talents.

Understandably, the advent of 15-second spots as a viable alternative to 30-second has been greeted with little enthusiasm by the creative community. A survey at the Art Directors Club showed a nearly absolute consensus that such a constraint would adversely effect creative quality, worth mentioning that 30-second spots (vs. 60-second) had met a similarly hostile reception about ten years ago, in the face of the fact that this commercial length is 70% more cost-effective as its 60-second counterpart.

Small-space print ads, too, are viewed with a jaundiced eye by the creative. When the high-concentration *Reader's Digest* lifted its half-century opposition to running advertising, and media buyers rushed happily to include the magazine on their schedules, art directors were less than enthusiastic. It took a concerted effort by the publisher to convince them that it was possible to create a graphically viable ad in a smaller than standard-sized publication.

This is not to imply that the creative impact of an advertising campaign should be dealt with casually when planning the media schedule. On the contrary, contributions from both art and copy as to execution should add greatly to the effectiveness of the campaign. The product may lend itself more to a live demonstration on television than to simple description print. Or the message may call for lengthy and carefully crafted copy in which case print may be more appropriate. Still other products, say, a piece of music or a speech lesson, may be best sold on radio.

What follows is a discussion of the advantages and disadvantages of each major medium from a creative point of view.

Television

Advantages. Sight, sound, and movement all combined. Maximum attention value in what has long since become an overwhelmingly visually oriented society. High credibility; the screen does not distort the truth. Opportunity to be creative. Color. High retention value; research shows that commercial spots are remembered a long time after they appear, sometimes for years.

Disadvantages. Not much time to convey specific information, particularly in view of trend toward shorter commercials. Air clutter; almost 25% of airtime consists of nonprogramming material (ads, promos, announcements). Over 20,000 commercials are shown a year. The fact that they are usually viewed in one's own home only adds to the feeling that they are intrusive. New technology (remote control, VCR) now makes it possible for the viewer to change channels or tune out the commercial altogether. Fleeting nature of the image; unless it is on tape, the viewer is hard put to go back to the commercial for better comprehension, the way he could with a printed ad (i.e. complicated instructions, cooking recipes, fine copy points). Lack of accurate demographic data. Capricious censorship. Relative lack of merchandising support.

Magazines

Advantages. High-fidelity reproduction, both in black and white and in color. Accurate demographic and psychographic data. Controllable editorial environment. Use of coupons in ads. Opportunity to have long copy and explain. Reader can tear out the ad and retain it. Imaginative use of the medium (i.e. scented stock, pop-outs, foldout pages, customized [i.e. silver, gold] inks, special transparency, bound-in plastic records and other inserts) allows advertiser to change pace. Excellent graphic opportunities. Color. Strong merchandising support.

Disadvantages. Smaller page size than newspaper or a poster. Long lead time (as much as three or four months) gives messages less immediacy (compared to radio, newspaper, or television). Tendency to bunch ads. "Positioning" (at what section of the magazine does the ad appear?) may be a problem. Left-hand page attracts fewer readers but at no reduction in space cost. Diffused geographic distribution. Difficulties in making last-minute changes. Need to catch the eye instantly; the average reader spends 3.2 seconds on a magazine page.

Newspapers

Advantages. Almost unlimited number of ad sizes available to the advertiser at short notice. Impact of black against white (still one of the most powerful color combinations). Four-color available in some newspapers. Close rapport with readers; newspapers are perceived as a "hometown" medium. Sense of immediacy. Quick response to an offer; calls and/or coupon returns may start coming in the next day. Last-minute modifications are handled expertly; the newspaper can make them through their own production facilities and easy-to-change computer-generated page layouts.

Disadvantages. Loss of fidelity, especially in reproduction of halftone illustration and color. Editorial environment is only partially controllable, as is position on the page. Possibility of "show-through" (ink seeps through the stock and shows up on reverse side). Variance in column width among individual newspapers (though there is an ongoing effort to standardize). Poorer readership above the middle horizontal fold. Short life. Ad clutter on the page. Hurried reading. Relative lack of merchandising support.

ANNCR: The Apple IIc is the perfect computer
to give your kids.
KID 1: This should be good.
KID 2: Yeah.
ANNCR: Because Apples are the leading
computers used in schools.
KID 1: Remember your bike last Christmas?
KID 2: Uh-oh . . .
ANNCR: Yet it can run thousands of business
and home-finance programs. And it's so
simple to set up and use, virtually anyone
can do it.
KID 2: Another Christmas miracle.

**Of all media, it is television that best
records human emotions. Here's how
Apple IIc reached millions of hearts in a
Christmas commercial.**

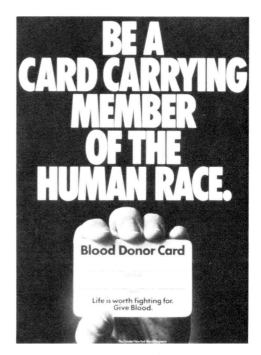

**One of the advantages of print advertis-
ing is that it can be referred to as often as
necessary. If this is an important part of
the advertising message, consider print.**

AUTHORITY

**The authority of words on paper — most
of us learn to respect the power of the
written word in childhood — is one of
the intrinsic values of the print media.**

**Direct mail most effectively reaches a
target audience, and lends itself to innovative, creative advertising.**

Ads above and below have taken optimum advantage of the print media. Copy on the Hearing Dog Center (Hill Holiday Conners Cosmopulos) makes for fascinating reading. Nary a word should be lost — as it could, say, on television. The ad below (Doyle Dane Bernbach) brings a specific message to specific people.

(SFX: UNDER THROUGHOUT)

MALE VOICE: *Um, Um, Um, Um, I don't worry, no I won't feel bad.*
Got the 501 Blues
They gonna feel glad.
Got to have them every day so they fit my way.
Uah, I'm talking to Levi's buttonfly 501 blues.

(SFX: CLAPPING SOLO)

MALE VOICE: *Blue as the sky with a buttonfly—y—y—y.*
You got to understand I'm a Levi's 501 natural bluesman.

(SFX: CLAPPING SOLO)

MALE VOICE: *You know I've got the moves always feels just right.*
In my natural blues got 'em day and night.

(SFX: CLAPPING SOLO)

MALE VOICE: *Easy kind of fading, ain't nothing complicated.*
You got to understand I'm a Levi's 501 natural bluesman.

(SFX: CLAPPING SOLO; CLAPPING OUT)

In radio advertising — one way to reach the elusive young — images can be conjured up through use of sound only. The song, 501 Blues, promoting Levi's 501 Jeans, reaches its jeans-wearing audience not only demographically but also psychographically.

Coupon

Only in print can the advertiser have coupons — one of the most cost-effective response-mechanisms in advertising.

POPULAR MUSIC
THE MACHINE AGE

Annie Lennox lets out a wild scream at the beginning of "I Need a Man," on Eurythmics' latest album, "Savage" (RCA) .... Her haughty demeanor and clipped speech, her close-cropped hair and fashionable leathers never hold out the possibility of androgynous openness that she was tagged with early in her career. Rather, they are the trappings of a perky, efficient career woman– say, Julie Andrews on Vivarin– for whom this silly pop music is just a stepping stone on the way to a good, solid profession, like Hollywood.

From a review by
Mark Moses
appearing in this week's issue of the best-written, best-read magazine in America.
Yes, The New Yorker.

An especially creative use of media. This full page newspaper ad (prepared by Lord Geller Frederico Einstein) not only makes interesting reading, but is also a visual stopper. The trick is done not with mirrors, but with use of white space.

Radio

Advantages. Immediacy. Opportunity to make literally last-minute changes if message is delivered live by station's announcer. Sound. Loyal listeners (the average person listens to only about two stations and rarely switches). Good retention. Relatively strong merchandising support.

Disadvantages. Lack of graphics (though this can be partially overcome by expert use of sound—more and more art directors are asked to participate in the making of a radio commercial). No opportunity to visually demonstrate the product. Wavering attention span (audience often listening to radio while distracted by other activities, such as reading, housekeeping, driving). Clutter on the air. Fleeting nature of the message; inability to hear the commercial again when listener misses some of the words.

Outdoor (Highway Posters)

Advantages. Large size, good visibility. Color. Excellent reproduction. Graphic opportunities. Nature of medium is such it invites bold, simple advertising of long staying power.

Disadvantages. Lack of opportunity to go into details (an average of less than six words appears on outdoor posters). Message must be conveyed visually; if set in type, that must be visible anywhere from 100 to 300 feet. Few people bother to stop and look to make out the message. Susceptible to graffiti and other forms of vandalism. Wear and tear during showing. Inadequate qualitative audience research. Relative lack of merchandising support.

Direct Mail

Advantages. Opportunity to use both graphics and copy imaginatively; no rules and restrictions other than the creator's own personal ethics and postal regulations. Unlike in most other media, size and color are in the eye (and pocketbook) of the maker. Intimacy. Measurable results. Use of response mechanism makes "selling off the page" possible at about the cost it would take to go through normal retail distribution.

Disadvantages. Lack of "guaranteed" audience. High accountability can stifle creative experimentation; direct mail writers tend to play it safe and rely on proven formulas.

Which Medium Is the Best Buy of All?

With each type of media having its own unique characteristics in reach, audience selectivity, geographic flexibility, and costs, it is no wonder that choosing one can be a complex undertaking. A clear marketing strategy, however, will make selection easier. Remember, there is no such thing as "best media"; it all depends on the advertiser's goals—short and long range.

Based on national spending, the most popular of media with advertisers is newspaper, with television (network, local, and cable), direct mail, radio, general magazines, business papers, national outdoor, local outdoor, and farm publications following it, in that order.

Certain Types of Advertisers Show Marked Preferences for Certain Media Categories

Advertisers selling widely distributed products often choose network *television* as their favorite media vehicle. More regionally inclined advertisers may find local spot buying via independents, affiliates, or cable (they have close to 20 major cable networks to choose from, reaching over half of United States homes) more efficient. Combination of national and local television is often used by large packaged goods advertisers, with the latter gaining in popularity. Advertisers using television as their prime advertising medium are food, drugs, telephone service, toiletries, cosmetics, wine, beer, liquor, soft drinks, gasoline, soaps, cleansers, rubber tires, toys, and public service.

Newspapers are the media choice with advertisers reaching geographically definable trading areas. Major users are department stores, entertainment, restaurants, airlines (destination advertising), automobile dealers, local financial and insurance services, real estate, tobacco.

Magazines are popular with advertisers trying to reach identifiable demographic and psychographic segments of the population. Major users are fashion, toiletries, cosmetics, appliances, automotive, airlines, tobacco, electronics, office equipment, financial services, banks, telephone, farm equipment, health products and services, hotels, credit cards.

Radio does not call for large up-front investment and permits the advertiser to act expeditiously. Audience segmentation is possible by using different dayparts. Major users are retail stores, restaurants, entertainment, soft drinks, the U.S. government, retail, fashion, airlines.

Outdoor posters offer very specific geographic coverage. Advertisers appealing to a mass population within a given area opt for this medium. Major users are automotive, rubber tires, banks, real estate, soft drink, beer, airlines, hotels.

Direct Mail enables the advertiser to target his audience geographically, demographically, and psychographically as well as to seek out heavy and medium users and nonusers through the process of elimination. Major users of direct mail are retail stores, credit cards, insurance brokers, airlines, travel agencies, financial services.

Fix 'em, Then Mix 'em

Rarely do advertisers use a single medium to get their message across unless budgetary restraints force them to do so. Mixing media can be synergism at its most efficient.

Contrary to popular belief, repetition does work in advertising; people are accustomed to hear and see the same message more than once. At some point, of course, repetition becomes counterproductive, depending on the nature of the message, degree of exposure, and the creative approach. As a rule, a soft-sell, less intrusive commercial wears better than its more brazen counterpart. There are those who maintain that repetition helps the recipient to retain the message. Let your common sense be your guide. In today's environment, viewers show a lesser tolerance level, and they often have a remote control in hand to zip out or zap on to something else on the air. When reach/frequency reports suggest (how many people reached with each schedule how many times) the average viewer had been exposed to your message more than six times in a month, think about creating a new one or a change in schedule.

The chief advantage of showing the same message in different *types* of media is that such a mix allows the advertiser to expose his message several times but each time in a different environment. His advertising is reinforced and yet less likely to offend the sensibilities of the reader or listener.

This is why so many advertisers today prefer to advertise in several media. Often-used combinations are:

Television and Magazine. One shows the product in motion, the other does not. One conveys few specifics, the other provides opportunity to explain.

Magazine and Newspaper. One offers excellent color reproduction, the other does not. One "lasts," the other is more fleeting but has more immediacy.

Radio and Print. The audience hears one, sees the other.

Direct Mail and Television. Perhaps because the two media reach human consciousness in such different ways, this can be a powerful combination. Research shows that response to direct mail can be increased more than tenfold if supported by television messages during the mailing period.

Direct Mail and Telemarketing. A telephone call before or after the mailing greatly enhances the effectiveness of the mailing piece.

Media Mix Reach

60% REACHED   40% NOT REACHED

TELEVISION ONLY

30% REACHED   50% REACHED   20% NOT REACHED

MAGAZINES ONLY

60% REACHED   20% REACHED

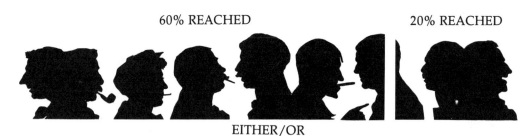

EITHER/OR

Combining media has several advantages. One is that groups not reached through one media may be tapped through another. And those who did see the message in one will now see it again, perhaps in another form (i.e. with coupon or recipe or long copy), receiving positive reinforcement. Media buyers have experience with various combinations and make professional cost-analysis comparisons.

	SEP	OCT	NOV	DEC	JAN	FEB	MAR	APR	MAY	JUN	JULY	AUG
PRIME AND FRINGE 10's (1100 GRPS)	600	300		-		100		100				
PRIME AND FRINGE 20's (800 GRPS)	300	200	100	-		100		100				
PRIME OR FRINGE 60's (1900 GRPS)	200	200	250	-	250	250	250	250	250			
DAYTIME 60's (1700 GRPS)	100	100	250	-	250	250	250	250	250			
TOTAL GRPS PER MONTH	1200	800	600	-	500	700	500	700	500			

DOLLAR TOTALS	Sept. - $541,062 Oct. - $361,228 Nov. - $245,837	Dec. - (Hiatus) Jan. - $181,563 Feb. - $291,954	Mar. - $181,563 Apr. - $291,954 May - $181,563		
BY QUARTER	$1,148,127 (50.4%)	$473,517 (20.8%)	$655,080 (28.8%)		

NEWSPAPERS
Roll-Out Area #1

	SEP	OCT	NOV	DEC	JAN	FEB	MAR	APR	MAY	JUN	JUL	AUG
LINEAGE* TOTAL: 10,200	FIRST QUARTER 2400			-	1200	600	1200	600	1200	1200	1200	600
FREE-STANDING INSERTS** (Sunday Papers)				-		X		X				X
CO-OP ADS (BG-25%) *** 13,545 Lines				—		4515		4515			4515	
COSTS	FIRST QUARTER $98,280			Dec. Hiatus Jan. - $49,140 Feb. - 70,792			Mar. - $49,140 Apr. - 46,222 May - 70,792			June - $49,140 July - 49,140 Aug. - 70,792		
COSTS BY QUARTER Total: $556,356	$98,280 (17.68%)			$119,932 (21.56%)			$169,072 (30.38%)			$169,072 (30.38%)		
COVERAGE	a. 59 markets (56 in top 175 - 3 in supplementary b. 11,057,000 total circulation c. Covering 70% of food sales and 90% of TV households d. 70% (avg.) penetration metro households in each market											

* Lineage shown by month to be distributed according to ad size.
** Insert in Sunday newspapers carried by 74 papers in 56 markets.
*** Bonus Gifts 25% share amounts to $46,222 each insertion.

All media schedules include such important data as reach, total linage, frequency, costs, gross rating points, circulation, size or length of ads, percentage of households covered in the area, and other information, if needed. Breakdowns may cover six months to a year. Such plans are important to media buyers who must look for buys or "avails" in advance.

Now You See It, Now You Don't

An important consideration in the preparation of a media schedule is the exact timing of the commercials or print ads. These are the factors to take into account:

Timeliness. This usually has to do with sales trends; i.e. air conditioners are more in demand in the summer, electric blankets more in the winter. But opportuneness also comes into play when advertising relates to a particular event (nation's 200th birthday, Christmas, back to school), selling peaks (riding on a fad, tying in with a hit song), or synergism with other selling efforts (special promotions, store sales).

Flighting Patterns

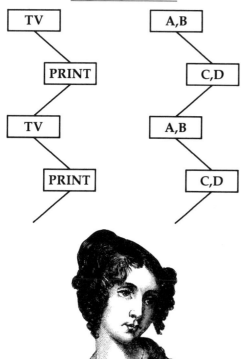

One of the best ways to increase advertising mileage is to alternate media — using either different stations or publications in the same campaign, or changing from television to print and vice versa.

Strategy of "Flighting" vs. "Continuous" vs. "Pulsing." These terms refer to the advertiser's method of scheduling his messages. No break occurs in a continuous advertising schedule. Using the flighting method, the advertiser alternates between activity and inactivity in his advertising. Total inactivity may last from a few weeks to several months. Pulsing refers to the combination of the two concepts. Continuous base of advertising is augmented by periods of intense advertising activity. It should be emphasized here that the impact of advertising does not cease immediately with the discontinuation of the campaign. Depending on the impact of the creative, messages may linger on in people's minds for a long time, perhaps longer than it is generally thought.

Take these slogans, for example:

You have a friend at Chase Manhattan.

Does she — or doesn't she?

Winston tastes good, like a cigarette should.

Getting there is half the fun.

Good to the last drop.

It's the real thing. "Coke."

Join the people who joined the Army.

Promise her anything, but give her Arpège.

These campaigns had their successful runs years ago. Yet they are still remembered. The same holds true of outstanding advertising campaigns. Commercials such as Wendy's "Where's the Beef?," Alka Seltzer's "I can't believe I ate the whole thing," Mennen Skin Bracer's "Thanks, I needed that," Federal Express's fast-talking pitchman, and print ads such as those done for Volkswagen, Hathaway Shirts, Maidenform Bra, Blackglama ("What becomes a Legend most?") make a long-lasting impact, giving the advertiser maximum return on his investment.

Flighting vs. Continuous Advertising

A

B

Advertising does not have to be continuous to achieve optimum effectiveness. On the contrary, a brief hiatus may build up to a strong "comeback" as well as affect important savings at the same time. Memories have surprisingly long staying power.

To Advertise Where Business Is — or Where Business Is Not?

Obviously, this question comes up early in media planning. Decisions on the right approach must be made on practical, not philosophical grounds. Either approach can be used successfully if the circumstances are right.

Sales are easier (and less expensive) to generate where the business is. This is essentially a defensive posture; the advertiser simply gains more customers where the product is already established.

Opening a new market is altogether a different matter. Here the advertiser is trying to change basic buying habits, perhaps induce major brand switching, and there is a good chance competition will fight the intrusion. Retailers must be persuaded to carry the product, and this, as pointed out before, can be an expensive proposition. Intensive media backing is usually necessary. The stakes are high, however, and expense notwithstanding, marketers are often willing to take the risk. There is no faster way to increase sales than to find new, hitherto unexplored markets for the product.

Measuring Media Effectiveness

The best source of information on media effectiveness has always been media itself. This is collected both by in-house research and syndicated outside services and is made available to advertisers, ad, and advertising agencies. Some of the best-known research firms to furnish syndicated data are A. C. Nielsen, Arbitron, Simmons (SMRB), AGB Television Research (people meters), Market Opinion Research, SRI International, R. L. Polk, Starch INRA Hooper, Birch Radio, and Market Facts.

The annual figures on net paid circulation supplied by the Audit Bureau of Circulation (A.B.C.) are routinely used to substantiate the publisher's statement for the preceding 12 months. This organization uses its own editors to verify claims made by its member publications. It also audits direct mail "response" lists and poster plants.

Other sources furnishing information (in case you are unable to get it through your media representative) are Business Publications Audit of Circulation, Traffic Audit Bureau, National Association of Transportation Advertising, Direct Mail Advertising Association, American Newspaper Publishers Association, Advertising Research Foundation, American Business Press, the American Association of Advertising Agencies, and various libraries.

Miscellaneous information also appears on the rate cards issued by media: mechanical requirements, method of printing, acceptability of mats and duplicate plates in the case of magazines and newspapers; time costs for various hours, station facilities such as library services, newsroom and talent-bureau service, identity of stations comprising the network in the case of radio and television; copy regulations, types of products and services not acceptable for advertising, discounts, and related details. The data is

235

reproduced in Standard Rate & Data Service reference volumes.

Some of the projects measuring media effectiveness are ongoing; others are ad hoc, or customized to the needs of the user. Each research organization uses its own system in gathering data, to which it has proprietary rights. The focus may be on various aspects of audience composition, quantitative or qualitative, gained through telephone surveys, focus group interviews, sales movements, scanners that read UPC bars on packaged goods, household diaries, coupon redemption, polls, controlled mail panels, home and field interviews, and readership studies. Many of the organizations maintain their own software systems to analyze the data; others make use of common data bases; still others use both methods.

For the most part, advertisers are interested in finding out if their advertising in a medium has been

— noticed

— comprehended

— remembered

— induces product purchase

— is identified with the sponsor

The advertiser's ability to measure response varies with the medium. Quantitative data is easier to obtain than qualitative data, especially in case of mass media. The following provides some insights in this respect:

Television audience is the most difficult to measure qualitatively. The traditional Nielsen ratings provide only desultory demographic and no psychographic information. A more accurate viewer profile is available through the people meter method, where information is fed into computers via phone lines and can be read the following day. The method reveals *by whom* (mother, father, children), *when* (is the viewer in the room during commercial breaks?), and *how often* the program is watched. Techniques are available to correlate viewing habits with product purchases.

Such an approach to measuring viewership is the product of our times. As mentioned earlier, narrow-casting and home video ownership enabled viewers to become more selective in programs. The old nose-counting method has been met with increased criticism by advertisers looking for segmented special-interest audiences.

Magazines and newspapers offer both quantitative and qualitative information. In addition, it is possible to measure readership of an ad in comparison to others in the same publication. The best known research group furnishing these reports is Starch INRA Hooper with its Advertisement Research Service. Through techniques of "instant recognition" and "aided recall," the effectiveness of ads in the publication are rated by their "attention values": noted, seen-associated, and read-most. Ratings are given in terms of percentages.

Radio listenership is difficult to measure. In general, radio reaches about 92 million adults, radio network about 28 million. The best research about the audience composition is prepared by the medium itself.

Posters are evaluated on the basis on "effective circulation"; i.e. the estimated percentage of people passing by the display per day. Values are also given to space positions. High-traffic areas command a higher price.

Direct mail is the most measurable medium of all. Number of responses and size of orders in relation to advertising costs indicates effectiveness of the mailing.

Six Money-Saving Caveats for the Astute Media Purchaser

While information about media is highly regulated by the industry, not all is gold that glitters in the media world. Competition is keen and in the heat of negotiations, facts and fiction often become one.

Here are just some of the gray areas:

Circulation Figures. Circulation figures may comprise both "paid" and "unpaid" (given away free) magazines. Be wary of figures that include pass-along readership. While this can be important, "total" readership (the sum of paid and unpaid circulation) does not lend itself to easy verification. Some publications claim two or three times as many readers as indicated in their A.B.C. audited figures. That may be so. Then again, it may not.

Subscription vs. Single-Copy Sales. In most cases, subscription figures are the most accurate criterion to the advertiser looking for guaranteed readership. Single-copy sales — most of which occur at newsstands — fluctuate, depending on the news, weather, economy, and vacation schedules. Magazines with large newsstand circulation will present their case in a positive light ("Our readers go out of their way to buy the magazine so they are sure to read it" or "Who knows what happens to the magazine at home?") but listen to their story carefully. How many issues have they really sold? What is their average return rate (it could be as high as 40% to 50%). Are they using print runs as the basis for their circulation claim? Is a one-time offer or a special premium responsible for the sudden upsurge in sales? Ask about rebates paid when the publication is unable to live up to its guaranteed circulation figure. The trend is away from newsstand sales; the proportion of copies sold through subscription almost doubled in the last ten years.

Be Skeptical of Too Many "Firsts." Almost any publication can claim leadership in this area or that. But how important is their "first in . . . " to you? Do you really care if a certain gardening magazine can show a higher percentage of miniature-poodle owners among its readers than any other gardening magazine? Probably not — unless you sell miniature poodles.

There's no substitute.

Media advertising is an excellent — and by and large reliable — source of information about the media itself. Almost every advertising vehicle has its own unique claim to fame. The question to ask: How important is media's claim in *selling* your product.

GENERAL
DISPLAY RATES

	B&W	2-Color	4-Color
Full Page	$36,215	$43,340	$48,735
2/3 Page	25,350	30,935	36,530
Digest Page	21,810	25,900	31,695
1/2 Page	21,810	25,900	31,695
1/3 Page	13,605	17,760	24,380
1/6 Page	7,650	13,260	—
Second Cover			58,155
Third Cover			51,220
Fourth Cover			63,215

Maximum earnable volume discount: 30%.

Bleed: Covers and 4-Color units: +15%. Black & white and 2-Color units: +10%. No additional charge for gutter bleeds.

Discounts on cumulative pages within a 12-month consecutive period:

6 Pages— 5%	30 Pages—22½%	54 Pages—28%
12 Pages—10%	36 Pages—25%	60 Pages—29%
18 Pages—14%	42 Pages—26%	72 Pages—30%
24 Pages—18%	48 Pages—27%	

Consecutive page discount: Contact nearest sales office for eligibility requirements and applicable discount.

COSMO
STYLE &
SUBSTANCE

Bold, graphic, powerful, new. Cosmo is the leader in the young women's field.

- 23 years of consecutive revenue and circulation increases.
- More single-copy sales at a higher cover price than any other magazine.
- #1 best seller on college campuses for the last six years.
- 2,864,343 total paid circulation—greater than any other young women's magazine.
- Cosmo's readers spend nearly $5 million at the newsstand every month.
- They spend 106 minutes—at home—reading Cosmo every month.
- Guaranteed delivery: Cosmo delivers a bonus circulation of 364,343 monthly.
- The Cosmopolitan girl has power: She knows more, does more, earns more, spends more.

Credible, complete Cosmo: The refreshing, original lifestyle magazine for today's young women, giving monthly inspiration for expanding life's possibilities.

REGIONAL RATES

		JUNE 1987			
REGION		ABC	B&W	2-Color	4-Color
1.	Northeast	176,186	$ 9,655	$10,835	$14,310
2.*	Mid-Atlantic	721,738	18,805	21,090	24,445
2a.	New York State	232,336	15,260	17,125	19,165
1&2.	Combination	897,924	20,620	23,135	29,570
3.	South	470,680	9,655	10,835	14,310
1-2-3.	Combination	1,368,604	29,570	32,840	41,095
4.	Central	519,252	18,805	21,090	24,445
5.	Mountain	164,814	9,655	10,835	14,310
6.	Southwest	325,786	9,655	10,835	14,310
7.*	Pacific Coast	485,887	18,805	21,090	24,445
7a.	California	360,900	17,760	19,930	21,475

*2. includes Foreign and Canada (except below).
*7. includes Alberta and British Columbia, Canada.

Only full page units accepted.
15% discount on two or more regions in same issue
(combinations excepted).

MAIL ORDER DISPLAY ADVERTISING RATES

	B&W	2-Color	4-Color
Page	$31,930	$36,285	$44,135
2/3 Page	22,355	25,900	33,065
1/2 Page	19,250	21,690	28,695
1/3 Page	11,995	14,865	22,075

All mail order units smaller than 1/3 page must run in the Shopper Section or take the General Display rate.

All mail order advertisers, except those selling personalized services, agree to refund the full price of any item they have advertised to dissatisfied readers who return that item promptly and unused.

Advertisers using post office box numbers must supply COSMOPOLITAN with their business office street address for its files.

The publisher's decision is final on eligibility of mail order copy to appear in COSMOPOLITAN.

SHOPPER SECTION
Available to eligible advertisers. Contact nearest sales office for details.

SPECIAL RATES

FASHION RETAIL, STORE/DEALER LISTINGS
Available to eligible advertisers. Contact nearest sales office for details.

TRAVEL & HOTEL
Available to eligible advertisers. Contact nearest sales office for details.

HEARST WOMAN POWER
Additional discounts over and above regular volume discounts can be earned by COSMOPOLITAN's national advertisers who qualify for Hearst Magazines Woman Power and cross-over programs. For details, contact your nearest sales office or The Corporate Advertising Sales Department. (212) 262-5775.

SHORT RATES & REBATES

Advertisers will be short-rated if the space upon which billings have been based is not used within the 12-month contract period. Advertisers will be rebated if they have used the space required within the 12-month contract period to earn a lower rate.

COMMISSION & CASH DISCOUNTS

Agency commission: 15%.

Cash discount: 2% of net if paid by 24th of month preceding cover date. Net due 30 days from invoice date.

Billing: Bills rendered 10 days prior to cash discount date. All advertising payments acceptable in U.S. funds only.

Direct orders: Orders direct from advertisers subject to payment before closing date of issue purchased.

Advertising agencies are fully responsible for all advertisements ordered by them.

CLOSING DATES

January	October 23, 1987
February*	November 24, 1987
March*	December 23, 1987
April*	January 22, 1988
May	February 25, 1988
June	March 25, 1988
July	April 25, 1988
August	May 25, 1988
September	June 24, 1988
October	July 25, 1988
November	August 25, 1988
December*	September 23, 1988
January	October 24, 1988

*Earlier Closing Dates

All insertion orders and materials must be at COSMOPOLITAN by closing. Requested positions could be affected by late arrival of materials.

MECHANICAL REQUIREMENTS

Publication trim size: 8" x 10-7/8".
Binding: Perfect.
Column depth: 143 agate lines, 3 columns to a page.
Minimum display space: 35 agate lines, single column.

FILM SIZES

Non-Bleed	Width	Length
Full Page	7"	10-3/16"
2/3 Page Vertical	4-5/8"	10-3/16"
1/2 Page Horizontal	7"	5-1/16"
1/2 Page Vertical	3-7/16"	10-3/16"
Digest Page	4-3/8"	6-1/2"
1/3 Page Vertical	2-1/4"	10-3/16"
1/3 Page Square	4-5/8"	5-1/16"
Spread	14-3/4"	10-3/16"

Bleed		
Full Page	8-1/8"	11-1/8"
2/3 Page Vertical	5-1/4"	11-1/8"
1/2 Page Horizontal	8-1/8"	5-9/16"
1/2 Page Vertical	3-15/16"	11-1/8"
Digest Page	5-5/8"	7-11/16"
1/3 Page Vertical	2-3/4"	11-1/8"
1/3 Page Square	5-1/4"	5-9/16"
Spread	16-1/4"	11-1/8"

Necessary clearance for live matter on top, bottom and sides is 3/8" from the bleed edge. Hairline precision of folding, binding and trimming is impossible; these clearances are essential.

Specifications for Web Offset Printing (SWOP) standards are to be followed.

Film required: Offset Negatives Right Reading Emulsion Side Up. Negatives should be hard-dot contacts with no corrective etching. All film should be a dimensionally stable base, .004".

Screen lines: B&W halftones should be 110 line screen. 4-Color should be 120 or 133 (maximum) line screen.

4-Color density: Total density of shadow areas not to exceed 280% with only one color being solid.

Crop marks: In film and on proof. One ruled proof showing cropping instructions should be included.

Proofs: Four (4) proofs and four (4) progs with color bars should be submitted with the film. Proofs must be pulled head to foot. Proofing sequence is yellow, magenta, cyan and black. Ink densities to match SWOP color reference bars with a plus or minus tolerance of no more than .05.

5th Colors: Day-glo, gold and silver available. Contact nearest sales office for details.

SPECIAL UNITS & SPLITS
Postcards, gatefolds, booklets and other special units available in limited numbers. Perfect A/B splits, A/B batching, random, geographical splits available. Contact nearest sales office for details.

Inquiries regarding mechanical requirements and reproduction and specifications for furnished cards and inserts available from the Production Department. (212) 262-6962.

All offset materials should be sent to the Advertising Production Department, COSMOPOLITAN, 224 W. 57th St., New York, NY 10019.

All material not ordered returned, in writing, will be destroyed 12 months after last use.

CONTRACT CONDITIONS

1. Orders must specifically state issues and space to be used.

2. Orders may not be cancelled or changed after the closing date without acknowledgement of the publisher.

3. All covers and special units are non-cancellable. Postcards and inserts may not be cancelled less than 60 days prior to regular closing date.

4. The publisher shall not be bound to requests for specific positions other than covers and special units and has the right to determine actual position.

5. Advertising orders and schedules are accepted for a specific product or line of products and may not be substituted with other products or subsidiary companies without the publisher's consent.

6. Copy resembling editorial will be labelled "advertisement" by COSMOPOLITAN, at its discretion.

7. COSMOPOLITAN reserves the right to decline or reject any advertising for any reason at any time without liability, even if said advertising had been previously acknowledged and accepted.

8. COSMOPOLITAN will not be bound by conditions of any nature on order blanks or copy instructions submitted by or on behalf of the advertiser when such conditions conflict with any provision in its Rate Card or with its policies.

9. The advertiser and its agency, if there be one, each represents that it is fully authorized and licensed to use (i) the names and/or the portraits or pictures of persons, living or dead, or of things, (ii) any trademarks, copyrighted or otherwise private material and (iii) any testimonials, contained in any advertisement submitted by or on behalf of the advertiser and published in COSMOPOLITAN and that such advertisement is not libelous, an invasion of privacy or otherwise unlawful as to any third party.

As part of the consideration and to induce COSMOPOLITAN to publish such advertisement, the advertiser and its agency, if there be one, each agrees to indemnify and save harmless The Hearst Corporation, publisher of COSMOPOLITAN, against all loss, liability, damage and expense of whatsoever nature arising out of copying, printing or publishing of such advertisement.

10. All orders are accepted subject to acts of God, fires, strikes, accidents or other occurrences beyond publisher's control (whether like or unlike any of those enumerated herein) which prevent publisher from partially or completely producing, publishing or distributing COSMOPOLITAN.

11. COSMOPOLITAN is not responsible and will allow no rebate for errors in key numbers.

12. Quoted rates do not include merchandising allowance.

13. Rates and conditions subject to change without notice.

In addition to rate cards, media is usually well-equipped to provide conventional information to advertisers, such as mechanical page requirements, statistical information about the audience, closing dates, and contract conditions. Rate structures call for careful scrutiny. Size, color, regional coverage, mail order display discounts, special rates, rebates, commission, and cash discounts are important factors. Shown here are pages of Cosmopolitan's pocket-sized ten-page rate card brochure.

Frequency in Itself Does Not Necessarily Connote a Larger Audience. For the cost of a single 30-second commercial shown during a successful prime-time program it is possible to buy over 300 one-minute spots in the wee hours of the morning. But what about the number of viewers?

Don't Let the Medium Talk You into Making Apples-and-Oranges Comparisons. Circulation vs. circulation is meaningful only if the medium reaches exactly the same kind of audience. But that rarely is the case. Readers of *Playboy* are not the same as those of *Penthouse,* at least not psychographically; viewers of car races not the same as viewers of horse races; readers of *Prevention Magazine* not the same as *Let's Live; Ms.* not the same as *New Woman.*

Ask About Rebates. More and more media offer credits to advertisers when the audience reached falls below the guidelines of the original purchase, whether in circulation (in print) or viewership (on television). Fewer copies sold in a given areas is the basis for the former, ratings shortfall for the latter.

Rate Cards Are Never Carved in Stone. Prices are almost always negotiable, both in broadcast *and* print. Try buying in bulk. Or up front. Then sit down with your representative and try negotiating the lowest rate available.

To Sum It Up

By far the largest part of advertising expenditure is spent on purchasing media. Increased segmentation has made selection more exacting than ever. Buying the right communication vehicle is left almost completely in the hands of experts today — the media buyers.

Comparing one medium with another has become increasingly complex, an art that calls for both personal experience and highly sophisticated computer science. Reach, coverage, and circulation are still key factors but by no means the sole criteria of media effectiveness. Qualitative data — the geographic, demographic, and, most of all, psychographic composition of the audience — are just as important in judging the CPM and other criteria.

"Major" media are television, newspaper, magazine, radio, outdoor posters, and direct mail. The last group is not "commissionable" and for that reason, agencies were slow in embracing it. Its fast growth, however, has changed all that. Today it is getting top attention, and deservedly so.

Each medium type has its own creative advantages and disadvantages. Writers and artists are quick to take note of this, and in some cases, it pays to solicit their opinions.

Sophisticated research tools are available in this day and age to measure the impact of media not only on the consumer's psyche but also his or her propensity to buy the advertised product as a direct result of advertising. Media usually provides well-researched and detailed background of its audience; much information is available through syndicated service organizations. Along with this data, advertisers develop research projects of their own to verify media effectiveness. Sales figures, still, are the most important yardstick.

12
People Are Products, Too

The marketing of an individual is, deep down, really not that different from that of a product. In the hands of an expert, the two approaches show striking similarities.

The PPP formula mentioned on page 157 applies here as well, only at this time it stands for Person (*not* Product)—Perception—People.

As with the product, the connecting "P," Perception, offers the marketer the greatest flexibility.

Can Perception of a Person Be Changed at Will?

Yes, except for this reminder: it is easier to change people's impressions of a product than of a person. That is because people know people. We learn about products by way of books, articles, television, and hearsay. But when it comes to people, we learn to rely on our own judgment of signals received from others: their facial expressions, speech mannerisms, body language, and last but not least, verbal messages. From infancy on, we have been programmed to form opinions about people, beginning with Mom, Dad, and the family, and then extending to everyone we meet. All of us become people experts; we are not easily fooled. Nature has given us that gift.

Your Company Spoken Here

The person you choose to represent your company (or product)—model, actor, spokesperson, person on the street—must reflect its image, whatever that is or should be. He or she must be a correct choice to deliver the message. Thus, a maker of a high-priced car wishing to address affluent buyers—say, the "old money" set—may use a person in his forties or fifties who is obviously comfortable with his wealth to deliver the message; while someone reaching the young and upwardly mobile would do better with a babyboomer in his thirties. Old rich and new rich are interchangeable demographically (they both have money) but not psychographically.

Thoughtful selection of characters should not be confused with stereotyping. The old-rich representative does not have to look like the "typical" old rich; he may be a devil at heart with a gleam of mischief in his eyes, for example, wearing sweatshirt and jeans. A beer-guzzling "type" may be wearing a necktie and display a vocabulary exceeding two dozen words. Effective commercials are as subtle in their choice of talent as they are in all other aspects of execution. Always, there is plenty of room between one obvious choice and another. The beef industry has hired Cybil Shepherd and James Garner to represent its "real food for real people"; a likeable pair obviously admired by nearly everyone on the demographic ladder. In a commercial with an egalitarian message, it is all right—sometimes even preferable—for the announcer to be a nondescript personality. Isuzu hired little-known actor David Leisure to act as a consummate dispenser of the hyperbole in his pitch. In such cases, it is not really the spokesperson who dominates the scene, but rather the message itself. Typically, television director Joe Sedelmaier, known for his uncanny knack of discovering talent, keeps a file of over 1,000 "ordinary" people, most of them without professional acting experience; his commercials for such clients as Federal Express, Subaru, Wendy's, and many others, lack all class consciousness.

Here are a few reminders for those casting a spokesperson:

Older People Carry More Authority. Depending on the message, you may want a voice of maturity. There is comfort in the avuncular likes of the Walter Cronkites of the world.

The Male of the Species Still Rules the Rostrum. Feminists will disagree but research tells us that both male and female viewers prefer a spokesman over a spokeswoman when it comes to delivering factual information. Women do better when appealing to emotions, as for example in promoting a social cause, family, or products for children.

Peers Attract Peers. In some cases it is imperative that the performer show intimate familiarity—real or imagined—with his audience's preferences. Young people, for example, may want to see one of their own speak for them about vacations or fashion trends.

Beauty and the Beast. There is a school of thought that an ordinary-looking housewife is more likely to appeal to the average person—himself or herself less than glamorous. However there is evidence that this is by no means true in the majority of cases. Both men and women would rather see the person of their dreams. Ratings of soap operas, sitcoms, and variety shows climb under the influence of beauty on the screen. Most television viewers have no particular desire to watch a replay of events they have experienced in the office, factory, or on the street. Not surprisingly, glamour cuts across differences in gender. Women are fascinated by the beauty of their own sex, too, and readily identify with it.

Look at the Total Person. Appearance is one thing; personality is quite another. An actor should be able to be what the script calls for; that is the mark of the profession. Clothes, makeup, and quality of voice all work toward the creation of a character. Speech does not have to be overly polished; ours is a nation of accents and dialects. At times, it actually helps to sound less than perfect.

Go for First Impressions. Not much time to develop a character in 15 to 30 seconds on television; the first few seconds set the tone.

How "Real" Should Real People Really Be?

"Slice-of-life" commercials were discovered more than two decades ago, and have lost little of their popularity. Today, they are more apt to appear in form of testimonials given by "real" people. All things being equal, such cinéma vérité commercials rank high on believability.

Testimonials, of course, rarely are given unsolicited. More often than not, they are the product of several rehearsals, careful coaching, and generous editing—much like the "spontaneous" happenings on prerecorded television game shows. It bears mention that as deliberate as such commercials may be, they are wholly within the letter of the law (and self-regulatory restraints of the industry) as long as they do not misrepresent the product. The difficulties, if any, with the approach are rarely conceptual; rather they can be traced to faulty or indifferent execution. The power of the testimonial commercials lies in their straightforwardness. Viewers are quick to spot pretense.

A few pointers to keep in mind:

Actors Are Usually Better at Conveying the Sense of a "Real" Person than Is a Real Person. Inexperienced subjects may freeze in the presence of the camera and crew or tend to overact to instructions in trying to please. Smiles grow too wide, voices rise to a high pitch, gestures become as sweeping as the diva's at curtain call. Trained actors have learned to overcome these all-too-human tendencies and so turn in a more authentic interpretation of a person caught unawares.

Pick Your Interviewer as Carefully as You Do the Interviewee. Techniques vary among interviewers; nervousness begets nervousness, shouters beget shouters. The Johnny Carsons, Larry Kings, and Diane Sawyers are hard to find but it pays to look for their type. The best interviewers are those who know how to relax and have an innate sense for fun. Genuinely curious about what others have to say, they make good listeners.

Four Ways to Set Your Guest's Mind at Ease. Chat with him before the interview. Tell him he is on tape and the "bad parts" will be edited out. Offer a cup of coffee, or even a glass of wine, to eliminate stage fright. Always laugh at his jokes, on- *or* off-camera.

Have a Limo Pick Him Up. Looking for the address of the studio adds stress to an already stressful situation. Besides, if he doesn't find the place, you're reduced to a monologue.

Take at Least Five Times the Footage You Plan to Use. That will give you a chance to edit out the bloopers. Ten times is even better.

Hide the Camera If at All Possible. That goes for the crew, too. Look for the Alan Funts and Frederick Wisemans of the industry, masters of the technique.

Check the Conditions Before the Shot, Not After. That includes lighting, camera angles, and sound—even "white" background noise. (Sometimes, you may want that for realism.) Go through the motions with the actor.

Don't Follow a Script to the Letter, Unless You Have to. Let things "happen." You may be pleasantly surprised. Actors are especially good at improvising.

The Great American Celebrity Hunt

In our people-oriented culture, most of us thrive vicariously on big names, be they in entertainment, athletics, business, or politics. We tend to bestow almost magical powers on those we put on the pedestal, soliciting opinions on secrets of a happy marriage from a seven-times-divorced actress, solutions to our growing crime rate from a lifer, and insights on literature from a quarterback collaborating on his autobiography.

No question, notoriety—which by the fact itself generates media exposure—sells products. But here again, the demographics and psychographics of the audience must be taken into account. Not *every* viewer believes *everything* he or she hears, no matter how rich and famous the source.

High-income (and presumably better-educated) viewers can be a particularly skeptical lot. Words of many baseball players, race car drivers, bowling champions, soap opera stars, and practitioners of unconventional medicine may fall on deaf ears here.

Performers listed in order of their ability to convince the largest segment of television audiences are shown (the most effective ones are on top) next. Both lists are a composite of findings published in *American Demographics*.

ATHLETES	PERFORMERS
Golfers	TV news anchors
Olympic winners	TV show hosts
Gymnasts	Beauty queens
Tennis players	Country singers
Track stars	Actors
Hockey players	Animal trainers
Car racers	Magicians
Football playcrs	Dancers
Baseball players	Singers
Basketball players	Comedians
Boxers	Rock musicians
Wrestlers	Hypnotists

A number of surveys have been conducted to find out which profession rates the highest with the U.S. public in terms of credibility. Results change regularly, but usually doctors, the clergy, and scientists lead the pack. Near the bottom are used-car salesmen and retail store operators. Others with credibility above the median are accountants, teachers, police officers, business executives, and pharmacists. Below are factory workers, salespersons, clothing store operators, and auto mechanics. Lawyers (and legislators, too) move up and down the line in roller-coaster fashion, depending on yesterday's news.

The Art of Being Oneself

The most effective spokespersons are those who represent their own personal attitudes, feelings, life-styles. If their views are widely known, so much the better. Alert advertisers are quick to spot heroes in the making whether or not their achievements happen to be covered by major media at the moment. Newspaper and magazine articles (even in the *National Inquirer*), talk shows, local newscasts, or even everyday gossip help locate such people.

Tie-ins between the product and a particular deed do not always have to be directly related; as always, a touch of subtlety adds to the intrigue. The well-publicized climber of the tallest skyscraper in town could be your next spokesman for a breakfast cereal; a designated kicker on a football team could speak of remedies for athlete's foot; a 100-year-old man or woman for yogurt; a Japanese driver for an American-made car.

Authors, scientists, inventors, and other experts usually receive less media exposure, perhaps because of their own sense of privacy. Nevertheless, they too can be powerful movers of products. Possible lack of slick presentation skills is more than made up by the authority that comes from their knowledge of the subject. The president of SpokesSearch, a firm that specializes in finding expert spokesmen, regularly visits bookstores to find out who has written a book on what. "Almost everybody can be bought," she says with a smile.

Successful ads have also been built around imaginary but well-known characters, such as the Road Runner, Flintstones, Count Dracula, Peanuts, Popeye, King Kong, and even the hunchback of Notre Dame. The past is heavily populated with heroes and nonheroes waiting to be cast. Samson is available to opine on hair growth as is Lady Godiva riding through town; Cleopatra is ready to offer her services for eye makeup; William Tell and Sir Isaac Newton know their apples; Mary Poppins is an expert on umbrellas; Rip Van Winkle is surely the world's greatest authority on getting a good night's sleep.

Famous people are usually known for their political, religious, professional, or humanitarian beliefs by way of media coverage. Entertainers often espouse social causes that are close to their hearts. Sensitive to the feelings of others and in a profession that bases much of its material on the human condition, their statements have the ring of truth.

The PPP theory (page 157) holds its own, if in a slightly modified version, in the promotion of people, too. "P" on the left stands for the Person, not the Product. Most amenable to change, as always, is the center "P" symbolizing Perception. Personalities can be positioned in public conciousness by way of consistent advertising just as products are. A word of caution: people are more sensitive to people than inanimate objects, and quickly sense chicanery.

One of the most effective spokesmen for his company in recent times has been Lee Iacocca, CEO of the Chrysler Corporation. Though reluctant at first to appear on television, it soon became apparent that his was just the right personality to embody all that his company stood for. A scrappy, second-generation American, the "car guy" executive had become a genuine folk hero. His first book sold nearly 7 million copies worldwide, bringing him over 70,000 letters from readers identifying with his point of view. Sensing his immense popular appeal, agency Kenyon & Eckhard insisted that he return to the television screen again and again, even after Chrysler's miraculous recovery from near bankruptcy. No one else would be able to duplicate the impact of his appearances; his was an impossible act to follow.

Wilt Chamberlain Cardmember since 1976
Willie Shoemaker Cardmember since 1966

Membership
has its privileges."

Don't leave home without it."
Call 1-800-THE-CARD to apply.

Who is using the product is as important to some people as *how* and *why* it is used. In its "portraits" campaign — the ultimate in simplicity and restraint — American Express takes full advantage of this human trait. Ogilvy & Mather created the campaign, one of the most successful of its genre.

"Lingerie does a lot for a woman. Not to mention what it does for a man. I love a woman who says how she feels. But I also love a woman who has secrets. In fact, it's what she keeps to herself that says the most about her. Lingerie. That's a secret she doesn't share with the world. So sometimes you don't find out. But, then again, sometimes you do."
Maidenform offers women over 150 ways to express themselves. And obviously, people are listening.

MAIDENFORM

No product shot here — just a succinct explanation of what it "means." The fact that a good-looking guy like Corbin Bernsen is offering the explanation doesn't hurt the cause, not in the least. A man is presenting *his* point of view, but in a way she likes to hear. Levin, Huntley, Schmidt & Beaver explored the approach; Maidenform had the courage to run it.

"I have no excuses. I just wear them."
—Donna Rice

Notoriety—in any form—gets attention. Never-missing-a-beat, Kirshenbaum & Baum quickly cashed in on this in their wordly-wise ad for "No Excuses" sportswear. Publicity surrounding Donna Rice's encounter with presidential aspirant Gary Hart inspired the line: "I have no excuses." When the dust had finally settled for good, the agency chose another spokeswoman to speak for the product.

Having established herself as America's favorite pop-psychologist and everyone's dream mother, Dr. Ruth seemed as good a choice to speak to young users of Smith Corona typewriters as anyone. Says she in her distinctive voice: "You think you've got problems. I've got one, too. It's psychological—I just misspelled it . . ." Rosenfeld Sirowitz & Humphrey put her and her words on television.

What Every Advertiser Should Know About the Likeability Factor

Important to advertisers is the fact that according to various polls some personalities are more popular than others (even in the same field) with the general public. Such people are the most persuasive. The performer's intimate knowledge of the subject is not necessarily what dazzles his audience, but other factors, most having to do more with the heart than the head. It is difficult to define exactly what makes these people—or anyone else, for that matter—"likeable," but some common traits emerge:

Relaxed Attitude Before the Camera. Some performers are "born" with the knack of establishing contact with their television audience; all television announcers have it.

Indisposition to Take Oneself Too Seriously. Sense of perspective about oneself, even while in the limelight, is an endearing quality.

Being Yourself. We mention this again because it is so important. Viewers know the difference between put-on acting and the real person.

Consistently high on television commercial popularity charts at this time are Bill Cosby, Bob Hope, Alan Alda, Johnny Carson, Michael Fox, Lionel Ritchie, Willard Scott (the weatherman), Karl Malden, Cliff Robertson, O. J. Simpson, and Arnold Palmer.

Putting the CEO on Television

More and more companies have their own top executive speak for them. There are two reasons for taking this approach or, rather, "allowing" it, as one creative director puts it. One is personal ego, pure and simple. Mass media promises mass exposure. Television has an allure all its own; a single commercial on national television may reach over a million times as many people as does the average play in a Broadway theatre and about five times as many as an average movie. For a business executive seeking recognition for personal, business, or political reasons, the home screen could yet be his best window on the world.

The other reason lies in the ability of a CEO to "humanize" the corporation he represents, by his presence to turn an abstraction into a flesh-and-blood reality. Few executives can match the flair of a Frank Perdue or Lee Iacocca and yet they can still do remarkably well in their new role. They rank high on credibility; the average viewer is grateful for the opportunity to see the head of the organization. Few actors are able to hold viewers' attention as well as corporate presidents, though this may have more to do with the top executive's office than with showmanship.

Good delivery and ability to memorize a script, to move with authority, and to redo the same scene over and over without showing signs of fatigue or impatience can expedite the shoot, of course, but slickness does not guarantee success. Here, too, personality is more important than professional polish.

Many commercials featuring a top executive have succeeded on the basis of the likeability factor alone. Sentiment is laid on thick at times, with scenes showing the CEO with his family or among his employees, but that is hardly the point. If he comes across as a warm human being, devoid of the trappings of his office, then chances are he will be liked—and heard.

Interestingly enough, the average viewer has some fairly fixed (and biased) notions as to the kind of executive he feels comfortable with. When Allen G. Rosenshine, then president of BBDO International, showed pictures of men with all possible combinations of facial hair, baldness, and eyeglasses, he found that those considered the best leaders were older, without facial hair (no beards, no mustaches), and, with only one exception, glassless. The same study showed that on changing one man's hair color from black to gray, his aggregate score for presidential ("I believe him") went up from 33% to 67%.

It should be noted here that dignity counts, but not for every product. The histrionic—sometimes downright rowdy—performance of, say, the owner of a local car dealership may seem hokey amateur theatre to some, if not all, viewers. But that does not mean he does not reach them. If they accept the person on the screen for what he is—and people usually do—they may still end up driving the car out of the showroom. As an advertising man once said of just such a commercial: "He is so bad, he's good."

Finding the right designer is difficult.
Let us select one for you.

The **Designer Referral Service** can save you the time often wasted meeting with designers who are as inappropriate for you personally, as they are for your budget, style and taste. We offer a no cost home or office interview to assess your particular needs and recommend the best **Interior Designer** or **Architect** for you and your project.

- Representing over 100 of NEW YORK and FLORIDA'S finest design professionals
- Placed over 15 million dollars in residential and commercial decorating budgets
- Winners of the Warner Communications "Best New Business Award"
- Designer Coordinators for the Spring '87 Interior Design Showhouse
- Profiled in the New York Times, Interior Design, Money, Newsday, Better Homes and Gardens, House Beautiful, Metropolis, Savvy, Glamour and Working Woman

Whether you've worked with an Interior Designer before, or are now approaching your first design project, our company can provide the most appropriate designer for you!

Designer Referral Service, Inc.
the best way to find an Interior Designer.

(212) 971-9681   (914) 747-0851   (516) 868-7864

The more personal the service, the more helpful the personal touch. At Designer's Referral Service, Judy Block and Sharon Dietz, are meeting the readers of the Sunday *New York Times* magazine section.

249

The Politics of Political Advertising

In the center of all political advertising is the candidate. Political analysts will discuss the views of the candidate on the issues (perhaps more so than the candidate himself). But this is largely because issues lend themselves to meaningful interpretive analysis more readily than people do. In the "open marketplace"—among the actual voters—the focus is more apt to be on the candidate as a person: his looks, his manners, his personal life, his background. The likeability factor is hard at work here.

Qualities like standing up under pressure or trustworthiness rank above experience and knowledge in the polls.

History bears this out. In the last few decades, most of the nation's presidents have been charmers; among them were Franklin Delano Roosevelt, Harry S Truman, John Fitzgerald Kennedy, and Ronald Reagan. All were reelected for another term except John Kennedy, who probably could have been had fate not intervened. All were immensely likeable.

The personality of the candidate has become even more important with the advent of electronics. Television makes it possible for the voter to observe the candidate firsthand and not have to rely on the interpretation of a third party. Telegenic personalities almost always win out over those inhibited by studio lights.

Positioning works with personalities just as it does with a product; the character of the person has to be easily definable and "come across" instantly. Franklin D. Roosevelt was perceived as a politically savvy leader; Harry S Truman as a nononsense, salty Midwesterner; John F. Kennedy as a young, dynamic ideologue; Ronald Reagan as a determined, stay-in-the-course but congenial individual with a genuine liking for people. These leaders were able to convey the sense of being unabashedly themselves and able to deal with the world on their own terms.

Politicians with less clear-cut personalities fare less well. Even though they may have valid and substantive ideas, their way of expressing their ideas, or rather themselves, proves their downfall. Walter Mondale, who had good credentials, failed to impress voters because of his paradoxical television (but not private) personality. George Bush, a leading presidential candidate at the writing of this book, had to find his own personality while on the campaign trail; voters learned to accept him.

It behooves every political consultant to help his candidate develop his own distinctive video image. It is one thing to shake hands with voters on the stump, and it is something altogether different to talk to millions from a television studio. Perhaps Bruce Babbitt, former governor of Arizona with presidential ambitions, put it best when asked about performing in front of the camera. "Television is an acquired taste," he said, then added: "If they can teach Mr. Ed to talk on television, they can teach me."

Should Issues Be Forgotten?

No political campaigner can hope to succeed without a clearly articulated platform, of course. Once voters have had a chance to meet him (in person or through the media), the time has come to articulate his views.

It may be worth repeating here that the eyes have it when it comes to making an impression. Most messages are received visually. In dreams, we replay visual images first and foremost. Perhaps equally telling is the policy that networks follow in "make-goods" for commercial blips; they offer a 30% rebate for audio but 80% for video problems.

Many brilliant public servants failed to realize their full potential because of their lack of communications skills. Their style of presentation had simply gone over people's heads, or they had mistakenly chosen to talk down to their audience.

Creation of a clear-cut, memorable image is especially important in the political arena, where the product is the person (the issues come second). All successful presidents, without exception, are remembered as much for their strong, distinctive personalities, or even mannerisms, as they are for their deeds.

Walter Mondale, again, is a good example of this. At first, his messages were laden with platitudes and sweeping generalizations. In response to criticism that his approach lacked depth, he made a complete turnaround and brought out the charts and maps, statistics galore, and presented them on prime-time television with the air of a professor speaking to his pupils. His ploy worked against him. His audience perceived his metamorphosis as nothing more than an opportunistic attempt to solicit their votes. Less apparent but just as real was their confusion about the candidate; one newspaper called his performance "chameleonlike."

Similarly, Adlai Stevenson, found that his profound intellect and erudition made it difficult for him to reach the voting public. Because he spoke the language of the highly educated, he found himself labeled an "egghead." He gave the vernacular a try, but it didn't become him.

More fortunate in reaching his public was Lieutenant Colonel Oliver North testifying at a hearing in Washington years later. Straightforward, plain-spoken, and highly telegenic in his winter uniform (chosen to support his medals, according to some critics) in July, this can-do Marine became a national hero almost overnight. Nature gave him the talent to reach the hearts and minds of the people. All three networks carried the hearings to as many as 55 million spellbound viewers, a better than 10% increase over normal TV daytime performance. His most often quoted remark? "I thought it was a neat idea."

Few presidents have understood the importance of effective one-on-one communication as well as President Ronald Reagan. In his eight years in the White House, he has taken upon himself on several occasions to talk directly to the nation. He far prefers this form of communication to that of a press conference (with its share of rambunctious reporters). An experienced actor, he knew the significance of every word, every gesture, every sign of emotion. His explanations of current events were simple enough for everyone to follow but not to the degree of sounding condescending. Many critics insist that his speeches were pure showmanship, without substance; this we had best leave to political pundits to decide. Suffice it to say here that his manner of presentation has been beyond all praise among advertising professionals.

The Advantages of Being an Incumbent

As a rule, an incumbent is in a better position to sound off on issues; his is an established personality. He has built up a record to back up his points and he gets free media coverage for simply being in the right place at the right time. Year after year, over 90% of the incumbents in Congress get reelected. While an incumbent's opponent does not enjoy such status, he does have one advantage. He is in a better position to base his attack on the incumbent's past performance. He should bear in mind, however, that the public will not be satisfied with criticism alone; they will also want to hear solutions to problems.

Use Media Wisely in Running for an Office

A quick overview:

Television. Best way to introduce yourself as a personality, to show your human side. On a paid commercial, issues must be kept down to their merciless minimum. If used for fund-raising, include a toll-free telephone number.

Newspaper. One of the best media to explain issues, but with no chance to establish one-on-one contact with your readers. Basically a local medium, so the message must fit the audience profile. Nearly impossible to cover all voters nationwide; only about 40% of the population buy a newspaper on a regular basis. Almost everyone watches television.

Magazine. Has most of the advantages of newspaper but long lead time makes it an awkward medium for politics. The audience is highly segmented.

Posters. Outdoor billboards serve as excellent reminders. Wide exposure.

Direct Mail. A powerful medium for candidates for its ability to reach a targeted audience (i.e. Republicans, Democrats, voters, activists, young, old, well to do, middle class, etc.). For purposes of raising funds, it is better than television. Responses can range from 5% to 20% or more.

Telemarketing. This in conjunction with other media (especially direct mail) is a relatively new and effective way to support ongoing advertising.

Madison Avenue, Meet Pennsylvania Avenue

The business of political "media consulting"—i.e. advertising—is big: over $2 billion was spent on national, state, and local elections in the last few years (a 50% increase since 1980), and the end is not yet in sight. It takes an average of $3 million to elect a senator and almost as much to gain a seat in the lower House. To reach the presidency can cost as much as $50 million, counting the cost of fundraising and winning primaries.

With 70% to 80% of the "billing" going into paid media (more than two-thirds of that to television), it is no wonder that some agencies show more than passing interest in the field. The 4A's report that fully one-third of its members have participated in such efforts in the last four years. Some agencies saw their first big opportunity working on political campaigns. It is generally agreed that Saatchi & Saatchi—one of the largest advertising conglomerates in the world today—got its first break in 1979 in helping Prime Minister Margaret Thatcher and her Conservative party to win the hearts of the British. The campaign (including the now famous "Labour Isn't Working" poster showing a line of unemployed men) gave the agency a chance to show its creative mettle.

As we mentioned earlier, incumbents may breathe easier — even when it comes to cash. William Proxmire, senator from Wisconsin, spent a total of $177.75 to be reelected in 1982. He won 67% of the vote, to the dismay of the community of political consultants who maintain that the more money the better the chances for winning.

Not surprisingly, political ad work has become more sophisticated. A typical national office seeker may have a phalanx of experts to show him the way; such a group typically consists of a pollster ("If you're spending more than $50,000, you'd better do polling" said one), media consultant, media buyer, and several direct mail experts, each with his own expertise and valuable proprietary mailing lists. Much of the creative work in this day and age is market driven, like any other type of advertising. Computers help weed out inefficient media buys and help target audiences on the basis of voting records and media preferences.

In some ways, it is unfortunate that so many agencies are passing the buck (literally) when approached to work on political campaigns. Political candidates do not always get the same high level of creativity in their advertising as does the private sector. Many of the 2,000 to 5,000 firms involved in the political packaging industry tend to rely on the tried-and-true "political advertising" techniques as if the basic rules were different from any other form of advertising. Dearth of fresh approaches is especially evident in television advertising. Candidates speaking into the camera — "talking heads" — is the standard formula, even with incumbents who could well afford to mix their advertising with issue-oriented messages suited to exciting visual interpretations. Advertising agencies with experience in handling a wide range of clients are probably more skilled in this type of selling. Some of the most memorable political advertising, in fact, has come out of advertising agencies — or consultants with agency backgrounds. Perhaps Ronald Reagan had the right idea in putting together his Tuesday Team task force to oversee his "Good Morning, America" campaign. As many as four commercials created by this group won important awards for creative excellence — as judged by panels of experts, both Republican and Democrat.

Politicians make exciting clients. Selling ideology stimulates the mind; many writers and artists are drawn to this type of advertising almost as much as they are to public service. Political campaigns also invite notoriety; they are visible and followed closely by the press. About the only problem with political campaigns is that an early association can — and often does — involve substantial financial risks. Losing candidates often run out of money, leaving the agency to fend off creditors.

Perhaps this is one of the reasons that more and more agencies opt to stay out of the race, tempting as the challenge may be. Della Femina Travisano, a large and highly creative agency, decided to pass on Ronald Reagan's second-term reelection campaign because it felt the work would need the attention of top talent in the agency and take too much time away from other, and more lucrative, accounts. Young & Rubicam and J. Walter Thompson are reluctant to handle political advertising for more or less the same reason. Says John O'Toole, director of the 4A's in Washington: "Agencies weren't set up for short campaigns. Clients disappear once the election is over, and then what?"

Where agencies leave off, others move in. An entirely new breed of image makers has entered the advertising scene as of late: political consultants. As do agencies, they too work on a commission basis, running anywhere from 7% to 15%. The average consultant handles from 10 to 20 campaigns a year, depending on the size of the "account." Big spenders get favored treatment, of course. There is profit to be made all year round; it is estimated that in an average year, about a half million candidates are running for elective office, spending as much money as they can get by way of contributions — and even some of their own at times. One aspirant spent more than $500,000 to be elected sheriff of Santa Clara County.

To Sum It Up

Increasingly, communications experts — many from advertising — are called upon to "sell" personalities much the way products are sold. The techniques used may be strikingly similar. As always, the focus is on the public's *perception* of the person, more than on any other factor.

A company's spokesperson represents both the company and himself. He or she can be a professional performer, an "average person," or someone from the company, such as a CEO. Be that as it may, this person must reflect the company's philosophy and have a special appeal to the company's target audience.

So-called "real" people do not necessarily have to be nonprofessionals for the sake of authenticity. Professionals often prove to be more relaxed often in front of a camera, whatever the role.

"People selling" takes on an added significance when the center of attention is the person. Such may be the focus in a political campaign. The personality of the office seeker — as perceived by the voters — could yet be the most important factor in deciding the outcome of the election, often more important than the causes espoused. That's because the average person is more confident in judging his fellow beings than complex issues.

13

Tools of the Trade: Words and Pictures

As stressed consistently in all the chapters leading up to this one, at the end it is still the creative product that counts. Perhaps editor and poet, James Russell Lowell put it best: "It is not the finding of the thing, but the making something out of it after it is found."

The word *creativity* means many different things, depending on who's using it. To an illustrator or photographer it may mean an artistic innovation; to a writer the birth of a headline; to a typographer the insertion of a dropped initial at the beginning of text; to a casting director a fresh face on the television screen. But whatever the definition, it usually boils down to either (1) the basic idea itself or (2) the way it is implemented, or, as some say, substance and style. Neither works without the other.

What's the Big Idea?

All successful campaigns have a strong underlying theme, a creative platform. Just as does a blueprint in the construction of a building, the theme shapes and guides all that follows.

Just exactly what it is that constitutes a *basic* concept (i.e. a "big idea") probably defies hard-and-fast definition, and yet the big ideas are as obvious to experienced advertising professionals as the "correct" combination of form and color is to an artist. They feel it in their blood. A common denominator of all "Big Ideas" is that they can be explained readily—usually in 25 words or less and without the aid of a layout. It could be said that all good basic concepts lend themselves to an explanation over the phone.

The writer of this book himself had a personal experience with just such a concept, which was the basis for a series of television commercials. He received the encouragement of an unusually open-minded and receptive client: "Call me any time at home if something really good pops into your mind.") The author did just that. He gave a brief verbal outline of the idea over the phone and asked for a few days to prepare storyboards to show ways of putting it on the screen. "That won't be necessary," the client said. "I like your idea. Let's get cracking." The next thing the advertiser saw was the finished commercial.

Big ideas are nearly always based on distinct, well-thought-out product attributes—either ones already perceived or those waiting to be perceived. A quick sampling of "Big Ideas" of the past helps to make the point:

- The presentation of Avis as the "Number Two" underdog in the rental car business.

- The selling of bran as a health food.

- The presentation of Marlboro as a favorite smoke with the macho cowboy (sales of the cigarette to women increased too).

- Pepsi-Cola's identification with each succeeding new generation.

- The positioning of Chivas Regal as the Scotch for self-proclaimed snobs.

- The building of a "sad" saga around the lonely repairman complaining of lack of calls to service his Maytag dishwashers.

- The use of a bull by Merrill Lynch to symbolize bullishness on America.

The best of "Big Ideas" usually represent genuine creative breakthrough, profoundly affecting perception of the product. The transformation of jeans from working clothes to a fashion designer's item was a brilliant move by both the manufacturer and his advertising agency, one that literally spawned a whole new industry. From the beginning, Volvo had focused in on the long life of the automobile, and had the record to back up its claim. In the land of rugged roads — Sweden — the average model of the car lasts for eight years, a unique selling proposition if there ever was one. All ads in the United States have been built around that theme: the "Big Idea."

Duracell has firmly established itself as the battery that simply outlasts its competitors. Here, the "big idea" is to get the most out of an important, easy-to-understand product feature — and then back up the claim unswervingly with a brilliant advertising campaign. Hewitt Ogily is behind this campaign.

In this advertisement, headline goes with the pictures — or to be more precise, a lack thereof. Execution, as much as the product itself, is the idea here. Doyle Dane Bernbach's London office created this masterpiece.

No doubt, most "big ideas" flow from the product. It is up to the advertiser to ferret out differences.

To most drivers this is a repair bill.
To Peugeot drivers it's just another road.

PEUGEOT

Peugeot sells high performance with a vengeance. The story lends itself to a vast array of creative interpretations.

Red Lobster Inns of America know exactly what it is they're dishing up to America: fresh, succulent seafood, starting with that old standby, the red lobster. Backer Spielvogel made this campaign so appealing.

258

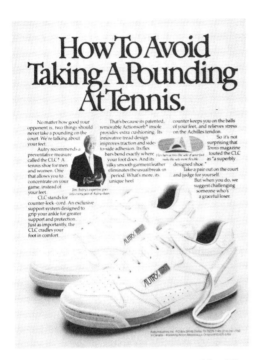

How To Avoid Taking A Pounding At Tennis.

No matter how good your opponent is, two things should never take a pounding on the court. We're talking about your feet.

Autry recommends a preventative measure called the CLC.* A tennis shoe for men and women. One that allows you to concentrate on your game, instead of your feet.

CLC stands for counter-lock-cord. An exclusive support system designed to grip your ankle for greater support and protection. Just as importantly, the CLC cradles your foot in comfort.

That's because its patented, removable Actionsorb® insole provides extra cushioning. Its innovative tread design improves traction and side-to-side adhesion. Its flex bars bend exactly where your foot does. And its silky smooth garment leather eliminates the usual break-in period. What's more, its unique heel counter keeps you on the balls of your feet, and relieves stress on the Achilles tendon.

So it's not surprising that Tennis magazine touted the CLC as "a superbly designed shoe."

Take a pair out on the court and judge for yourself.

But when you do, we suggest challenging someone who's a graceful loser.

Ad for Autry's sneakers, created by The Richard Group, states the problem clearly and then offers the solution.

You're looking at the most respected designer in the clothing business today.

Recently, the American Society of Quality Control held a survey to find out consumers' confidence in American products. And using the word quality as a benchmark for confidence, they asked more than 7,000 American consumers to select products and companies they associate with the word "quality."

Of the Fortune 500, thirty companies were selected. Twenty-two of which were American. But only one of which was a clothing designer. And you're looking at him.

His name is Levi Strauss. And even though his designs date back to the 1850's, to this day, they still are able to put rivets in the pockets of jeans, Levi Strauss used then to keep the pockets from falling apart.

And while fancy stitching in jeans may be trendy today, Strauss used the bar which is now his trademark just for stitching at the seams.

In fact, this spirit of endless commitment to quality led to 12 new improvements to his jeans in just the past year alone. And as Levi Strauss himself used to say, "Levi's denim jeans are the standard of quality that all Levi's clothing must be judged against."

So while the man in the funny suit may not look like a respected clothing designer of today, just remember that no other designer earned the same respect from American consumers. Besides, you're looking at the first man to ever wear a pair of designer jeans.

Levi's QUALITY NEVER GOES OUT OF STYLE

Ad focuses on Levi Strauss' preoccupation with breeches that would outlast their wearers, be they cowboys, farmers, or golddiggers.

Un-Fare.

It's tough to beat Piedmont's low fares to any of the cities listed below. Or, in fact, to any city we serve.

But, what really makes things unfare is that you can fly for these low prices, and still receive the kind of service that other airlines look up to.

In fact, a recent independent survey appearing in *USA Today* reports that frequent travelers rate Piedmont's service the best in America.

So, next time ask your travel agent to book Piedmont. Or call toll-free, 1-800-251-5720.

BALTIMORE	$54⁰⁰	JACKSONVILLE, FL	$99⁰⁰
BOSTON	$66⁵⁰	LOUISVILLE	$59⁰⁰
BUFFALO	$59⁰⁰	MIAMI	$109⁰⁰
CHARLOTTE	$66⁵⁰	NAPLES	$119⁰⁰
CHICAGO	$89⁰⁰	NEW YORK (LGA)	$59⁰⁰
CINCINNATI	$49⁰⁰	NEWARK	$49⁰⁰
DALLAS/FT. WORTH	$99⁰⁰	ORLANDO	$99⁰⁰
DAYTONA BEACH	$99⁰⁰	PHILADELPHIA	$54⁰⁰
DENVER	$109⁰⁰	TAMPA	$99⁰⁰
FT. LAUDERDALE	$99⁰⁰		

PIEDMONT

Fares shown may require up to a 30-day advance purchase and one half of the required round-trip purchase where applicable. Minimum/maximum stay, ticket time limit, seat limitation, time of day and day of week restrictions, and/or other restrictions may apply. Voluntary refund service charge penalties, cancellation penalty, or itinerary change penalty may apply. Fares may change or expire without notice. Fares shown may not be available on Mar. 21-23, Mar. 26-31, and Apr. 1-2. Fuel surcharge $2.50 per person from Boston. Fuel surcharge $1.00 per person from all Florida cities.

© Piedmont Airlines 1988

This ad for Piedmont appears unassuming at first — not the stuff art directors gloat about. Yet thanks to the judges of The One Show, it took its rightful place among the print finalists. The message is straightforward: Piedmont's low fares *are* tough to beat. McKinney Silver & Rockett is responsible for bringing this message the right way to the right audience: the frequent flier who knows a bargain when he or she sees one.

A trademark, in itself, may be an important — and lasting — creative breakthrough. The CBS "eye" designed by William Golden has become as much a part of the corporate psyche as the evening news.

Old techniques gain new life in new settings, surprising the eye. Rubber stamps have a century-old history. Used in this sign, with the illustration appearing in black, lettering in green, they lend immediacy to the message. In their own way, innovations such as these may pass for a "big idea."

Attention-getting ideas come from all corners — agencies, creative services, clients, friends, the family. In this house promotion, miniature pencils inside a matchbook ignite like a match. Any group capable of siring an idea like this can do the same for anyone else. This one is from Resource Manhattan.

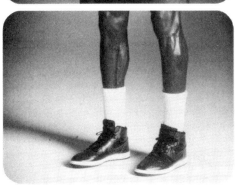

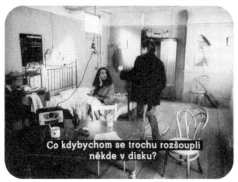

ANNCR VO: On September 15th, Nike created a revolutionary new basketball shoe. On October 18th, the NBA threw them out of the game.

(SFX: METAL SOUND ALA DRAGNET)

ANNCR VO: Fortunately, the NBA can't stop you from wearing them. Air Jordans. From Nike.

VICTOR: Oh dear, this film is obviously in need of some refreshment.

MAN (IN ENGLISH): (SILENCE) . . . Let's face it, Olga. No way are we going to crack the meaning of life tonight.

WOMAN (IN ENGLISH): Suppose not.

MAN: What say we give it some down the disco?

WOMAN: Can we have a curry after?

MAN: Yeah.

VICTOR: Apparently film buffs, Heineken can even refresh the Part Twos other beers cannot reach.

As pointed out before, distinctive technique in execution may in itself be part of the "big idea." In the Nike commercial, it is the unusual camera movement that separates it from the others. In the Heineken spot, it is the sound that grabs you. She speaks Czech.

261

If you missed it on this empty page, imagine how easy it is to miss it in your kid's Halloween candy.

There. Up in the left hand corner. A pin. Just like the one your kids could bring home in a piece of their Halloween candy.

If you're going to find it before it finds your kid's mouth, you're going to have to look very carefully. Then look again. And not just for pins. For any breaks in a candy wrapper's surface.

Remember, when in doubt throw it out. Or your kids could get stuck with some Halloween candy they'll never forget.

The Boston Globe
A Public Affairs presentation of The Boston Globe

Here again is the execution of a concept that stops the reader from turning the page. Wooding & L Housley is the agency.

262

Same Theme, Different Execution

As said earlier, strong campaigns are built around strong themes, and they can be implemented in a variety of ways. It is not absolutely necessary to follow the same graphic approach or the same writing style throughout the same campaign. Different media lend themselves to different techniques; different audiences call for different interpretations.

Art or Copy—Which Is More Important?

Advertising always works on two levels —words and pictures. Even when there are no pictures, graphics comes into play on a subconscious level by way of typography, layout, lighting, and color selection. Even the most skilled of writers would find it difficult to produce an advertisement without the knowing hand of an artist.

It is an old and well-cherished maxim that one picture is worth a thousand words, but sometimes just the opposite holds true: A few well-chosen words are worth a thousand pictures. It is possible to describe an object much more precisely than to show it. Always, a picture—even a photograph—is open to interpretation. Words can be less ambiguous.

Admittedly, there are two sides to the coin. Picture talk is quicker, an important consideration in a culture as fast paced as ours. What's more, in the absence of interpretation by a third party (the writer), the viewer is allowed to make up his own mind, based on his own set of values, beliefs, and attitudes—all of which make the illustration or photograph all the more persuasive.

Obviously, each approach has its own advantages. Some products, like food, fashion, vacations, home furnishings, cosmetics, soft drinks, and entertainment, lend themselves to pictorial representation. Others, like insurance, investment programs, banking, and computers, call for verbal support. In the final analysis, it is for the advertiser to decide which if any position to take in the picture vs. words debate. Both work in the fine hands of the creative even for the same product if need be.

In some cases, three, four, or even five senses can be called to act on an advertisement. Examples are scented magazine inserts; samplings of food, drinks, or cosmetics; or packages appealing to the touch. The Gestalt view that an entity is so unified that it is perceived as a whole works hard in the selling of a product where two impressions are better than one.

The experience you seek

SURGEON GENERAL'S WARNING: Smoking
By Pregnant Women May Result In Fetal
Injury, Premature Birth, And Low Birth Weight.

The experience you seek

SURGEON GENERAL'S WARNING: Smoking
Causes Lung Cancer, Heart Disease,
Emphysema, And May Complicate Pregnancy.

Art — Michael David Brown's cut-and-torn paper style technique — was chosen for this series of ads to set them apart from the photo-realistic campaigns so prevalently used by competitors. Richard Savean at BBDO art directed the campaign.

The experience you seek

SURGEON GENERAL'S WARNING: Cigarette
Smoke Contains Carbon Monoxide.

Kent III. Experience it.

SURGEON GENERAL'S WARNING: Quitting Smoking
Now Greatly Reduces Serious Risks to Your Health.

Geoff Hayes and Michael Roux of TBWA shuttled back and forth in their technique of choice — between art and photography — in this campaign for Absolut Vodka, a product of Carillon Importers. Visually surprising, surrealistic, artistically satisfying, this campaign proves that the camera and brush can be used interchangeably at no loss of continuity, provided the grapic theme is well established.

There are many ways to achieve graphic continuity — and experienced art directors know them all. Consistency in type selection too creates a "family resemblance" among ads, enabling the reader to recognize them at a quick glance. In this campaign for BMW of North America, Ammirati & Puris — an agency known for its high creative standards — uses bold Gothic type to help in establishing a format.

Finding the Photographer You Need

Some photographers show a special talent in photographing people. Others prefer to take pictures of products (some specializing in glass, jewelry, automobiles, and interiors) or reportage (unposed, unrehearsed photos, showing "real" people). Some may have a way with babies or animals. Still others like to go on location, shoot cityscapes, seascapes, nature as created from above. Fashion and beauty photographers enjoy the beauty of women, and know how to best display clothes on the human figure. Food photographers are the chefs de cuisine of the industry; they may have their own test kitchen and can make food look good enough to want to lick it off the page. Picture snappers with a sense of comedy are the "cartoonists" of the profession. And today there is a new breed: the state-of-the-art photographer who uses special effects in manipulating images. They give the saying "done with mirrors" a whole new meaning. Techniques run the gamut: aerial photography, microphotography, telephotography, old-fashioned tintype, stroboscopic photography, infrared photography.

Obviously, it makes less than good business sense to ask a "still life photographer" to convey the spirit of a wild teenage party on the beach, say, in the tradition of the "Pepsi Generation." Conversely, a "people photographer" may be stumped by trying to make cars look longer and sleeker, the way Detroit likes to see them in its collective fantasy.

IN TODAY'S LOW-TAR, LOW-TASTE CONFUSION ONE CIGARETTE REMAINS TRUE TO RICH RELAXING FLAVOR

F L A V O R · T O · S A V O R

AD: *Marleen Fusaris*; Photog: *Rod Cook*; Agency: *Dancer Fitzgerald Sample*; Client: *True Cigarettes*.

When should photography be chosen over illustration? In most ads, the theme probably lends itself to more than a single interpretation, depending on the art director's judgment at the moment. Photography lends a sense of reality to this ad, helping to reinforce the message. Blurry images suggest helter-skelter, fast-lane activity; in contrast is the smoker in clear focus, in a state of cool repose. Rod Cook proves, in this ad, that it is possible for a photographer to use film as freely as a painter uses his canvas. Dancer Fitzgerald Sample is the agency for True Cigarettes.

Starting A Softball Team At Della Femina
Was A Natural. Most Of Our People Have Been
Out In Left Field For Years.

This startling announcement was created by — who else? — Della Femina McNamee, an agency known for the irrepressible, dare-to-be-different founder Jerry Della Femina, himself an ardent baseball fan, and a proud Brooklynite. Photography was chosen here to heighten the surprise.

YOU MAY HAVE SEEN OUR FASHIONS ON THE STREETS OF PARIS.

New and used military clothing and equipment so reasonably priced, maybe the Pentagon should be shopping here.
AMERICAN SURPLUS STORE
1st Avenue No. & 2nd Street in Minneapolis.

This documentary approach lends support to the story; take away the "proof" and the headline falls flat. Agency Martin/Williams wisely chooses photography (a stock photograph at that) to dramatize the message.

A potato has nutritional value.

It takes an exceptionally skillful illustrator to match the mouthwatering impact of photography. This is a lifelike replica of a steaming baked potato for the Potato Chip Snack Food Association.

Photography is especially popular among fashion and beauty advertisers — and for good reason. Realism — in detail and color — is an important part of the message. This picture was snapped by Nancy Ney of the Source Force.

It's not a dog.
It's a guinea pig.

How does it feel
to tell yourself
it's only a game?

Sports Illustrated
Get the feeling.

Both illustration and photography can evoke human emotions, but the straightfor-wardness of the camera — real or perceived — lends a special believability to photo-graphs. A black-and-white photograph of a puppy reaches many a heart. Leonard Monahan Saabye created the ad. It is doubtful that a drawing of an embattled football player could have been as effective as the photograph used in the Sports Illustrated "Get The Feeling" campaign by Ogilvy Mather.

Photography works well when the per-son in an ad is an integral part of the message. As president of the company, a photo of Susan Wallace frequently ap-pears in campaigns for People Re-sources, a private club for singles.

This lovely soft-focus photo of a bride, by Yonkers' Vin Gaudio, is as profes-sional as most of its counterparts taken by long-established photographers whose fees reflect their years in busi-ness. Talent is where talent lives.

Finding the Illustrator You Need

Here is an overview of types of artists:

Caricaturist. A sharp eye for distinctive features in people's faces, his forte is to exaggerate them. The artist of choice when recognition counts and the approach is whimsical.

Cartoonist. Lets his pencil fly, too, but his people are born out of his imagination.

Realistic Illustrator. Best to replicate nature, sometimes with surprising fidelity. Almost always works from a photograph or other reference.

Portrait Artist. A realistic illustrator whose specialty is to put people on paper (or canvas).

Fashion Illustrator. An authority on fashion, he knows what "details" to include—or, more important, leave out. Many have developed their own style, instantly identifiable.

Designer. Basically an abstractionist, his world is filled with shapes, forms, spatial relationships, patterns. All art directors have a solid sense of design. Most apt to view his work upside down or in the mirror to gain a fresh impression of the overall design.

Fine Artist. The most independent of all, he works toward developing uniqueness in style. Personal expression can become an issue here; that is why it may take years for painters to "find themselves." Least apt to follow an art director's roughs, space requirements, or deadlines. The line between commercial illustrators and fine artists often blurs, even in the eye of the beholder.

Animator. Has his drawings come to life on the screen; a highly specialized skill.

Some artists are "good" at drawing people—they know anatomy, movements, facial expressions. Others gravitate toward painting inanimate objects—they excel in product illustrations, for example. Still others specialize in landscapes, seascapes, still lifes, cityscapes, architectural renderings, mechanical drawings, humorous illustrations, animals, children, glamour, science fiction, decorative drawings. Talent for still life does not guarantee the same degree of competence in other forms of art—product illustrators often feel at a loss rendering a human figure and solicit the help of a colleague whose forte is drawing the species.

Designers and artists should not be lumped into the same group either; they do not come from the same ilk. Many designers do poorly in illustration, particularly when realism is called for. A package designer, for example, may need help in rendering a lifelike portrait of a meowing cat on his pet food box. He may turn to an illustrator to complete his design, perhaps one at home with drawing animals or, more specifically, cats. (There are at least two illustrators specializing in delineating domestic cats.

On the other hand, a "sketchman" (the artist employed by agencies and studios to help art directors render realistic comprehensives) would probably have to rely on the fine Italian hand of a "designer" to indicate type or a decorative strip in a layout.

Giving the artist a feel of what is expected can save money—not to mention grief—later on. Discuss technique with him, if you can, size, and color. This need not inhibit creativity. Use pictures—samples of someone else's work, a magazine page—to get your ideas across. "One picture is worth a thousand words" certainly holds true in artist/client relationships. But never try to impose your own taste, superseding his. Grizzled art buyers solve this problem the easy way, by making an effort to find an illustrator whose own natural technique is the closest to what they are looking for.

271

Animation 2 West 47th Street, New York, N.Y. 10016 (212) 869-1630

In this house ad, not surprisingly, the advertiser opted for art. Execution is part of the message. The Ink Tank's "product" is artistic talent with expertise in animation. This drawing is Mark Marek's, a member of the firm.

Full page newspaper ad (opposite page) was prepared by BDA/BBDO for Delta Airlines (the official airline for conventioneers during the presidential race). Choice between art and photography favored the former for ease in creating characters, logistics and sharper newspaper reproduction.

One Thing Both Parties Agree On.

Democrats and Republicans stopped debating long enough recently to appoint Delta the official airline of both of their national conventions.

The choice is logical, rather than political.

Delta and its partner airlines, The Delta Connection, are now one of the largest airline systems in the U.S.,

with over 3,900 flights a day to over 240 cities worldwide.

This means Delta will be able to fly thousands of the delegates from both parties to their conventions in Atlanta and New Orleans, and still be able to take care of you.

Whether you're a Democrat. Or a Republican. Or Undecided.

DELTA

The Official Airline Of The Democratic And Republican National Conventions.

As is evidenced here, the size of an ad is not always proportional to its impact.

Four ads (illustrated by Tom Bloom and John Marciuliano) make up a small sample of an extensive campaign for *The New York Times*. Most were two columns wide. They are shown here for their judicious use of white space, bold use of blacks and whites, and unusual illustrations. All this helped them stand out on the page regardless of their size.

TAKE 20% OFF SOLID PRIVATE LABEL HOSIERY
TAKE 20% OFF CALVIN KLEIN, HOM AND MANSILK UNDERWEAR
"MORE POWERFUL THAN A LOCOMOTIVE"

TAKE 20% OFF ALL SOLID PRIVATE LABEL DRESS SHIRTS
30% OFF GEOFFREY BEENE SOLID DRESS SHIRTS.
"FASTER THAN A SPEEDING BULLET"

In retail store ads especially, technique is of vital importance. Different artistic treatment — or an established style used in a different way — makes the difference. Bloomingdale's, one of the most successful department stores in the nation, tried the unexpected in this two page newspaper ad when it used comic strip technique in announcing its 20% off/"Command Performance Sale."

I Trè Merli.
(ˈī ˈtrê ˈmê ˈrlɪ)

Why and Where:

*"…the unpredictable
is predictable."*

"…it's formally informal."

*"…thousands of bottles of family wines
are stacked from wall to wall."*

"…you are going to feel good. Simply."

*"…it tastes like there.
But it's here."*

*"…even the buttoned down
can loosen up."*

"…real Italians go for real Italian food."

*"…isn't that bzz-bzz
sitting with bzz-bzz-bzz."*

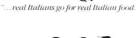

i tre'merli

"Where to enjoy
Northern Italian Specialities…
special atmosphere included."

Restaurant & Bar • 463 W. Broadway, "The Heart of Soho", NYC
For Reservations Call • 212-254-8699

Production techniques can open up a treasure-trove of new creative opportunities, some at little additional cost. In this full-page newspaper ad, the same trio of birds appear nine times but each time in different feathers (Ben Day screens, really). Copy is broken into short captions, making the message inviting to read. The owner of this fine restaurant was pleased enough with the results to have the ad appear again and again in the New York Times and other upscale publications.

ONE

SHHHHHH!

THREE

The Cuisinart® Little Pro is much quieter than the other small food processors.
Much, much better, too.

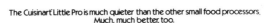

SIX

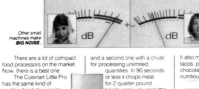

Other small machines make **BIG NOISE.**   dB   +   dB   Our small machine makes small noise

FIVE

There are a lot of compact food processors on the market. Now there is a best one.

The Cuisinart Little Pro has the same kind of quality, direct-drive motor as our larger food processors—strong, but quiet. The others use inexpensive, noisy universal motors.

Tests show that the motors of these other machines are 30 to 100 times noisier.

BIG RESULTS

The Little Pro makes quick and easy work of chopping, kneading, mixing and makes perfect slices and shreds.

You get both a standard work bowl

and a second one with a chute for processing unlimited quantities. In 90 seconds or less it chops meat for 2 quarter-pound hamburgers, mixes batter for 6 muffins, or a dozen chocolate chip cookies, or prepares more than a cup of chicken salad.

It also makes dips, fillings for tacos, pizza, ice cream, chocolate sauce and fresh nutritious baby food.

SMALL SIZE

The Little Pro is so compact it will fit on a copy of TV Guide. It's easy to store or leave on your counter. Easy to use and clean, too.

BIGGER WARRANTY

The Little Pro is protected for 3 years and the principal motor parts are warranted for 15 years (includes parts and even labor).

For more information, please write: Cuisinarts, Inc. 15 (N) Valley Dr. P.O. Box 2150, Greenwich, CT 06836-2150

Cuisinart
LITTLE PRO

TWO

FOUR

Eye movement studies show that readers read ads at their own pace, and in a haphazard fashion at that. Their eyes wander all over the page. In this ad, the headline catches our attention because of its dominance on the page, and the unique wording. The next stop is the picture of the product, more or less to find out quickly the main thrust of the message. Subheadline, smaller illustrations, and logo, follow in that order. The whole process may only take a few seconds. It is only after this quick preliminary study that the reader may — or may not — scan the text, but once again, not necessarily in proper sequence. Cost, availability of the product, and location are facts he or she wants to know the quickest. Then, and only then, will the reader work his or her way through the entire message.

Lay It On, Lay It Out

A layout (or storyboard) is the blueprint for a print or television ad. Contrary to what some people believe, experienced art directors do not view a layout primarily as a design product. Cryptic comments like "balance," "white space," "high tech look" still creep into exchanges around the conference table; nonetheless, these are not — or at least, should not be — the prime concerns. The challenge is more apt to lie in any of these areas:

1. To catch attention.

2. To get the basic idea across.

3. To guide the reader's eye if in print.

4. To integrate picture and sound if on television.

No layout is created for its own sake. An ad that advertises itself belongs in a museum, not the pages of a publication or on the television screen.

Many different graphic devices are available to the art director that he can use to draw attention to various elements in a print ad. Readers do not examine a page in a "logical" fashion, i.e. left to right and from top to bottom; rather, they prefer to browse. As shown on page 000, their eyes wander from here to there, depending on the art director's subtle "instructions" as to emphasis.

Visual Persuasion: The Effect of Pictures on the Subconscious

More than anything else, it is the subject matter that catches attention. If the reader (or viewer) is interested in buying a car, a picture of this year's model is likely to draw him into the ad. Home buyers like to learn about homes, vacationers about vacation places, lovers of good food about food.

But there is more to picture-talk than that. Just as "clothes make the person," graphic techniques can make an ad.

Here are a few general observations:

1. As a rule, the realism of a photograph carries more conviction than a drawing or painting, which is why photography dominates the advertising scene today. It should be remembered, however, that the average reader, less attentive to the nuances of communications, is not always aware of the difference between a photograph and a realistic illustration. For all practical purposes, a Norman Rockwell type of illustration carries the same conviction with the public as a photograph.

2. An "unrealistic" illustration (or animation) still may be the technique of choice. A loose, casual fashion sketch suggests sophistication, a humorous cartoon gets a laugh, an art deco style of figure connotes elegance. Animation (including computer-generated graphics) enters the realm of fantasy, and lets the artist go as far as his imagination will let him.

3. Size, shape, color have a life of their own, as any art director knows. Large size (in relation to surroundings) implies power and dominance. Round, flowing shapes appeal to passive instincts ("feminine") while angular objects signify decisiveness ("masculine"). Lines convey movement, dots stand still. Red and yellow stir the blood, green and blue steady the nerves, white cheers, black saddens (which is why the walls of hospitals are often painted shades of green and blue, while sports arenas and nurseries are rich in reds and yellows). Package designers are acutely conscious of the impressions colors make and the fact that preferences change with age, sex, income, occupation, and even regions. For example, "cold" colors reign in the northern

parts of the United States, "hot" colors are more likely to appeal to the young in California and Florida. Campers and boaters like green more than any other color; the fashion conscious find red intriguing; blue appeals to intellectuals and those in need of an organized life; yellow connotes excitement to risk takers at any age. Yellow and red are favorites with infants but their preferences change as they get older; purple is an acceptable hue to the over-fifty crowd, but less so to the under-thirty. Men prefer browns and primary colors while women go for pink, light blues, and pastels.

4. In print there is a limit to the number of pictures the reader will be willing to study in an advertisement. Unless the subject has exceptional intrigue, interest will wane after four to six pictures. (Captions help to hold interest.) A single large picture is more likely to grab attention but for a shorter time than a series of pictures.

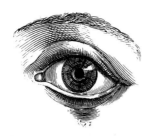

5. Advertisers' signatures (logotypes) are often needed for sponsor identification. It should be noted, however, that they suggest the presence of paid commercial space. Editorial techniques work better (incorporate the name of the headline or body copy, show a package instead) but not if the reader feels he has been baited into reading the text.

6. Borders make an ad appear smaller.

The larger the illustration, the larger the ad seems. It is possible to simulate bleed by judicious use of white space; i.e. with nothing standing between the outer edges of the ad and of the page, (the former spills over the entire area).

7. Coupons are more apt to be clipped if placed at outside bottom (preferably the right) corner of the page. But a coupon on top of the ad (or anywhere else, for that matter) can also be effective given the right emphasis.

8. Full-sized ads can be justified by the sense of importance they create in the reader's mind. However, there is no indication that two pages invite proprotionately higher readership than one.

9. Slightly less than full-page newspaper ads — with an editorial column running down one side — get the same, if not more, attention than their full-page counterparts. Which means the former can be more cost-effective.

10. Editorial environment has an effect on readership and, more important, on the reader's state of mind. The nine-page insert on vacation cruises placed in the *New York Times* immediately following a 508 point drop in the stock market lost much of its luster because of its timing.

11. Two-color ads do not necessarily get more readership in a magazine than their single-color counterparts. Black and white is still among the most effective combinations; readers associate such pictures with editorial news. If another color is added, it should be done mostly for emphasis. One color (preferably black) should clearly dominate over the other.

12. A square photograph is more believable than one that is silhouetted.

13. Poor placement of illustrations (as haphazard insertions of vignettes in the midst of text material) inhibit readership.

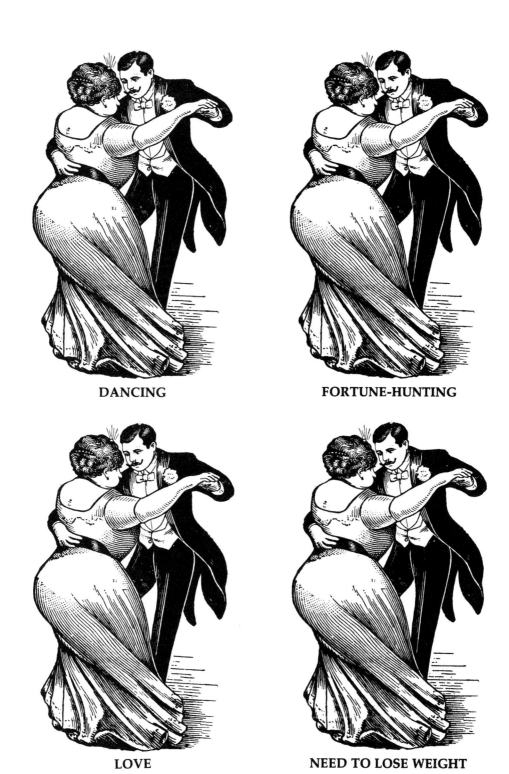

DANCING

FORTUNE-HUNTING

LOVE

NEED TO LOSE WEIGHT

An illustration — any illustration — lives in the eye of the beholder. The advertiser's interpretation may be substantially different from the person he is trying to reach. Perceptions vary for reasons demographic, geographic, psychographic, or other reasons. A good clue as to the nature of the audience is the media in which the picture is carried.

©1986, COMPAR, Inc. Photograph by Joel Baldwin.

Hello?

Is this the man with the secret tattoo?

Now that you know about it, it's not a secret anymore, is it?

Your tattoo is safe with me. Were you able to get a taxi?

I walked home.

And how was Paris while all the sensible folk were still in bed?

It was grey and drizzling and bloody marvelous. I kept making up poems with your name in them. Also a love song that, for rhyming reasons, ended up being all about your right elbow. I don't think my feet touched the ground once all the way home.

I meant to tell you. I love the way you smell. Most men's colognes make them smell like they take themselves too seriously.

I thank you. My Paco Rabanne cologne thanks you. My mother thanks you.

Your mother would never approve of what you and your Paco Rabanne do to me, so let's leave her out of this. Am I going to see your tattoo again tonight?

That's up to you, isn't it?

Paco Rabanne
For men
What is remembered is up to you

Shown here (left) are "no-layout layouts" — a term that connotes absence of conscious effort to arrange elements on the page to piece together a "composition." Knowledgable art directors know, however, that an ad often "designs itself." Restraint (no part of the text receives special emphasis, not even the logo) can go a long way, as this ad created by Ogilvy Mather shows. Not surprisingly, it was the founder of the agency, David Ogilvy, who first advocated this type of "editorial" treatment in advertising. History proved him right. The layout may be quiet here, but not the message of the ad.

283

Today, the most successful transactions
grow out of merchant banking relationships.

Yesterday, it was not unusual for banks and clients to form temporary alliances.

Today, an increasing number of corporations believe that their interests are best served by long-term, in-depth banking relationships.

So does Bankers Trust. A cornerstone of our merchant banking philosophy is the maintenance of multi-level, multi-service relationships.

We have become a trusted financial advisor to many clients, providing everything from cash management to risk management. This keeps us constantly abreast of your overall financial plans.

So when special opportunities arise—a recapitalization, a merger, an acquisition—we are perfectly positioned to help you take advantage of them. There is no learning curve to climb, no long-term objectives to be identified.

Solid merchant banking relationships have never been more productive than in the uncertain world of today.

◻Bankers Trust Company
Because today isn't yesterday.

Classic may be the best way to describe this layout for Bankers Trust Company. Created by Doremus & Company, it breaks through the newspaper clutter by virtue of its simplicity. When everyone shouts, the soft-spoken often stands out.

The headline you can't read says, "A few drops of blood can completely obliterate a microsurgeon's field of vision."

Years of medical expertise can be rendered useless when a tiny leakage of blood covers a surgical site that is sometimes only 3/8 of an inch in diameter.

To prevent this problem during microsurgery, a special instrument was developed by a Mount Sinai doctor.

It safely seals off blood vessels. So the field of surgery remains bloodless during an operation.

And doctors can take full advantage of two of the most important tools they own: their eyes.

The ramifications for patients and doctors alike have been profound. The risk of serious side effects from some forms of brain surgery, for example, has dropped from 50% to a heartening 2%.

But then, looking beyond existing procedures to discover safer, more efficient ones has been our goal for 135 years. In fact, Mount Sinai has such an exceptional record of discoveries and achievements that it's recognized today as one of the most respected medical centers in the world.

Hospitals routinely employ many of our advancements in treating their own patients.

Which isn't surprising, since we're committed to providing more than just concern for patients' problems. We're committed to finding solutions.

MOUNT SINAI.
TAKE GOOD CARE OF YOURSELF.
The Mount Sinai Medical Center, 1176 Fifth Avenue, New York, N.Y. 10029

1-800-MD-SINAI

In this full page newspaper advertisement created by Grace & Rothschild, illustration and headline is one and the same. Copy explains: "The headline you can't read says: A few drops of blood can completely obliterate a microsurgeon's field of vision." It's hard not to go on reading the message after this statement.

SEVEN

THINGS THAT GO BETTER WITH

CORVO

The difference between having dinner, and dining with pleasure.

KETCHUM/MANDABACH & SIMMS

Headline is the body text.

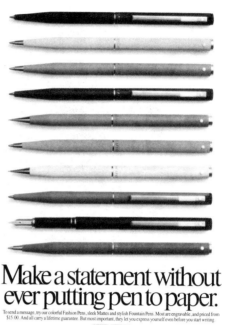

Make a statement without ever putting pen to paper.

To send a message, try our colorful Fashion Pens, sleek Mattes and stylish Fountain Pens. Most are engravable, and priced from $15.00. And all carry a lifetime guarantee. But most important, they let you express yourself even before you start writing.

SHEAFFER.

TOLSON COMPANY

Headline at the bottom of ad but large enough to be seen.

MERCEDES-BENZ ANNOUNCES A NEW LEASING PROGRAM BASED ON THE IDEA THAT YOU'D LIKE A SHREWD FINANCIAL PROPOSITION AS MUCH AS YOU'D LIKE A NEW MERCEDES-BENZ.

SEE YOUR AUTHORIZED MERCEDES-BENZ DEALER

McCAFFREY & McCALL

Headline is set on eight separate lines.

EMPORIO ARMANI

IN-HOUSE

Headline *is* the logo.

Different headline treatments appear in these ads — and they all work, which again proves that in advertising graphics good taste and common sense set the pace.

Words, Too, Pack Emotions

The photograph of a woman with tears running down her cheek evokes sympathy; the U.S. flag inspires patriotism; the sight of a clown brings laughter. It would appear that the eyes have it over the ears when it comes to speaking to the heart, but that, too, depends on context. Ask any writer (including an advertising copywriter) and he will testify that words also have the power to appeal to the tender susceptibilities of the reader or even the viewer.

Our language is rich enough to describe all shades of emotions, perhaps even more accurately than pictures. Tears running down a face connote sadness, but what kind of sadness? Is the person deeply depressed, simply out of sorts, happy enough to cry, or peeling onions? Words tell the *complete* story. Read these words and listen to your feelings:

LOVE	LAUGHTER
BABY	MUSIC
FLOWERS	HATE
POWER	WAR
MONEY	GOD
TERROR	MOTHER

Accomplished copywriters use a verbal brush to create an image on paper. Listen to this description of a Mercedes-Benz in a magazine ad:

MANY AUTOMOBILE MAKERS ITCH TO BUILD THE PERFECT CAR. THE MERCEDES-BENZ S-CLASS IS PROOF THAT SOME SIMPLY ITCH MORE THAN OTHERS

It is a curious fact that not everyone who seeks the very best in a large sedan is fully aware of just how much sedan this entitles today's buyer to demand.

Some still opt for the overbearing "luxury" sedan in all its bulk and ostentation, unaware that big today can also mean fast, agile, and responsive. Somewhat better off are those who have moved up to vivid big-sedan performance — but then go no further.

Then there are those who choose the sedans of the S-Class. The Mercedes-Benz overview is their overview: a large sedan — sufficiently well engineered — can balance triple-digit performance with hushed driving ease. Agile handling with an unruffled ride. The fragrance of leather upholstery and the richness of handworked woods with the tactile pleasures and keen precision of a true driver's car.

And the rewards that follow are theirs to enjoy every mile: swift and sure-footed automotive travel on vast highways and unpaved byways alike. Experienced amid sumptuously comfortable surroundings. And in a blissful state of near silence.

The rewards continue — because the S-Class is, after all, built by Mercedes-Benz. And thus is welded, brazed, filed, sanded, polished and nitpicked to completion along an assembly route lined with enough inspections (and inspectors) to make this the most demanding trip of its life, if not any car's life. The S-Class aims not only for the glamour of high technology but also the reassurance of high technological reliability. And reflects almost 50 years of basic Mercedes-Benz safety research and engineering.

You can choose from three S-Class sedans — the 560 SEL and 420 SEL V-8's and the stunning six-cylinder 300 SDL Turbo. Their character subtly differs from one to another; their blend of high performance and high-driving civilization differs from all other large sedans in the world.

Note how expressions like "hushed driving ease," "handworked woods," "with the tactile pleasures," "the fragrance of leather upholstery," "in all its bulk and ostentation," "sumptuously comfortable surroundings," "blissful state of near silence" are made to give free play to at least four of our senses: sight, hearing, smell, and touch. With all its factual content the copy succeeds in creating a vivid palpable imagery.

Factual vs. Suggestive

There are those who tell it straight, and those who stroke before they strike. Either approach has its place in advertising. Getting to the point quickly saves time but does not give the consumer a chance to sort out his feelings and arrive at a solution he feels most comfortable with. This copy written for a miniature computer capable of storing names and numbers leaves little to the imagination:

THE
LITTLE
BLACK BOOK
. . . COMES OF AGE

- Holds up to 150 names/numbers
- Keeps addresses and memos, too
- Fast forward/reverse feature
- No memory loss battery system

Now, the legendary little black book has come of age. At the touch of a button, the combination of names, addresses, telephone numbers, memos and even dates relating to specific "to do" reminders appear on your display screen of the Calling Card's flexible 2,024 character memory. How does it work? Simply type in your information and it automatically is filed in alphabetical order. All in the size of a credit card. The Calling Card will become your most productive and convenient asset for your daily information needs. Only $35.

Protect your Calling Card with a custom-fit, butter-soft leather case. A perfect companion, featuring a magnetized card pad. — $10.

Add $3 per piece for postage/handling.

Call Toll Free 24 hours a day, 7 days a week.

1-800-346-6000

California residents add 6% sales tax.

Information-packed text like this works especially well in direct response ads. In space no larger than 2¼″ × 5″, the advertiser succeeds in telling a great deal about his product in the hope that his "Calling Card" will sell itself.

In contrast, here is a two-page magazine color ad extolling the virtues of the Concord Saratoga wristwatch. On the left-hand side, a beautiful soft-focused shot of a young romantic couple sets the tone.

"NEVER TRUST A MAN WHO LAVISHES EXPENSIVE GIFTS UPON YOU," MY MOTHER ALWAYS SAID. "UNLESS YOU REALLY LIKE HIM."

She told me a lot of things about men, my Mother. And she was almost always right.

But this man was no typical man. This was a man in a million. A man who seems very fond of me.

It had started only six weeks ago when I was stuck in row 12 on one of those seemingly endless flights that stop in Guam on their way to Tokyo.

In seat 12F, alongside of me, was an elbow that seemed intent on straying across the armrest the entire flight. It was his elbow.

By the time they served lunch I was halfway to falling in love.

Over the next two weeks I saw him just about every day. So when he asked me to join him for a trip out of town, it wasn't really a surprise.

After a long and leisurely lunch at a remote Country Inn, my man took me for a walk into the garden.

"This is for you, and for our days to come," he whispered in my ear as he handed me a package about half the size of a shoe box.

I undid the wrapping paper and revealed a beautiful calfskin jewelry box. With bated breath I lifted the lid.

And there it was, the diamonds glistening in the late afternoon country light, the most exquisite watch you've ever seen.

The name on the textured face identified it as a Concord Saratoga.

"There are sixteen diamonds locked snugly into that polished eighteen-carat gold

and brushed steel bezel," he informed me with a smile, "one for every day I've known you."

The curve of the linkages on the bracelet matched my wrist as though it was designed just for me. And it felt solid and substantial.

This was a watch for a lifetime.

Admiring the way the raised gold numerals seemed to shimmer in the reflected sparkle of the diamonds, I suddenly recalled my Mother's advice.

"There must be strings attached to a gift as beautiful as this?" I asked my man, perhaps a little hopefully.

He let go of me and knelt down on one knee, "I was rather hoping it would help get you to the church on time."

The story is told in the best of heart-throbbing Gothic Romance tradition, with the product allowed to only tick quietly in the background. The ad is aimed at a sophisticated audience who know — and enjoy — the difference between tongue in cheek and true to life.

The question of factual vs. fanciful often comes up when crafting clever captions for products advertised in a retail ad or a catalogue. For the copy to be successful, it must be consistent with the art treatment. This is the no-nonsense approach Macy's used in its Spring Sale Catalogue, describing the item:

OLGA'S CHRISTINA COMFORT-BACK contour bra woven of soft, cool cotton with polyester/Lycra spandex to add shaping and support. Size 32–36 A,B,C, #36142. Reg. $18.50. Sale $14.80.

Bloomingdale's, on the other hand, chose to wax poetic in describing its lacy little things on the glossy full-color pages of a 10-page catalogue:

Beyond dreams and desires there is a vision of innocence and expectation. Part yearning. Part poetry. Beautifully expressed by Miss Dior in rich, gleaming satin of nylon/rayon/poly with exquisite, pale blue embroideries. The fitted tie-back satin gown is one long sweep of tender temptation from bodice to hem in white for XP (4–6), P (6–8), S (8–10), M (10–12). Its matching bed jacket has puffed sleeves and the richest of embroidery. The set #7191 $95.00.

When Headlines Make Headlines

About five times as many people read — or more accurately, perceive — a headline in a print advertisement than read the body copy, or even part of the body copy. That is why headlines are important, and have, for the most part, become one of the basic elements of a conventional print ad. (On television, it is usually the "tag line" at the end of the commercial that serves as the headline.)

There are two schools of thought as to the functions of a headline. One is that it is put there for intrigue and to make the reader read the body copy. The other is that, along with the illustration, it should be able to "explain" the essence of the message to those going through the publication in a hurry. Both are commendable goals, but while the headline should invite careful scanning of the entire ad, this is often wishful thinking on the part of the advertiser. The best headlines are those that stand on their own. If they succeed in enticing the reader to study the ad further, so much the better — consider that an extract bonus.

Research shows that headlines are often absorbed the moment they enter the field of vision, however brief that may be. (As any speedreader knows, the eye does not read words, but entire lines). Accomplished art directors have developed the knack of making a reader "read" a headline on a subconscious level. Size of type is one way to have an impact on a wandering mind, but size — a graphic shout, if you will — is not the only way. Isolation on the page is another important factor; headlines away from other material and surrounded by white space have a better chance of being noticed. In view of this, headlines need not appear near the top of advertisements. There are as many ways to design an effective layout as there are art directors who design them.

There is no hard evidence to support the popular notion that short headlines (or book and movie titles) are more successful than long ones, except for the fact that they gain in visibility when set in large type (or are displayed on a marquee). Many two- or three-line headlines too have proved their worth; witness the lead-in to the text for the Concord Watch ad described earlier: *"Never trust a man who lavishes expensive gifts upon you," my Mother always said. "Unless you really like him."*

Some people have an innate ability to come up with pithy "one-liners." They are usually witty, word-crazy people who enjoy coining a phrase and tend to loose patience working on long, exacting copy for, say, mailing pieces, brochures, catalogues, publicity releases, and speeches. Conversely, writers with talent and tolerance for writing lengthy messages usually feel less tempted to go for the jugular with a single catchy phrase.

Seven "Do Nots" in Writing a Headline

1. Avoid puns like the plague, or trite expressions such as "like the plague." Playing on words is not the only game in town.

2. Cutesy headlines are cute. But do they sell?

3. Go easy on exclamation marks. Let your statements do the shouting.

4. Words like *best, most, greatest, first,* and *without peer* may be music to a client's ear. But is the consumer listening?

5. A headline your competitor can use is of no use to you at all.

6. Having to read a headline twice for understanding is once too many.

7. You can fool some people all the time . . . and so forth.

Good Thing, the Vernacular

Advertising is hardly the place for magniloquence (speech sprinkled with pompous polysyllables such as "magniloquence.") Clarity and brevity are the key; in-depth study of major newspapers shows that their stories contain an average of only five letters per word. Yet verbs rule over nouns (in our culture that values action—in the more meditative Orient nouns connote stability and permanence, and thus are preferred.) Simple declaratory statements are usually the preferred over the pushy predicative.

Some of the most inspired advertising messages are not much more than spoken words put to paper, but this takes nothing away from their eloquence. Much is to be learned from "ordinary," everyday speech. Verbal communication does not easily accommodate convoluted sentence construction, words without end, prose turned purple. It tends to be informal and unadorned, and not necessarily grammatical. Consider such slogans as "Winston tastes good like a cigarette should," "Nobody doesn't like Sara Lee," "What becomes a legend most?"

It is doubtful if the patter in this immensely effective California Cooler commercial would have pleased the likes of Mrs. Grundy:

"VO: You know, my friend Aldo came over today and gave me this California Cooler.
(SFX: POP, GURGLE, FIZZ)
Now, I hate California. You know what it is? It's what it does to your body. You move out there looking like me, then you come back with muscles. I don't need it. Your skin turns brown, your hair turns blond.

This is not good for you. Your teeth get whiter. And then the sun dries out your zits. Hey man, I'm a lifeguard. I have a totally awesome, bronze bod. Don't touch. Get outta here. You know, you move to California. First of all you stop eating American food. No white bread, no salami, no bratwurst. Everything's good for you. Bagels are like some rare treat from some foreign land. Meanwhile, you eat all this garbage, you live longer but so what, your mind gets soft. Then they pay money to chant along with Raji-oly-oxen-free. Who are these people? You know, I even hate what they drink. Aha, look at it. This stuff. California Cooler. I hate the name. You drink it ice cold, on a hot day. (POURING) I hate it. I really hate it. Heh, heh, just pretend you never saw me drinkin' the stuff, will ya?

ANNCR: *California Cooler.*

One more reason to hate California. California Cooler, Stockton, California."

Advertising copywriters are among the most prolific contributors to the ever-changing English vocabulary. Expressions like "middle-age spread," "tired blood," "diaper rash," "vitamin deficiency" all got their start on Madison Avenue.

Punchy, Crunchy, Raunchy Anglo-Saxon

Plain talk works best in advertising and that makes words with Anglo-Saxon roots the favorites with copywriters. Terms of Latin and Greek origin fare less well for their complexity (though there are, of course, many exceptions). All of which means that *go down* sounds more forceful in advertising copy than *descend* (from the Latin *descendere*); *get* is preferable to *receive* (from Latin *recipere*); and *burp* is more powerful than *eructate*.

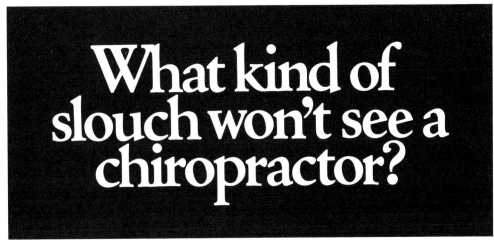

Delaying treatment for a back injury can be as harmful as the injury itself. Don't put it off. Call Mountain Chiropractic. Because if your back feels like it's killing you, maybe it is.

Mountain Chiropractic

104 N. Ash, Cortez, CO 565-7817 (T, Th); 3211 Main Ave., Durango, CO 259-6540 (M, W, F)

King's English is for Kings — too small of a market for most products. Chances are the advertiser will do better with vernacular as in this poster for Mountain Chiropractic.

How to write a personal letter

by Garrison Keillor

International Paper asked Garrison Keillor, author of the best-selling books, Happy to Be Here and Lake Wobegon Days, to tell you how to write a letter that will bring joy into the life of someone you love.

We shy persons need to write a letter now and then, or else we'll dry up and blow away. It's true. And I speak as one who loves to reach for the phone, dial the number, and talk. I say, "Big Bopper here—what's shakin', babes?" The telephone is to shyness what Hawaii is to February, it's a way out of the woods, *and yet:* a letter is better.

Such a sweet gift

Such a sweet gift—a piece of handmade writing, in an envelope that is not a bill, sitting in our friend's path when she trudges home from a long day spent among wahoos and savages, a day our words will help repair. They don't need to be immortal, just sincere. She can read them twice and again tomorrow: *You're someone I care about, Corinne, and think of often*

and every time I do you make me smile.

We need to write, otherwise nobody will know who we are. They will have only a vague impression of us as A Nice Person, because frankly, we don't shine at conversation, we lack the confidence to thrust our faces forward and say, "Hi, I'm Heather Hooten, let me tell you about my week." Mostly we say "Uh-huh" and "Oh really." People smile and look over our shoulder, looking for someone else to talk to.

So a shy person sits down and writes a letter. To be known by another person—to meet and talk freely on the page—to be close despite distance. To escape from anonymity and be our own sweet selves and express the music of our souls.

Same thing that moves a giant rock star to sing his heart out in front of 123,000 people moves us to take ball-point in hand and write a few

lines to our dear Aunt Eleanor. *We want to be known.* We want her to know that we have fallen in love, that we quit our job, that we're moving to New York, and we want to say a few things that might not get said in casual conversation: *thank you for what you've meant to me, I am very happy right now.*

Skip the guilt

The first step in writing letters is to get over the guilt of *not* writing. You don't "owe" anybody a letter. Letters are a gift. The burning shame you feel when you see unanswered mail makes it harder to pick up a pen and makes for a cheerless letter when you finally do. *I feel bad about not writing, but I've been so busy,* etc. Skip this. Few letters are obligatory, and they are *Thanks for the wonderful gift* and *I am terribly sorry to hear about George's death* and *Yes, you're welcome to stay with us next month,* and not many more than that. Write those promptly if you want to keep your friends. Don't worry about the others, except love letters, of course. When your true love writes *Dear Light of My Life, Joy of My Heart, O Lovely Pulsating Core of My Sensate Life,* some response is called for. Some of the best letters are tossed off in a burst of inspiration, so keep your writing stuff in one place where you can sit down for a few minutes and *Dear Roy,*

"If you like to receive mail as much as I do, here's one infallible rule: To get a letter, you've got to send a letter."

I am in the middle of an essay for *International Paper* but thought I'd drop you a line. Hi to your sweetie too dash off a note to a pal. Envelopes, stamps, address book, everything in a drawer so you can write fast when the pen is hot.

A blank white 8″ x 11″ sheet can look as big as Montana if the pen's not so hot — try a smaller page and write boldly. Or use a note card with a piece of fine art on the front; if your letter ain't good, at least they get the Matisse. Get a pen that makes a sensuous line, get a comfortable typewriter, a friendly word processor — whichever feels

ment: *I'm sitting at the kitchen table on a rainy Saturday morning. Everyone is gone and the house is quiet.* Let your simple description of the present moment lead to something else, let the letter drift gently along.

Take it easy

The toughest letter to crank out is one that is meant to impress, as we all know from writing job applications; if it's hard work to slip off a letter to a friend, maybe you're trying too hard to be terrific. A letter is only a report to someone who already likes you for reasons other than your brilliance. Take it easy.

write to, a *compadre,* a soul sibling, then it's like driving a car down a country road, you just get behind the keyboard and press on the gas.

Don't tear up the page and start over when you write a bad line — try to write your way out of it. Make mistakes and plunge on. Let the letter cook along and let yourself be bold. Outrage, confusion, love — whatever is in your mind, let it find a way to the page. Writing is a means of discovery, always, and when you come to the end and write *Yours ever* or *Hugs and Kisses,* you'll know something you didn't when you wrote *Dear Pal.*

An object of art

Probably your friend will put your letter away, and it'll be read again a few years from now — and it will improve with age.

"Outrage, confusion, love — whatever is in your mind, let it find a way to the page."

And forty years from now, your friend's grandkids will dig it out of the attic and read it, a sweet and precious relic of the ancient Eighties that gives them a sudden clear glimpse of you and her and the world we old-timers knew. You will then have created an object of art. Your simple lines about where you went, who you saw, what they said, will speak to those children and they will feel in their hearts the humanity of our times.

You can't pick up a phone and call the future and tell them about our times. You have to pick up a piece of paper.

easy to the hand.

Sit for a few minutes with the blank sheet in front of you, and meditate on the person you will write to, let your friend come to mind until you can almost see her or him in the room with you. Remember the last time you saw each other and how your friend looked and what you said and what perhaps was unsaid between you, and when your friend becomes real to you, start to write.

Tell us what you're doing

Write the salutation — *Dear* You — and take a deep breath and plunge in. A simple declarative sentence will do, followed by another and another and another. Tell us what you're doing and tell it like you were talking to us. Don't think about grammar, don't think about lit'ry style, don't try to write dramatically, just give us your news. Where did you go, who did you see, what did they say, what do you think?

If you don't know where to begin, start with the present mo-

Don't worry about form. It's not a term paper. When you come to the end of one episode, just start a new paragraph. You can go from a few lines about the sad state of rock 'n roll to the fight with your mother to your fond memories of Mexico to your cat's urinary tract infection to a few thoughts on personal indebtedness to the kitchen sink and what's in it. The more you write, the easier it gets, and when you have a True True Friend to

[signature: Garrison Keillor]

Copy or pictures? Which should be the advertiser's choice? The fact is that either form of communication works if used at the right time, the right place, and for the right reason. Long copy is certainly justified in International Paper Company's "Power of the Printed Word" series. So far, over 30 million people have asked for reprints of these ads.

Name That Name

Finding a name for a product or a service can be a major undertaking. Sometimes, the responsibility falls squarely in the lap of the advertising agency, but not always. Several specialty companies are also available to lend a hand, as are graphics and identity firms who supply names along with design recommendations. The charge may be (but does not always have to) anywhere from $10,000 to $60,000 for the name only—more if a design is needed. Computer wizard Stephen Jobs paid $100,000 to designer Paul Rand to develop the name and logotype for a new line of electronic hardware: NEXT. And NBC paid almost ten times that to an art studio to come up with a signature different from the one the network executives had grown tired of.

To a large consumer-oriented company, naming a product is rarely a hit-or-miss proposition. Usually dozens of names, perhaps even more, are explored (with and without the aid of computers). They are tested with panels of target audiences and finally incorporated into the overall creative strategy.

Some law firms specialize in "name searches"—a check to see if the name has already been registered and used by someone else. While the process of finding that out is quite simple, the ramifications are not. The law is quite specific in this area. Registration and even copyright (a name cannot be patented) in themselves are not always sufficient to protect the owner against infringement. He must prove priority-in-use; i.e. that he has in fact used the name commercially. Degree of usage, geography, the product itself are all taken into consideration. The same name may be used for different products, as has "Blue Ribbon" for ammonia, mixed nuts, margarine, housing materials, automotive cleaners, paper products, beer, and a restaurant.

Once you have found a name you like —and at times, that may be the result of long and tedious searches—ask yourself these questions:

1. *Does the name suggest a product attribute?* Proctor & Gamble's Duz does. So do Day-Glo fluorescent colors, Krazy Glue, and Kwik-Kopy. Avoid, however, the sledgehammer approach, i.e. Hollywood Shoepolish or Best Kosher Sausage.

2. *Will it please the target audience?* King Cobra malt liquor, Virginia Slims, Yugo cars, Lava, and Manpower do.

3. *Does the name lend itself to easy graphic interpretation?* Apple Computers, Flying Tiger Line, Green Giant, Dutch Boy come to mind.

4. *Is it memorable?* Tongue twisters— like Müeslix (European cereal sold by Kellogg) or Häagen-Dazs—work some of the time (they're so difficult to remember that people remember them) but simple names work better as a rule. Nobody has problems recalling appellations like M&M's, McDonald's, Piper Aircraft, Swiss Air.

5. *One name or two names are better than three or more.* For one thing, they make for simpler package and ad designs. Long names like Transamerica Delaval Incorporated, Trust Life Insurance Company of America, Merrill Lynch Pierce Fenner & Smith (now wisely reduced to Merrill Lynch) take up graphic space and throw tongues into a twitter.

6. *Watch subtle associations.* Sales of Ayds (an appetite suppressant) dropped nearly 50% because of publicity about the deadly disease AIDS. The company changed the name to Aydslim. Other possible negative connotations: Castro Convertible (though the brand is well established), Citizen Watch (the name is less elite than the product it represents), Zero Corporation.

7. *Will it fly in other parts of the world?* The Japanese may have a problem with the "r" in Retroflex. Burrito does not translate *burada* in Spanish as one company thought (in that language the word means "big mistake").

8. *Some names just don't mix.* Combinations like Cadillac Plumbing, Chappel Chairs, Imperial Nurseries sound awkward.

9. *Be an original.* Crown, King, Diamond, Executive, Federal, First, General, Gold, Globe, Liberty, Life, World, Ideal, Victory, Ambassador, Apex, Hollywood, Atlas, Prime, Imperial, Hercules, Prestige are words that have lost much of their force through usage. Think twice before using them, and then only in circumspect combinations. The "brag-and-boast" approach is as out of place in naming products as it is in writing a headline.

These are general rules only. All can be broken under the right circumstances. Names alone do not make a product; it is the *total* image that counts. That includes package design, shelf display, the reputation of the company making the product, the advertising and promotion surrounding it, and the service that goes with it.

Even the commonest of designations will be remembered favorably if other factors are at work. The name Smith certainly carries no particular distinction (the New York Telephone Book in itself lists over 3,000 Smiths), and yet the patronymic solid millions of cough drops with the help of the faces (and reputation) of the two brothers on the box. Coca-Cola practically invented itself; the name made history because of the drink itself, not the other way around. The fact that it also became known as "Coke" (listed in most dictionaries as a trade name) only argues for its general acceptance.

Names are as flexible as any part of the language. They can be adopted, borrowed, coined, or thrown together, spelled backward, forward, and sideways. The world is filled with names, they come from everywhere. Look around you. All living entities have names — including other people; so do objects, and places. Feel free to enjoy the riches. The words are yours to put on your package.

Take apples, for example. They come in almost a hundred varieties, including Streaked Pippin, Early Harvest, and Red Delicious. In the public domain are designations of over 40 species of butterflies — the likes of Skippers, Pearl Crescents, Viceroys. Even chemical elements can sound like titles of a song: terbium, phosphorus, xenon.

Name giving really isn't so difficult once you get the hang of the process. Horses of fame (Phar Lap, Whirlaway,

295

Sun Beam) all have names that became them. Entertainers, dissatisfied with names on their birth certificates changed them without further ado; just ask Woody Allen (who once was an Allen Steward Konigsberg), Anne Bancroft (Anne Marie Italiana), or Cary Grant (Archibald Leach). Even street gangs — notorious as their activities may be — show signs of new founded literacy when it comes to finding their identity: Red Peppers, Car Bar Bandits, The Wild Bunch, Mollie Matches. Have they perhaps hired an advertising agency too to come up with a few suggestions?

To Sum It Up

Creativity is by far the most important ingredient of advertising — and the hardest to measure. It cannot be expressed in numbers, or any other hard-and-fast criteria; even computers become perplexed by it. The process is so immensely complex that only the human brain can hope to cope with it. That will never change, except perhaps in the unbridled imagination of science fiction writers, in whose worlds anything goes.

Every campaign starts with an idea. Those remembered the longest start with a Big Idea which any advertising professional worth his drawing board, word processor, or executive desk recognizes on sight. Such a concept stands out by virtue of originality, drama, and its unswerving emphasis on a true product difference.

That is not to minimize the importance of execution — the way the idea is carried out. Technique itself can constitute a Big Idea, as many recent campaigns show. But the rules are still the same.

Two of the advertiser's major tools are words and pictures. Both play a role; neither is more important than the other, per se. If they work in close tandem, so much the better.

The richness of the English language makes for quick and easy communication, to the delight of those in advertising. There is a word for every shade of action, thought, or emotion; in some ways, even an object can be more precisely described than shown by way of an illustration. Our language is among the most hospitable in the world, welcoming input from any and all sources: the young and the old, the rich and the poor, the educated and the uneducated, the native and the newly arrived. Choice of words in advertisements in themselves preselect their audience, providing another sophisticated method of market segmentation.

But ours is a visual society, so we cannot ignore picture-talk either. Advertising visuals begin with the layout or storyboard — the art director's province. He can catch, keep, and guide the audience's attention at will. His weapons are illustrations, overall design, and type on the printed page. Add movement, sound, and cinema to this on the television screen.

Use of words and pictures calls for subtlety and very special finesse. The message must be understood, of course. But there is more to it than that. A shout should be as good as a whisper; a whisper as good as a shout.

14
Know Thyself

It has become a truism in psychology that we are the product of two forces — Nature (heredity) and Nurture (environment). In a corporate setting, the terms Personality (who we are) and Position (the powers that reside with the office) may be more appropriate. Our work, the way we operate, is an amalgam of both forces, whether we admit it or not.

It is no easy task to be able to tell the difference between our own accomplishments and the credit accorded to us by our position. Is it true self-confidence that gives us a sense of power over others — or is it our standing in the company? Are we really as decisive in our everyday life (say, at home with our teenage children) as we appear behind the huge mahogany desk? Are we as generous with our own money as we are with the company's princely expense account?

The more loftly the office, the more onerous it becomes to draw the fine line between our individual and corporate persona. It is all too common to hybridize the two: to bestow magic powers upon the individual befitting his job description. The person then becomes a symbol of authority, an omnipotent being devoid of everyday human frailties. Can you imagine the Pope taking a shower?

Hello, Person

Behind the office trappings hides the real person, and it is good to know *who* that person is, not only *what* he or she does during office hours. Yes, the employer maybe different from the rest of us, in way of the size of his paycheck, the position of his seat at the conference table. But still he is a human being. He bumps into things, argues with the spouse, and takes the dog out for a walk. A warm handshake makes him feel warm all over; chilly glances chill his soul, no matter where they come from. He gets upset when stuck in traffic and buys everyone a drink with a score of 90 on his golf card for the first time in his life.

With such nebulous distinctions between Person and Position, a little soul-searching now and then shouldn't do anyone harm. What follows is just a quick reminder of how to better understand the actions of others — and perhaps, ourselves.

Family Background. Personalities are formed in childhood. It takes an effort to live down a childhood. Fortunately, it is not impossible.

Values. In the heat of conducting business (often a reenactment of one tribe of cave men fighting another in another era) it pays to stop and reflect on these once in a while. Business has its own set of rules.

Education. The knowledge we possess not only affects our intellect but our total being. The intellect often governs our emotions, and vice versa. Even our instincts are based on information, one way or another.

Business Experience. That, too, is part of the learning process. It follows us wherever we go, even as we change employers, or even careers.

Aspiration. No two people ever have exactly the same goals, even if they sound the same when explained. The word *manager* means different things to different people. To one person, the position connotes higher income; to another it symbolizes power; to still another, it promises security.

Self-Image. This is among the most important legacies parents can pass on to their offspring. Our capacity to withstand reverses in life is based on our inner confidence, probably more than any other single factor.

ADVERTISING MANAGER'S
KNOW THYSELF QUIZ

	YES	NO
1. I prefer to look at a campaign vs. single ads.		
2. If I lose my job, it's not the end of the world. There are plenty of other companies that need my talents.		
3. I believe it is best to share with others the information I have.		
4. Sometimes I think I know more than my boss.		
5. I'd just as soon suggest to the art director the layout I had in mind.		
6. I let my creative people explore all the possibilities and have them arrive at a solution one step at a time.		
7. To save embarrassment for my agency — and myself as I present an idea to others in the organization — I prefer to see three or four solutions to the same problem. There is safety in numbers.		

298

8. I mainly depend on our company research and my own insights as to knowing our customer's mind.

9. I believe the best way to keep an ad agency on its toes is to invite frequent presentations from competitive agencies.

10. Advertising is a gamble. Sometimes you win, sometimes you lose.

11. Advertising is too expensive for what it produces.

12. I believe most people work best under strict daily supervision.

13. The closer the deadline the more attention creative people pay to the work.

14. I wish I could leave my job and join an ad agency. Life is more exciting on the "other side."

If you answered "yes" to the first four questions and "no" to the other ten, you like what you are doing — and probably do it well.

Analysis of the Quiz

Statement No. 1. *"I prefer to look at a campaign vs. single ads."* Those who prefer the former usually take the "big picture" approach, a sign of a good executive. Theme is as important as every detail of execution.

Statement No. 2. *"If I lose my job, it's not the end of the world. There are plenty of other companies that need my talents."* Fear of losing one's job can be destructive; self-confidence will help you to ride through uncertain times.

Statement No. 3. *"I believe it is best to share with others the information I have."* The information you have accumulated could be of great value to others working on your account. Many corporations have proprietary research they keep under lock and key in fear of its being borrowed by a competitor. Discuss the situation with your agency; there are ways to forestall breach of confidence.

Statement No. 4. *"Sometimes I think I know more than my boss."* Let's hope so. His area of expertise is probably not identical with yours.

Statement No. 5. *"I'd just as soon suggest to the art director the layout I had in mind."* Few art directors take kindly to others interfering with their work. It is best not to insist on precise visual solutions, much as they may intrigue you. Talk around your ideas until they become the art director's. If you don't like his work, then either (1) he is failing at his task or (2) you are not giving him a chance.

Statement No. 6. *"I let my creative people explore all the possibilities and arrive at a solution one step at a time."* Logical, but time consuming—and often discouraging to those who must go through the motions. It is better if creative people are given an in-depth factual briefing *before* they sit down at their word machines and drawing tables. The term *creative freedom* must not be confused with a hit-or-miss directionless expedition into the unknown.

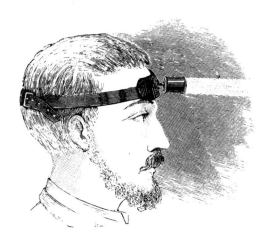

ONE	TWO

THREE

Statement No. 8. *"I mainly depend on our company research and my own insights as to knowing our customer's mind."* Corporate research is invaluable. However, agencies are especially skilled in plumbing the depths of human nature; they could be more attuned to human psychology than your company. Take advantage of both sources of information: yours *and* theirs.

Statement No. 7. *"To save embarrassment for my agency—and myself as I present an idea to others in the organization—I prefer to see three or four solutions to the same problem. There is safety in numbers."* Poppycock. A single good idea is worth more than a bagful of mediocre ones. You are not paying for concepts by the pound. Encourage your agency to concentrate on developing only a few ideas, perhaps only one. If you feel theirs is a flawed solution, ask for another. As a client, that is your prerogative.

Statement No. 9. *"I believe the best way to keep an agency on its toes is to invite frequent presentations from competitive agencies."* Agencies are used to competition, but there is a limit. Fear of losing an account is not conducive to the best of creative work. Talk to other agencies if you feel the need, but if at all possible, offer your incumbent agency every chance to compete on even terms.

Statement No. 10. *"Advertising is a gamble. Sometimes you win, sometimes you lose."* There is an element of chance in all business activity, but as a whole, advertising is becoming more accountable, more predictable, more part of overall corporate strategies.

Statement No. 11. *"Advertising is too expensive for what it produces."* Research shows that advertising is among the fastest ways to increase corporate profits. It is almost always a less expensive activity than addition of labor, machinery, or the introduction of a new product line. Advertisers who cut back on their budgets during recession and depression times (as in the early 1930's and 1960's) learned a costly lesson; they have lost their market share, sometimes irrevocably. This is why the level of advertising expenditures has fluctuated less in recent times.

Statement No. 12. *"I believe most people work best under strict daily supervision."* It depends. Some people look to receiving instructions, the more complete, the better. (Especially the left-brainers.) Others become more inspired left to their own thoughts. Still others feel psychologically inhibited in the omnipresence of a Big Brother, and leave.

Statement No. 13. *"The closer the deadline the more attention creative people pay to the work."* Again, it all depends. Pressure stimulates some, but unsettles others.

Statement No. 14. *"I wish I could leave my job and join an ad agency. Life is more exciting on the 'other side.'"* You may be the type that thrives on the hectic pace of an agency, the constant competition from within and without, the challenge of satisfying difficult clients. Then again, you may be happier in your present environment. The grass is *not* always greener on the other side. It may only seem so.

Working Is a State of Mind

It is a wonder how differently people go about accomplishing their tasks, even if they hold the same jobs. Some prefer to solve problems in a cold, methodical fashion. Others invest their emotions in every project. There are those who prefer to work slow or fast, straight or in a convoluted fashion, even-pacedly or unevenly, alone or as a member of a team, with the help of modern technology or only their wits, in a structured or loose environment. There are as many ways to work as there are employees and employers.

Yet, despite this variety of approaches, it helps to have set working habits and follow them regularly. The word *discipline* may be an anathema to many, yet without it the work gets harder, not easier. All successful business people have well-established working routines. They know that to get the best results they need to know the following *before* solving a problem:

What must be accomplished

The purpose of it all

The time it will take to complete it

Scope of their authority

Available assistance, outside and inside the company

The approval process (who, how many, when)

Costs involved

Everybody Is Creative

In the writing of this book, an attempt was made to show the close interplay between the left and right sides of the brain. In doing so, we hope we have not created the impression that every individual is hopelessly mired in a given pattern, his karma, as it were. The fact is that any left-brainer can turn into a right-brainer at will, and the reverse holds true as well. Rigid distinction between the two kinds of thinkers is an artificial one, cultivated mostly by the turf keepers (their own turf) of the profession. To say that a business executive called upon to solve complex problems every day, that a scientist inventing new technology, are less "creative" than a writer or an artist—or any advertising professional for that matter—is absurd. Sparks fly in everybody's mind. Only not everybody goes about lighting up his own fire in exactly the same way.

To Sum It Up

"Corporate culture" is often so strong that it can overwhelm those who work for the company. The true personalities of men and women are put on hold, not always encouraged to assert themselves in this kind of environment.

This is why it pays—especially for those in advertising, which so depends on individuality—to pause once in a while and ask: Who am I? What am I doing here? What are my likes and dislikes? What do I do best? What are my natural talents? Why am I solving problems the way I do? Am I primarily a left-brainer? Or is it the right hemisphere that guides my decisions?

It is important to know what our strengths are, so we can use them to full advantage. The logic of a left-brainer is as important in business as are the seemingly inexplicable creative flashes of a right-brainer. It is comforting to know that there is need for both types of problem solvers; there is no reason why the two cannot work hand in hand, "brain with brain."

And let us not forget that the human mind is a marvelously flexible instrument. It can be changed at will—by anyone, at any age. Proclivity to use one side of the brain or the other may be nothing more than a familiar routine that we became used to. Isn't it time to break the habit?

Index